Germany Speaks
by
21 Leading Members Of The
Party And State

With A Preface By
Joachim Von Ribbentrop

Germany Speaks

by

21 Leading Members of the Party and State

With a Preface

by

Joachim Von Ribbentrop

ISBN-13: 978-1-913176-08-2

Sanctuary Press Ltd
71-75 Shelton Street
Covent Garden
London
WC2H 9JQ

www.sanctuarypress.com
Email: info@sanctuarypress.com

Germany Speaks

by

21 Leading Members of the Party and State

With a Preface

by

Joachim Von Ribbentrop

"Germany is making every effort in reconciling the apparently conflicting social interests which threaten the integral unity of all nations, to give her people the happiness of a community held together in brotherly fashion; to assist those in poorer circumstances and to further all good and healthy instincts for the material and personal well-being of the people as a whole.

"With the same spirit which governs our actions at home we wish to establish our relations abroad.

"We believe that the tasks which Providence has set us all, if we are to dwell amicably side by side on this earth, must be solved in the same spirit; we wish, therefore, to co-operate sincerely and confidently with all Nations and all States who share these sentiments: and to put this our earnest striving into practice."

    — The Fuhrer and Chancellor of the
    Reich to the Diplomatic Corps.

    January 11th, 1938.

Contents

PREFACE

THE Fuhrer and Chancellor has repeatedly referred to the importance attaching to Anglo-German relations for the peaceful development of Europe.

As Reich Minister for Foreign Affairs I look upon it as one of my duties to assist in every way possible any movement genuinely desirous of promoting understanding between these two great nations. Thus I welcome the following chapters in which competent authorities have endeavoured to bring those problems and ideas which actuate life in Germany closer to the understanding of the English.

Joachim Von Ribbentrop

Reich Minister for Foreign Affairs.

Berlin,

April 2nd, 1938.

PUBLISHERS' NOTE

UNDERSTANDING and practical co-operation in the interests of peace between Great Britain, Germany, France and Italy, are the supreme desideratum of our day. It is therefore essential that the British Public should obtain reliable information on Germany's political and economic aims and aspirations, and a picture of the developments in that country since Adolf Hitler came to power.

This authoritative book is an endeavour to meet that crying need. In it almost all the Reich Ministers or their responsible representatives, Secretaries of State and leading Party Officials have furnished a carefully balanced account of their individual activities. The English reader is thus shown the attitude of Germany on things economic and political, foreign and domestic, her claim to colonies, and numerous other aspects of life in the Reich.

It is hoped that such a clarification of German policy, enunciated by those most intimately concerned, may contribute towards a clearer understanding of our neighbour's aims and aspirations.

Preparations for the publication of this book were already well advanced when the Publishers had the gratification of receiving the following message of approval and encouragement from Reich Minister Baron von Neurath, President of the Secret Cabinet Council:

This book should be looked upon as an earnest endeavour on the part of the Germany created by Adolf Hitler to explain in plain and simple language - as I think every reader will admit - to her neighbour across the North Sea her plans and achievements, her desires and aims. I therefore venture to express the wish that its thoughts and words may not pass unheard, but be received in England in a spirit of understanding and friendship. I personally believe that a frank discussion before the public of the world between these two great and kindred nations should constitute a valuable contribution towards the advent of peace to Europe and the whole world. It is in this spirit that I wish every success to Germany Speaks. It only remains to thank those who have contributed the various articles and particularly our Hamburg collaborator, Dr. G. Kurt Johannsen, who was instrumental in obtaining the entire material; and to state that, while we cannot be expected to agree with all the views herein expressed, we hope that by the publication of this book we may have contributed in some small measure to international goodwill.

PART I

The Fundamental Principles Of The New Germany

SECTION ONE

GERMANY AS A UNITARY STATE

Dr. Frick

Reich Minister Of The Interior

GERMANY has been centuries behind Great Britain and France in achieving her national consolidation; and many struggles, both internal and external, have been required to attain it. At a time when the principles of unification had long established themselves in the governance and administration of other European countries, Germany was still divided into a huge number of secular and ecclesiastical principalities, considerably differing in size, whose rulers were eagerly intent-even at the time when the medieval Empire was at the zenith of its power - upon their own aggrandisement at the expense of the Emperors. It was of great help to them, in that connection, that the Holy Roman Empire of the German Nation rested on an elective - as opposed to an hereditary - foundation, which made it all the easier for them to impose their own will upon the wearers of the Imperial crown. The Thirty Years War destroyed even the outward semblance of power wielded by the Emperors. What was left was a "shadow Empire," an utterly impoverished nation, and an almost innumerable number of rival States which, in time, became mere pawns in the political game of the non-German powers. Large tracts of country inhabited by a purely Germanic population, stretching from the Netherlands to Switzerland, detached themselves from the Empire, some permanently and some temporarily.

To Germany, the peculiar tragedy of this development lies in the fact that it coincided with the age of discovery and with the colonisation of the American continent the West Indies and Africa. When, therefore, the world was first distributed among the European countries, the political and national constitution of Germany was such as to make it impossible for the nation to take an active share in those great movements. More than two centuries had to pass before the spirit of national solidarity grew up again. In the course of time, the number of small and very small States was reduced to workable proportions; but even then a severe struggle for ascendancy - more particularly between Prussia and Austria-had to be waged before the Second Reich could be founded as a result of the policy conducted by Prince Bismarck.

It would be wrong to assume that the Bismarckian Empire of 1871 was a unitary State. It was, indeed, composed of 22 federal States, each of which had its own ruler, its own government, and its own legislative bodies. In addition, some of them had their own postal and railway administrations, and even their own armies. There were very important matters of internal organisation in which the authority of the Central Government in Berlin could only be exercised after innumerable obstacles had been surmounted, or in which it could not be exercised at all.

There was - above all - a lack of uniformity in internal administration, in the principles underlying municipal legislation, and in the police system.

In Great Britain, the work of political consolidation was started during the Norman period, so that - during the Elizabethan era - it could be used as the foundation of the world-wide Empire subsequently acquired by the Insular Kingdom.

In France, the development from a feudal to a national State dates back to Henry of Navarre and Louis XIII. By Cardinal Richelieu the administration of the country was completely centralised, all authority being vested in the king and his ministers and all legislation originating from Paris. Within a short time, the spirit of national unity grew so strong that it could successfully withstand not only the revolution of 1789, but also all the other political crises that have since occurred in France.

In Germany, events moved in the opposite direction. The Imperial Prerogative, still fairly considerable during the Middle Ages, decreased more and more, and after the Thirty Years War full sovereignty was accorded each of the territorial principalities. The final goal of that development was decentralisation instead of centralisation; and the process of political disintegration was accelerated by economic barriers of all kinds.

Notwithstanding its shortcomings, however, the Constitution drawn up by Prince Bismarck was a great improvement upon the preceding state of affairs. By it, the loose confederation of States previously existing was converted into a far more coherent federated State, of which Bismarck's North German Confederation was a kind of forerunner, both politically and economically. During the Franco-German War (1870-1), that great statesman's far-sighted policy in his dealings with the South German States resulted in the creation of a federated State which comprised both North and South Germany.

After the debacle of 1918, the monarchical Constitution was superseded by that of the Weimar Republic, but no fundamental change took place in the relations between the Central Government and the individual States. The part previously paid by the rulers of the latter was henceforth taken by their respective parliamentary bodies.

It was therefore not until the advent of the National Socialist regime under the leadership of Herr Hitler (1933) that the authority still wielded by the then existing seventeen federal States was so severely curtailed that it became subordinated to that exercised by the National Government.

Seventeen parliamentary bodies, each of which nullified the will of the German people by creating artificial antagonisms and fomenting party dissension, were swept away by the fervour of the National Socialist movement. Before that, the supreme authority of the Central Government was constantly weakened by its own instability, by its dependence upon shifting parliamentary majorities, and by the resulting civil disturbances. These conditions vanished as if by magic as soon as the triumph of Herr Hitler and the National Socialist movement became a reality. Party strife and class war came to an end. The menace of a Bolshevist revolution was overcome at the eleventh hour. Communism was suppressed, and the last traces of the always smouldering civil war were eradicated. A regime that was shaken by one crisis after the other, that lacked the confidence of the nation, and wearily continued its precarious existence from day to day, had to give way to that of Herr Hitler, which enjoys the support of the great majority of the German people. Since then, order and security prevail again, and economic conditions are continually improving.

The Leader and Chancellor has vigorously taken in hand the great work of political reconstruction. He is now converting the federated State into a unitary one, whose affairs are conducted as he directs. Thus, the century-old attempts at unification are at last within sight of being crowned with success.

Four years have elapsed since Herr Hitler's assumption of power on January 30th, 1933. Anyone visiting the country can personally convince himself of the immense improvement wrought in that short time. Within a few months, supreme power throughout the country was concentrated in the hands of the Leader. Since then, systematic steps have been taken to rebuild the State. The measures introduced to that end no longer depend for their success upon political accidents or the intrigues of political opponents. Recent elections and plebiscites have shown that not a mere majority, but actually 99 % of the electorate, support the Government and endorse its decisions, so that the Reichstag is now more fully representative of the nation's will than it has ever been before.

The victory of National Socialism has thus created the political conditions indispensable to the complete unification of Germany.

The Bismarckian Constitution succumbed to the onslaughts of Germany's internal enemies during the World War. It was sabotaged by those political parties which - as early as 1917 - had endeavoured to exercise a certain influence in connection with the conduct of the State. The ultimate reason for its failure to withstand these attacks upon it was that the Second Reich was not a unitary State. The twenty-two components of that Reich had retained a considerable amount of political sovereignty, and the authority of the Central Government was restricted to a few domains. The Constitution was bound to break down when parliamentary parties took the place of the ruling dynasties, and when its main pillar - the close connection between the Reich and Prussia in the person of the monarch - was withdrawn.

The Weimar Constitution of 1919 did not even restore this connection, which had proved so useful a bond of union so long as the monarchical Constitution existed. It made it compulsory for all the federal States - including Prussia - to adopt the parliamentary Republican regime. Under such a regime, the centre of political gravity must naturally lie in the parliaments of the federal States and in the Reichstag. In effect, however, all these bodies were dominated by a legion of political parties, the percentage representation of which in each State varied exceedingly. Hence, the Weimar Republic soon presented a picture of so much political disunion that it was found quite impossible to form a Government really capable of governing the country.

The Weimar Constitution is directly responsible for the open breach between the Reich and Prussia in 1932, inasmuch as - under its terms - that dispute was referred to a State Tribunal, which was by no means qualified to effect a just solution. In October, 1932, a decision was pronounced by that court: political authority in Prussia was divided up and an untenable situation was created which lasted until January 30th, 1933.

Herr Hitler's Government has turned the party-governed federated State existing prior to his coming-into-power into a unitary State. Three great measures had to be passed to bring about this transformation, viz., first, the Acts establishing uniformity in the political organisations throughout the country (1933); second, the Act of January 30th, 1934, governing the reform of the Reich Government, and third, the extension of the authority wielded by the Reich Governors in the individual States. These fundamental measures were supplemented by a number of others introduced for the purpose of ensuring uniformity in the State executive and administration.

The first Act establishing uniformity in the political organisations was passed on March 31st, 1933. It did away with the difficulties arising out of the discrepancy between the composition of the Reichstag and that of the parliamentary bodies in the various States. It was provided that party representation must be uniform in all these parliaments so long as they continued in existence. The second Act was passed on April 7th, 1933, and empowered the Leader and Chancellor to appoint Reich Governors in all States. They act as his personal representatives, and each of them is entrusted with the task of ensuring that Herr Hitler's political views dominate the policy of the State concerned. The same Act restored an arrangement wisely introduced by Prince Bismarck years ago, but thrown overboard by the makers of the Weimar Constitution, namely that by which the Government of the Reich and that of Prussia (by far the largest of its constituent parts) are conducted on identical lines. Herr Hitler achieved this purpose by appointing himself Reich Governor for Prussia.

After the dissolution of all political parties and the combined plebiscite and Reichstag elections held on November 12th, 1933, when the new Government secured an overwhelming majority throughout the country, it became possible for the new Reichstag to give its unanimous consent to an Act definitely establishing the unitary State, i.e., that passed on January 30th, 1934, governing the reform of the Reich Government. The five classical sentences expressing the nation's desire for the creation of the unitary State read as follows:

The parliaments of the individual States are abolished. The sovereign rights of the States are transferred to the Reich. The Reich Governors receive their instructions from the Reich Minister of the Interior. The Reich Government is empowered to create new constitutional law.

By abolishing the separate parliamentary bodies and assigning all sovereign rights to the Reich Government, this Act - to which the late President Hindenburg appended his signature on the day it was passed - has removed the ultimate causes to which Germany's political disunion was attributable.

By subjecting the State governments to the Reich, it has established the unquestioned supremacy of the latter. By empowering the Reich Minister of the Interior to give instructions to the Reich Governors, it indicates that these latter will be the future heads of the various States, which - at a later date - will be transformed into Reich provinces.

Additional legislation, more especially the act of January 30th, 1935, by which the authority exercised by the Reich Governors was further extended, directed these Governors (and along with them the Governors of the Prussian provinces) to ensure that the policy of the Leader is also adopted within the areas over which they preside and which need not be identical with those covered by the States, in so far as they still exist. To that end, they are authorised to make all the necessary arrangements in connection with the administrative bodies set up within their respective districts, including those of the Reich, those of the States, and all others exercising public functions. They are also entitled - if instructed by the Leader and Chancellor to do so - to promulgate the laws affecting their particular districts and to appoint officials in his name. In doing all this, however, they act as the representatives of the Leader and Chancellor and of the Reich Government. The Act passed on January 30th, 1935, contains some clauses that make it possible to establish still closer collaboration between the executive of the Reich and the States. Thus, it provides that the Leader and Chancellor may commission any Reich Governor to conduct the government of the State concerned. Up to now, this provision has been made use of in respect of Saxony, Hesse, Lippe, and Hamburg. In these States, therefore, the conditions have already been established that will prevail throughout Germany when the reform of the Reich Government has been completed: The Reich Governor solely and directly conducts the State Government and presides over the State administration so that the States named are in effect administrative units subject to the control of Governors appointed by the Reich.

Thanks to all the aforenamed measures, the individual States have already been transformed into constituent parts of the unitary State. This development has made especial progress in regard to Prussia - a country which comprises three-fifths of the population and the area of Germany, which can look back upon a long and proud history, and which therefore forms the main pillar of the constitutional structure of the Reich. Prior to 1933, the Reich Government exercised but few administrative functions of major importance, e.g., those in the domain of national finance. It was thus found convenient to bring about far-reaching co-operation between itself and the highly developed administrative system of Prussia. First, the competent Reich Ministers were entrusted with the executive functions of the corresponding Prussian Ministers; and later on, such amalgamation was extended throughout their respective spheres of work. Today, combined administrations of this type exist in the following departments: home affairs; justice; science, education: and popular instruction; labour; transportation; national economy, and forests. Thus, what may be called a "Greater Prussia" is being more efficiently merged with the" Greater Reich" than could have been achieved by the disintegration of Prussia, and one of Prince Bismarck's aspirations is nearing its realisation. Such a gradual merger will be the outcome of the "liquidation of the States," which Herr Hitler described in 1933 as the goal of the plans for the reform of the Reich Government. It will be further accelerated by the fact that the Governors of the Prussian provinces (each of which covers an area about equal to the average area covered by the other States) have been given authority - as already stated - similar to that granted to the Reich Governors. Like them, they are directly subject to the Reich Ministers, and represent the Reich within the districts over which they preside.

The unification of Germany has not only been brought about in regard to the political and administrative functions formerly reserved to the competent organs of the States and Prussian provinces, but also finds expression in the political status of the inhabitants and in the form of the national symbols. Under the Weimar Constitution, there was no German citizenship. Every German was a citizen of some particular State. All this has been abolished, and all Germans are now citizens, or nationals, of the Reich. Citizenship can be conferred by the States only if the Reich Minister of the Interior gives his consent. By his famous decree of March 12th, 1933, President Hindenburg made the swastika flag - the emblem of the victorious National Socialist movement - the national symbol of the Third Reich along side with the black-and-white-and-red flag of the Bismarckian Reich; and by the Act passed September 15th, 1935, the swastika flag showing the national colours - black, white, and red - was made the principal symbol of Germany's political unity and is now representative of the Reich, the nation, and the country's commerce.

The progress of unification has made itself felt in many respects. More particularly, the Reich is now the sole competent authority in matters concerning legislation, administration and justice. The States can only pass new legislation within the authorisation granted them by the Reich and with the co-operation of the Reich Governors.

The administrative sovereignty of the States, which formed the backbone of their political life under the Weimar Constitution, has passed over to the Reich; and their administrative functions are now performed in pursuance of the authority vested in them by the latter. The decree issued by the Leader and Chancellor on June 17th, 1936, subjected the important domain of police administration to the uniform control of the Head of the German Police. By the decree governing municipal administration (January 30th, 1935), genuine self government was restored to the municipalities, and their legal status was uniformly determined. Public officials - whose importance to the unitary State was specially emphasised when the new Act governing their status (January 26th, 1937) was passed - are today one of the main pillars of that State. All of them are the direct servants of the Leader and Chancellor and swear allegiance to him upon their appointment. He is responsible, in principle, for their appointment and dismissal. The administration of law and justice is the exclusive domain of the Reich, by which the whole of the legal system with all its accessories was taken over in pursuance of the Act passed January 24th, 1935. Accordingly, all courts of law are now Reich institutions. They administer justice in the name of the German people. The granting of pardons is solely vested in the Leader and Chancellor.

The reorganisation of the political structure of the Reich, as foreshadowed by the Act of January 30th, 1934, will be definitely completed when a number of internal territorial changes have been effected. The present distribution of territory - quite comprehensible in view of the country's past history - is largely due to purely accidental occurrences; and it will be necessary to remove existing anomalies and to make arrangements by which regions with a homogeneous population and with identical economic interests are amalgamated with one another, thus preparing the future division of the whole country into Reich provinces. The first step in connection with this difficult measure - difficult because so many traditions have to be respected - was made when the Act of January 26th, 1937, was passed. It deals with the future status of Greater Hamburg and a few similar matters. It provides that Prussia, Oldenburg, and Mecklenburg will make certain territorial adjustments among themselves, that the Hanseatic city of Lubeck will be incorporated with Prussia, and that the Prussian towns and rural districts closely adjoining Hamburg will be absorbed by the latter, with which they will henceforth form one administrative unit. By this Act the conditions have been created that are indispensable for the territorial reorganisation of North-Western Germany.

The National Socialist Government is well aware of its duty to preserve the special cultural features characteristic of each part of the country and to do everything that will encourage their growth and further development. Care will be taken to render this easily possible notwithstanding the unifying measures introduced in public administration, legislation and internal government. For that reason some of the great organisations of the German people have been closely associated with certain towns and cities. Munich is "the capital of the National Socialist movement," Nuremberg "the city of the National Socialist party rallies," Goslar "the city of the Reich Food Corporation," Frankfort "the city of German handicraft," and Hamburg will be "the Hanseatic city" entrusted with some tasks of nation-wide importance.

National Socialist Germany, however, is not merely a unitary State: it is also a unitary nation, and its governance is based on the principle of leadership. The nation constitutes the concrete substance of the National Socialist movement, and the State is merely a means for the realisation of its political aims. The National Socialist party is acknowledged to be the organisation with which by far the greater part of the German people have identified themselves. It is therefore best qualified to represent the nation, and the ultimate object must be to establish the complete unity of the party and the State. Hence, leadership must be vested in the party, and positive tasks must be entrusted to it. It is the embodiment of the German political idea and determines Germany's political activities. Its organisation is the supreme organisation of the German people. The State apparatus serves the purpose of giving effect to the political principles laid down by the party. It attends to all matters of administration through the instrumentality of the public authorities and public officials. Its only task is to be of service to the nation; but it is not fit for the exercise of leadership, Similar conditions have existed in all periods of Germany's national history. Leadership has always been the preserve of persons or groups of persons not directly connected with the machinery of State, such as the German kings and emperors, the Church, the estates of the realm, the princely houses, and - in our own days - the parliamentary bodies. In all these instances, the State apparatus was only a means employed by the ruling powers.

In National Socialist Germany, leadership is in the hands of an organised community, the National Socialist party; and as the latter represents the will of the nation the policy adopted by it in harmony with the vital interests of the nation is at the same time the policy adopted by the country.

The necessary unity of the party and the State is the subject of the Act passed December 1st, 1933, by which the National Socialist party is specifically described as the leading and moving force within the State. It does not follow, however, that the State as such has ceased to, exist or that it is intended to merge it with the party. The National Socialist party is the only political party in Germany and therefore the true representative of the people. It incorporates the German idea of the State and is indissolubly associated with the State.

The unity of the party and the State finds its highest realisation in the person of the Leader and Chancellor who - under the terms of the Act passed August 1st 1934 - combines the offices of President and Chancellor. He is the leader of the National Socialist party, the political head of the State, and the supreme commander of the defence forces. In this way, the authority of the party as being the highest political organisation in the country has received recognition. Whenever the proclamation of a new leader of the party takes place, the person thus nominated is at the same time the head of the State and the supreme commander of the defence forces.

Other means by which effect has been given to the unity of the party and the State are the following: the provision that the Leader's deputy is a member of the Government and that he takes part in legislative and administrative matters; the personal identity of Reich Ministers with Reich leaders of the party, and of Reich Governors and of Governors of Prussian provinces with district leaders of the party; the fact that party functionaries are also members of State and municipal councils and the appointment of party members in connection with the practical application of the Code of Municipal Law.

All the organisational measures, however, that have been introduced in order to ensure the unity of the party and the State, are dominated by the unity of the German idea of the State as embodied in the Leader. It has created the party, has brought about its accession to power, and will continue to inspire its actions, whilst it is the function of the State to give reality to that idea in accordance with the will expressed by the National Socialist party.

The German people are aware that the principal task before them in the domain of domestic policy is the further development of the unitary State on a national basis. I believe that I cannot close this account more fitly than by quoting the concluding sentences of the broadcast speech which I addressed to the nation on January 31st, 1934, immediately after the passing of the Act governing the reform of the Reich Government.

Our generation has been called upon to create the national unitary State. We are to succeed where our fathers failed and to bequeath to future generations the result of our endeavours. Let us rejoice that Fate has found us worthy of so huge a task. Let us also realise that this day is a turning-point in the history of our country, and that its importance can only be properly estimated by posterity. I ask everyone of you to contribute your share to this splendid achievement. Let the past be past, and - always conscious of your duty - envisage the future with confidence.

Pride yourselves on being privileged to witness so tremendous a change and to collaborate in the work of moulding our country's destiny. Everyone is needed for that noble purpose. And all those who love Germany must serve her to the limit of their power, so that the great work may be completed for the benefit of the whole nation.

SECTION TWO

POPULATION POLICY

Dr. Arthur Gutt

Head of the National Hygiene Department
in the Ministry of the Interior

IN most countries, neither the governments nor the peoples have so far paid much attention to the circumstances that account for the alternation of growth and decay in the history of civilised nations. The rulers of ancient Greece and Imperial Rome did not realise the need for a constructive population policy until the signs of decay and degeneration were too patent to be ignored. The position is exactly the same today. Statesmen everywhere have occupied themselves far too little with the valuable racial assets inherited from an untold number of past generations. They have been content to interest themselves in the promotion of material and cultural assets without appreciating the fact that there is always a close relationship between these latter and the hereditary racial characteristics of the nation. Moreover, the real value of those assets will be much impaired if the nation contains too small a number of thoroughly healthy individuals. If that number is subject to a continuous decrease because of the tendency on the part of married couples to remain childless or, at the best, to be satisfied with one or two children, the nation must renounce all hope of progressive development. Its civilisation will be doomed to ultimate destruction. It is not however, sufficient merely to realise the danger thus impending. What is wanted is an active policy consistently aiming at the preservation of racial health. Practical steps must be taken to prevent the further decline in the number of births.

When at the close of 1932, Germany found herself faced with national bankruptcy and the danger of racial disintegration the National Socialist Government resolutely put a stop to the policy of laissez-faire previously adopted. Due prominence was henceforth given to

25

the importance of the family, to the nation's special characteristics, and to its racial origins. The governments of all civilised countries are aware that it is not enough to safeguard the future of their respective populations by an adequate system of administration and by an adequate economic policy. They know that equal care must be given to the people's racial health. Notwithstanding this, there has been a failure to consider the effects produced by their endeavours in that direction - tinged, as they were - by Liberal principles. The object of the legislation governing sickness, disablement and old-age insurance, and of the various other measures taken to promote public welfare, has always been too much concerned with the interests of each unhealthy individual, and too little with the interests of the community as a whole.

The more sickness there was and the more a person conducted himself in an anti-social way, the greater were the efforts made by the State, the municipalities and the various associations to relieve him of his troubles and worries. Many apparent successes were thus achieved and the mortality index decreased more and more. It is quite true that the spread of infectious diseases was largely prevented, but in order to recover the cost of all those schemes, the healthy members of the community had to be increasingly taxed.

The more instinctively a man had preserved intact his feeling for the family, the nation and the race, and the more children he had, the more was he "penalised" by the indirect taxes levied on articles of every-day consumption, by social charges, and by insurance payments of all kinds. The "success" of this system was only too visible: The family sense, the sense of individual responsibility, and the economic foundations of the family were destroyed. The masses, influenced by Marxist and Bolshevist teaching, responded by selfishness, enmity to the State, a disinclination to marry, the loosening of all mutual ties, and a lack of ambition. The decline in the birth-rate began to assume menacing proportions in Germany as well as in Great Britain.

In Germany, in or about the year 1900, there was about one child to every four marriages each year, but in 1932 there was only one child to every fourteen marriages; and matters were not much better in Great Britain. The cause of this degeneration was believed to be connected with the economic conditions. It was not realised that the family is the nucleus of the State and that, without it, there can be no healthy political or economic conditions at all.

The aim of the population policy now pursued in Germany is to preserve the numerical strength of the nation and to ensure its racial health, our first thought, therefore, must be to maintain the very existence of our nation. Although it is generally assumed that the term "nation" is so clearly understood that it needs no further definition, it may be necessary to make a few remarks concerning it. It is a mistake, for instance, to think that it comprises all those who are citizens of the State concerned, irrespective of their race or their origin.

The science of heredity teaches us that such a view is but superficial, and that the term must be restricted to those persons who are racially akin to one another owing to their ancestry and to their physical and intellectual features. On the other hand, it should not be solely applied to those persons who are contemporary to one another at any given moment, but also to all their ancestors and descendants. It is essential, therefore, to remember that the term "nation" implies the element of timelessness, as this circumstance has an important bearing upon all the efforts made to preserve the national health, and the numerical strength of the nation. If the present decline in the birth-rate is allowed to go on unchecked in Germany, Great Britain and elsewhere, there is the grave danger of the nations concerned losing the very foundations of their existence and their civilisation.

Average number of children born per annum,
excluding those still-born, 000's being omitted.

Name of Country.	Population 1932	1905 to 1909	1910 to 1914	1915 to 1919	1920 to 1924	1925 to 1929	1932
Germany	64,912	1,748	1,628	985	1,408	1,202	978
Sweden	6,176	137	132	120	121	100	90
Norway	2,831	61	61	61	63	51	47
Denmark	3,590	75	74	71	76	69	65
England and Wales	40,201	927	882	725	815	673	614
Scotland	4,880	130	123	105	119	98	91
Ireland	4,230	103	101	90	93	87	81
Netherlands	8,116	171	171	169	187	177	179
France	41,928	841	790	446	784	751	722

Bad as these figures are, they do not yet indicate the position as it really is. The apparent excess of births over deaths is not due to any increase in the number of births, but rather to a decrease in that of deaths.

On account of the improved standards of living, the progress of medical science and the greater care bestowed on matters of hygiene, the age classes originating from the years during which the birth-rate was still high, die much later than the corresponding classes in the past.

The rate of mortality has gone down two and even threefold with the result that, in Germany and Great Britain, the number of persons now living exceeds the number of those living some sixty years ago by the equivalent of about twenty age classes. This circumstance effectively conceals the actual dying-out of the nations concerned. As soon as those age classes begin to die, the present illusion regarding the excess of births over deaths will be destroyed.

By that time, the numerically weak age classes dating from the present time of declining birth rates will have reached the marriageable age, and the death-rate will undergo a sudden and considerable rise. The offspring then born will be inadequate to maintain the numerical strength of the nations because of the reduced number of potential fathers and mothers.

If we want to obtain a true idea of the situation, we must allow for all these facts and adjust the figures accordingly. We shall then find that, as already stated above, the nations concerned are gradually dying out.

Burgdorfer has made the adjustment which the statistical figures demand in accordance with the foregoing explanations and has ascertained that in all the Germanic countries (except the Netherlands) the natural growth of the population has ceased altogether. In France, a certain stagnation may be said to exist, whilst in the Netherlands, Italy, Poland and the Ukrainian Socialist Soviet Republic the population still continues its natural growth.

The decline of the birth-rate, especially in the Germanic countries, may be clearly seen by a glance in the above table. In the Slavonic countries, the birth-rate is twice as high as, for instance, it is in Germany.

Name of country.	No. of births (exc. still births) per 1,000 inhabitants					Excess of births per 1,000 inhabitants.				
	1913	1927	1930	1931	1932	1913	1927	1930	1931	1932
Germany	27.5	18.4	17.5	16.0	15.1	12.4	6.4	6.5	4.7	4.3
Austria	24.1	17.8	16.8	15.8	15.2	5.7	2.9	3.3	1.9	1.3
Switzerland	23.1	17.6	17.2	16.7	16.7	8.8	5.2	5.6	4.6	4.5
Lithuania	-	29.1	27.4	26.8	27.3	-	12.0	11.5	11.0	12.1
Latvia	-	22.0	19.8	19.3	19.4	-	6.6	5.6	5.3	5.7
Estonia	-	17.7	17.4	17.4	17.6	-	0.4	2.5	1.2	2.7
Finland	27.2	21.2	20.6	19.5	-	11.1	6.7	7.4	6.2	-
Sweden	23.2	16.1	15.4	14.8	14.5	9.5	3.4	3.7	2.3	3.0
Norway	25.1	17.8	17.0	16.7	-	11.8	6.6	6.4	6.0	-
Denmark	25.6	19.6	18.7	18.0	18.0	13.1	8.0	7.9	6.6	6.9
Great Britain and Ireland	24.2	17.3	16.9	16.3	15.9	9.9	4.7	5.1	3.9	3.6
Netherlands	28.2	23.1	23.0	22.2	22.0	15.9	12.8	13.9	12.6	13.0
Belgium	22.4	18.3	18.6	18.2	17.6	7.8	4.9	5.4	5.0	4.8
France	18.8	18.2	18.0	17.4	17.3	1.1	1.7	2.4	1.1	1.5
Spain	30.4	28.6	29.0	28.3	28.3	8.3	9.7	11.7	10.5	11.9
Portugal	32.3	32.3	30.4	30.4	30.7	11.8	12.3	12.9	13.3	13.2
Italy	31.7	27.0	26.7	24.9	23.8	13.0	11.2	12.6	10.1	9.2
Greece	-	29.3	31.4	30.9	-	-	12.7	15.0	13.1	-
Bulgaria	41.0	33.2	31.3	29.4	31.3	18.6	12.9	15.2	12.5	15.1
Roumania	42.1	35.5	35.0	33.3	35.9	16.0	12.4	15.6	12.5	14.2
Hungary	33.8	25.7	25.4	23.2	23.0	11.5	8.0	9.9	6.7	5.2
Czechoslo-vakia	28.9	23.3	22.7	21.5	21.0	9.6	7.3	8.5	7.1	6.9
Poland	-	31.9	32.3	30.3	28.7	-	14.3	16.7	14.8	13.7
Ukraine (U.S.S.R.)	41.8	40.3				18.1	22.5			
White Russia (W.R.S.S.R.)	39.0	38.6				19.7	24.5			
Russia proper (R.S.F.S.R.)	49.8	44.2				16.3	21.9			

These tables indicate the extent of the danger to which the Germanic countries of Europe are exposed by the falling birth-rate. They also show the menace to which the racial and political independence of the Central and North European nations will be subjected in future by the incessant pressure exerted by the Slavonic peoples. The outward cause of the decline in the birth-rate is the desire on the part of many families to have but few, if any, children.

The two-child system has been largely adopted, and there are also considerable sections of the population that have adopted the one-child system. No more than 10 % of all families have now four or more children. It may be seen that a nationwide adoption of the two-child system would lead to the practical extinction of the nation after three hundred years. No statesman, least of all in Germany or Great Britain, can ignore these circumstances without grave injury to the country he represents.

Let us now consider the effects that will be produced by the present development. They may not be openly discernible just yet, but they will be distinctly noticeable after the lapse of another ten years.

There can be no doubt that these effects will make themselves felt in every branch of public activity, e.g., in the labour market, the production and consumption of goods, the building trade, school education, social politics, and the defence of the country.

Seeing that children are consumers only, and not producers as well, the shortage of children below 15 (which age class in Germany, for example, is now about 9,000,000 less numerous in proportion to the number of persons working for a living than it was before the War) is bound to upset the equilibrium between producers and consumers. During the second half of the present century, conditions will be almost entirely reversed. There will be such a shortage of workers not only in Germany, but in Great Britain as well, that serious inconvenience will result therefrom. History has taught us that conditions such as these invariably lead to a large influx of foreign labour; and as the situation in the Slavonic countries, more particularly Russia, is the exact reverse, the pressure exercised upon our population will become so great that we shall be unable to resist it.

The number of persons of 65 or more, which is about 4,000,000 at present, will rise to about 10,000,000 within the not too distant future. This will bring about an unhealthy disproportion between those who are the beneficiaries of our social and insurance legislation and those who have to pay the contributions. The country's social policy will then have to face a complete collapse. The position is exactly the same as regards the defensive forces of the nation, as may be seen from the following table:

Number Of Youths Aged 20 In The Years Named
(i.e., Persons Of Military Age)

Year.	Germany	England.	Italy	France	Russia	Japan
1930	630,000	391,700	426,400	_	1,752,900	_
1931	599,000	386,300	393,000	394,000	1,765,600	621,800
1932	630,600	388,500	417,300	354,000	1,753,100	652,400
1933	607,400	386,200	417,000	351,000	1,797,300	657,300
1934	595,900	391,900	406,800	279,000	2,102,100	659,500
1935	464,500	360,200	397,200	184,000	1,295,000	636,200
1936	350,900	343,600	311,500	165,000	1,400,500	645,300
1937	313,700	296,900	250,500	171,000	1,108,300	630,100
1938	326,300	304,500	239,800	197,000	1,583,700	618,200
1939	485,000	424,500	298,800	218,000	1,395,200	606,000
1940	636,300	433,500	454,900	360,000	1,422,600	739,700

The figures given in the foregoing table refer to the young people who have become (or will become) of military age in the years named. No deductions have been made in respect of those that may be physically unfit for military service. The minima reached in each of the six countries concerned are printed in italics. The figures plainly show the great numerical inferiority of the Western European countries to Russia and Japan twenty years after the worst year of the World War. The fact that in or about 1937 the figures are so exceedingly low is a direct, although belated, result of the War. Germany and France are the two countries where the shortage of births due to that cause is most pronounced. The corresponding shortage in Russia is attributable to the 1917 revolution. As regards the Western countries, the figures will be more unfavourable still in the years after 1940. By 1946, the age class here concerned will increase to more than 2,000,000 in Russia, and its average strength is expected to amount to four times that of the corresponding class in Germany.

It is evident from this development and from these statistics that the European nations cannot possibly afford another war among themselves. If such a war should come about, their fate would be sealed. Great Britain too, will not be able to retain her sway over her distant possessions and dependencies unless she can rely upon the support rendered by a Central European bloc. Germany, however, is not only the heart, but also the backbone of Europe; and Bolshevism, if victorious, would not stay its progress on the banks of the Rhine or the Seine, but only after reaching Copenhagen, Stockholm and London.

The numerical decline of the population, however, is but one aspect of the danger that confronts the nations and their governments. Its other aspect is the biological and racial degeneration that is becoming more and more evident as time goes on. It is a fact that the limitation of the number of children to one or two is practised by the physically and mentally superior members of all classes, including the working class, and that childlessness, too, is spreading among them to an alarming extent. The very opposite development is taking place among persons suffering from inherited physical or mental defects, including persons of a morbidly anti-social type and criminals. Statistics prove that three, four or even more children are by no means uncommon in these biologically inferior sections of the population. These facts indicate the extent of the danger we have to face today in Germany, and also in Great Britain. Once, however, the inferior sections actually predominate and the position is further worsened by wholesale racial mixture, it will be too late to apply a remedy. Our proud, race-conscious nations will perish, and European civilisation along with them. Their place will be taken, in all probability, by the Bolshevist mixture of Russian and Asiatic peoples that has sprung up in Eastern Europe owing to the dissolution of all family ties. During my internment as a prisoner of war, I became acquainted with the former Russia and the former Siberia; and I know that these countries are no longer now what they were then. The members of the upper strata, who were educated along Western European lines, have been killed or have fled the country; and a section racially foreign to the European Russians has replaced them.

We must bear in mind that a new generation of mixed racial origin is now growing up in Russia, that it is intellectually trained by Jews, that it does not appreciate our Western civilisation and does not understand our Western views. It will be a bad day for Europe when an army consisting of 17,000,000 members of that Russo-Asiatic mixture, allied with some European nations and supported by negro armies, is let loose on it and finally destroys it. No European nation can hope to be victorious against such opponents single-handed. A common front and a sense of solidarity are necessary to avert disaster. Will that necessity be realised in time? That is the decisive question which Europe will have to answer.

It appears to me that the deceptive technical progress of our age and the dominance of financial interests have given rise to a certain feeling of conceit among us. Old standards have made room for new ones. What was valuable yesterday, seems worthless today; and what was regarded as indispensable then is now thrown overboard. "Have not all the forces of Nature been tamed and subordinated to our will? Surely, it will soon be possible to subject to human interference the last of the secrets surrounding our knowledge of the origin and the decay of life! What, therefore, do we care for the past and for such things as family life, tradition, ancestry, racial up-grading, and racial ties?" Such were the views we had to listen to in this country before the advent of the National Socialist regime.

Moreover, we were asked, What is the use of proclaiming the kinship of the Germanic peoples and their sense of solidarity? All conceptions of this kind are rejected and ridiculed by the Liberalistic and Jewish-Bolshevist spokesmen. And yet, it is true that not only our own nation, but almost all the nations of Northern and Western Europe are - as the racial biologist sees it - on the brink of an abyss. The excessive hold of city life upon our civilisation and the excessive influence exercised by international finance and international intellectualism have created political and economic insecurity among the peoples. In our country, the disgraceful terms of the Versailles treaty, the material and ideal losses, the Jewish domination over everything, the currency depreciation during the inflation period, and the impoverishment of our middle classes - all these circumstances caused our economic system to break down completely and the number of unemployed to rise to seven millions. People felt disinclined to take upon themselves the responsibilities of married life; birth-control was practised to an unparalleled extent, and the German people were drifting towards utter ruin.

When Herr Hitler took over the Government in 1933, he was aware that, first of all, family life must be restored to what it was. That was indispensable if a brighter future was to be in store for the nation. On June 28th, 1933, Dr. Frick, the Minister of the Interior, announced the Government's programme in connection with its population policy. In the course of his speech he said, inter alia, that "the greatest task before the Government of the national revolution is to ensure the racial regeneration of our people and to preserve its numerical strength in the centre of Europe."

Much has been achieved since then - but much more remains to be done. Two requirements must be fulfilled in order to attain final success. First, the Government must intervene by adequate legislation; and second, each individual must regain due consciousness of his duties towards the country of his birth.

The Government, acting under Herr Hitler's direction, has done much by legislation. Trade and industry have been promoted and the unemployment situation has been improved. We have regained our internal and external liberty of action; and in addition to solving these and other important problems in the political and economic spheres, we have embarked upon a systematic campaign of practical population policy.

The nation and the race must be regarded as the pivot upon which all State activity hinges. "The nation as such," Herr Hitler has said, "is the eternal fountain from which new life is always emanating; and this fountain must be kept in a healthy state. "Hence, our struggle is concerned with the preservation of racial health and the encouragement of large-sized families. Measures aiming at the reduction of unemployment, the protection of the home soil, the provision of small holdings and settlements near the outskirts of large cities, and a suitable readjustment of our fiscal and population policies, have already been introduced; and others will follow. The results achieved, however, can only be of practical value and of a lasting character when the change of attitude is complete and makes itself felt in every branch of State activity. Moreover, there must be a uniformly directed administrative apparatus to assist in carrying out the necessary hygienic reforms.

In spite of the unsatisfactory economic and financial conditions ruling in 1933, the Ministry of the Interior succeeded in unifying the public health system of the country and in doing away with the wasteful decentralisation previously existing. By the Act passed on July 3rd, 1934, the various boards of health established by the subordinate public authorities were given over to central administration, and a new department - that for racial hygiene - was added. The new boards of health set up in every municipality or district are directed by a State appointed physician, assisted by an efficient staff. The scope of the work done by the Public Health Department has been extended by the addition to it of the Advisory Offices for Racial Culture and Heredity. Their functions are: to watch the natural growth (or otherwise) of the population, to safeguard the nation's inherited assets, and to enlighten persons intending to marry.

The progress of racial science has been very considerable in recent years; and much benefit to the community has been derived from it. Although it is not possible to influence the course of the racial development by direct methods, it can be done indirectly. Darwin explained the upward development in the animal and vegetable kingdoms by pointing out that those animals and plants which are capable of assimilating themselves to their surroundings more successfully than others are best fitted to survive in the struggle for existence and to pass their characteristic features on to their descendants. This is called "natural selection," and its opposite (in the domain of human development) is the artificial selection brought about by the influences of civilisation. The very progress of human knowledge produces an increasing amount of artificial interference with the influences that are at work naturally. The weaker elements - which, if Nature alone were at work, would soon be eliminated - are kept alive and are even specially cared for by the skill of our physicians and by the improved conditions of life. In the realm of Nature and among the uncivilised peoples, everything that is unhealthy speedily perishes. Among civilised nations, the opposite development takes place. The healthy and valuable individuals either refuse to marry or, if they do, largely practise family limitation.

During the Liberalist and Marxist regime in Germany, it was also believed that the human race could be improved by artificial means. It was thought that the characteristics thus acquired were hereditable; and this view is still largely advocated. But, we may ask, what useful purpose can be served by the constant extension of public welfare work, so long as the efforts in that direction fail to deal with the real causes of a nation's decay? It has been proved that the unhealthy traits are usually reproduced to a larger extent than the healthy ones; and Galton has already emphasised that this circumstance tends to increase the danger of racial degeneration.

We know that we cannot restore the natural conditions of life, and we do not intend to do so or to throw overboard the blessings of a higher civilisation. But as we are aware of the causes of degeneration, we can counteract the effects of an artificial environment by an artificial selection of the right kind, i.e., by promoting racial culture; and the final outcome will correspond to our intentions. If we facilitate the propagation of healthy stock by systematic selection and by the elimination of the unhealthy elements, we shall be able to improve the physical standards not, perhaps, of the present generation, but of those that will succeed us. Credit is due to the National Socialist Government for perceiving the danger of degeneration and for issuing legislation dealing with it, e.g., the Acts for the Prevention of Hereditarily Diseased Offspring, for the Restoration of Professionalism in the Public Services, for dealing with Habitual Offenders and Immoral Offences, and many others. It goes without saying that the medical activities carried out by physicians on behalf of individuals and on that of the community will continue to go on along the lines universally adopted in conformity with the researches of Koch, Lister, Pasteur, and other celebrated scientists.

It was a great achievement on the part of Robert Koch when he succeeded, many years ago, in discovering that various micro-organisms are the cause of anthrax, tuberculosis, cholera, etc. The result was that a systematic campaign against these infectious diseases was organised throughout the civilised world. Acts were passed by which the State was given the right to interfere with the private life of individuals, on the ground that such interference, although restricting individual liberty, would benefit the nation as a whole. It can hardly be denied that - in pursuance of such legislation - the State was not only entitled, but compelled, to issue regulations governing the duty of individuals to report all cases of infection, providing for the isolation of the patients concerned, and so on. The same right must therefore be claimed by the State for its activities in the wider domain of racial hygiene.

Germany has taken the lead in these endeavours by taking practical steps towards the initiation of a systematic population policy. The Advisory Offices already referred to are required, among other matters, to administer the Act for the Prevention of Hereditarily Diseased Offspring. Whenever it may be assumed, with a fair measure of probability, that a serious hereditary disease will be propagated, sterilisation may be resorted to. The scope of the Act is limited to the most important diseases, e.g., congenital imbecility or insanity, epilepsy, hereditary deafness or blindness, etc., and stringent regulations have been issued to prevent any misuse.

Special courts have been created to decide whether, in any given instance, the provisions of the Act are to be applied to it. They are composed of physicians and judges. Prior to making their decision, they carefully examine the circumstances of the case in question. It must be remembered, in this connection, that sterilisation is by no means identical with castration. It may be effected by means of X-rays or radium treatment, so that an operation is not necessarily required. The work performed by the courts is of a highly responsible nature, its ultimate object being to stamp out all hereditary diseases.

A clearly defined legal position has been created in every domain of racial biology. The interception of pregnancy for hygienic reasons - a difficult problem in every civilised country - has been dealt with in a satisfactory way by giving the necessary discretionary powers to commissions composed of medical men. Additional safeguards are provided by the Act dealing with Habitual Offenders and Immoral Offences, passed on November 24th, 1936. It empowers the ordinary courts to inflict adequate punishment upon habitual offenders and upon persons committing immoral offences against women and children.

It is obvious that the measures hitherto discussed are of a negative character only. Their chief aim is to remove the dangers that have arisen as the result of many decades of neglect. They must, of course, be supplemented by others intended to ensure a healthy offspring and the economic safeguarding of the family. Thus, steps have been taken to diminish unemployment and to protect the German soil. The Act of July 14th, 1933, providing for the improvement in the position of the rural population, has transferred to the Reich the whole domain of agricultural settlement. Similar objects are to be achieved by the Act governing hereditary farmsteads and by various laws granting tax relief to persons with large families.

The decree issued on July 1st, 1933, in pursuance of Section 5 of the Act governing the reduction of unemployment, provided for the grant of loans to persons intending to marry. Subject to certain regulations, the repayment of the money can be partly or wholly waived upon the birth of one or more children. The effect produced by this decree has been an immediate increase in the number of marriages (to more than 600,000).

Whilst not more than about 957,000 children were born in 1933, the corresponding figures for 1934 and 1935 were 1,197,000 and 1,265,000 respectively; and whilst, as already stated, the relation between the annual number of births and that of marriages was 1 to 14 in 1933, it had improved to 1 to 11 two years later.

However gratifying these improvements may be, they must not make us think that the dangers threatening the German people have now been completely overcome. Owing to the unsatisfactory economic conditions during the past few years, some 300,000 marriages had to be postponed until now. We may perhaps assume that, on an average, one child has so far resulted from each of these delayed marriages; and it remains to be seen whether second or third children will follow. In addition, the men and women born during the years of war (and therefore representing the numerically weak age classes) are now getting of marriageable age, so that there will presumably be fewer marriages and fewer births. It is a great mistake to believe that the German people has become a growing people again. Even the number of children born in 1935 is insufficient to ensure a numerical increase or even to maintain the nation's present numerical strength. Those critics, therefore, who contend that Germany's population policy is a menace to the equilibrium of Europe, fail to view the situation aright. We are surrounded by growing populations in the south and east; and it is our position as a people inhabiting the heart of Europe that is actually at stake. Even though it is true that Britain is not handicapped by such open and unprotected frontiers as is Germany, the statistics prove that the danger of a numerical decline in the near future is just as great in her case as it is in our own. The same remark, indeed, applies to other North and West European nations.

The decree providing for the grant of loans to persons intending to marry laid it down that applicants had to undergo a medical examination in order to ascertain that they were not suffering from some hereditary physical or mental disease detrimental to the nation's health. Apart from this provision, no similar evidence was demanded - until recently - in connection with the contraction of marriages, and even the diseases referred to did not constitute an obstacle to marriage. It is true that in Prussia and elsewhere, the registrar would advise the young people to interchange certificates of health; but there was no need for them to follow that advice. Since then, however, an Act has been passed (on October 18th, 1935) which makes it possible to prevent marriages that would be undesirable for reasons of racial health, thus protecting from untold misery and suffering not only the persons intending to marry, but also any possible offspring as well as the whole community.

In the course of the past thousand years or so, people had quite forgotten that they are the result of heredity and environment. Marriages, therefore, were frequently brought about by purely external reasons, such as the desire for a dowry, for social preferment, etc. Men of good physique did not hesitate to marry girls suffering from grave physical or mental defects; and healthy girls often regarded it as a work of Christian charity to choose for their partner in life a sick and unhealthy man for whom they could care and to whose needs they could administer.

No one seemed to mind that marriages thus contracted would tend to produce an offspring liable to the same grave defects. A mistaken sense of charity prompted people to commit acts of ruthless cruelty towards those who - being racially inferior or suffering from an incurable disease - furnished visible evidence of "the sin against the race." Statistical evidence of the great danger to which such an attitude must lead is by no means lacking. Up to now people have failed to see that the ultimate outcome of this development must be the decay and the utter ruin of our civilisation. They are still governed by too strong a faith in the doctrines with which they were conversant throughout their lives, without realising all their implications. It was therefore an event of the utmost historical importance when the National Socialist Government proceeded to enact the various legislative measures by which the evil could be tackled at its root.

The racial purity of a nation and its freedom from hereditary disease are just as closely related to one another as body and soul. The former is mainly concerned with the preservation of that which is good and healthy. To ensure the latter, the Act prohibiting marriages between persons suffering from hereditary disease makes it incumbent upon registrars to refuse a marriage licence if one or other of the following conditions obtains:

(a) If either the man or the woman is suffering from an infectious disease likely to inflict grave injury upon the other party or their issue.

(b) If either party is under restraint or tutelage.

(c) If either party, although not under restraint, is yet suffering from a mental disability which makes it undesirable in the national interest that he or she should marry.

(d) If either party is suffering from one of the congenital diseases specified in the Act governing the Prevention of Hereditarily Diseased Offspring. Clause (d) will not be considered an obstacle to marriage if the other party is sterile.

Thus, the contraction of a marriage can now be legally prohibited if its consummation would be certain to cause grave damage to the parties concerned. In drawing up these regulations, the legislator has wisely limited the scope of his interference to a minimum and has carefully defined their exact meaning. Even the most uncompromising opponents of National Socialism will probably admit that the prohibitions cover those circumstances only in which a citizen conscious of his responsibilities would abstain from marrying in any case. Foreign critics, indeed, have not found fault with any of them, well knowing that the propagation of infectious diseases and mental defects is bound to undermine the health of any nation.

Responsible parents have always felt that it is advisable to consult a physician before any of their children contract a marriage. It is therefore in harmony with this feeling that the issuance of a certificate of fitness to marry is described, in one of the new Acts, as one of the functions of the offices giving advice to persons intending to marry. A medical examination is compulsory upon all candidates for such a certificate. In order to be thus examined, they may either apply to a private medical practitioner or to the physicians appointed by the boards of health. The certificate itself will always be issued by the board of health within whose district the fiancee is domiciled. For the present, it has been provided that the certificate will only be demanded whenever the registrar or the board of health has reason to assume that one of the obstacles to marriage specified above applies to the case in question. Applicants are not compelled to produce any evidence on that point; but if they decline to give the information requested by the board, the latter will be unable to issue a certificate.

In the event of the medical examination being effected by a private medical practitioner, no charge will be made if the candidate is insured with an officially recognised sickness insurance society, either directly or indirectly, or if the cost of any illness he or she might contract would be payable by a public-welfare institution. Persons claiming this privilege must produce the necessary evidence. If the certificate is refused on the ground that one or other of the obstacles to marriage already referred to applies to the case, the applicant may appeal to one of the competent courts specially established to deal with matters of racial hygiene. If he or she is dissatisfied with the decision, a second appeal may be made (within fourteen days) to a superior court of like character, the decision of which will be final. Whenever recourse is had to this procedure, the demand for a certificate to marry may be waived. There are also cases in which the appeal against the decision of the board of health can only be lodged with an administrative official, such as, for instance, the Government President of the district (in so far as Prussia is concerned). These superior authorities may, in special instances, grant exemption from the ordinary rules. Lastly, there are certain cases in which the Minister of the Interior may be appealed to, whose decision will then be final.

All the biological information collected will be entered in special registers, so that - after the lapse of ten years or so - we shall have at our disposal an almost complete record of the state of our nation's racial health. When that time has come, the boards of health will be able to supply full hygienic details of every individual and every family in the country.

As regards actual practice, the prohibitions to marry will only be issued in a relatively small number of cases. Normally, the certificate will be drawn up by a private medical practitioner. If he is of the opinion that both applicants-though apparently in good health - are of an unhealthy hereditary disposition, he will urge them to abstain from marrying, but it rests with them whether they will follow his advice or reject it.

All competent and unbiased critics will presumably agree that the legislation governing racial hygiene cannot but be of great benefit to the national development. It is quite true that many of the measures now introduced are disliked because of the extent to which they may be thought to interfere with individual liberty; but after the lapse of a few decades they will probably be regarded, not only in Germany, but also elsewhere, as matters concerning which disagreement is no longer possible.

Marriages detrimental to the racial purity of the German stock have been made illegal by the Nuremberg Law for the Protection of the German Race and German Honour (September 15th, 1935). In the preamble, a concise statement is given of the objects aimed at by the National Socialist Government in the domain of racial policy. It begins as follows:

Fully convinced that the purity of the German stock is indispensable to the continued existence of the German nation and animated by the inflexible determination to safeguard its existence for all times, the Reichstag has unanimously resolved upon the following law.

The law prohibits all marriages between Jews and any German nationals who are of German stock or of kindred ancestry. Any marriages contracted abroad in order to evade this prohibition are illegal. Proceedings to have them annulled can only be instituted by the public prosecutor. The same prohibition applies to illicit sexual intercourse between the persons named. Any infringement of the law will be punished. It stands to reason, however, that all these measures - if isolated - will still fail in their objective unless steps are also taken to protect the vital rights of all healthy families by due recognition of their economic needs.

The political and social future of our country can only be definitely safeguarded on condition that the middle classes, the employees and the workers have their proper share in the national assets. The State is required to make it possible for all citizens to carry out their appointed tasks and to become part-owners of the means of production. Economic and social legislation will be needed to enable prolific families to purchase the means of subsistence. This can only be achieved by an adjustment of the burdens each family has to carry; and this, in turn, can be brought about by tax remission, by educational assistance, or other measures.

The problem we have to solve is this: How can we provide financial aid to all prolific and biologically healthy families by way of uniform and comprehensive action? It is evident that such assistance - if it is to benefit racial health - must be graded according to the income of the persons concerned. Its precise form will therefore vary, although the general principle underlying it will be the same. In the upper middle classes, the object aimed at may be attained by tax reform; those who are employed in the public services may have their salaries increased; the masses of workers and employees in private undertakings may be assisted by creating a "national family adjustment fund," whilst an altogether different method may have to be adopted in connection with the farming community, handicraftsmen, and others. In no case will this involve additional taxation. All that will happen will be a re-distribution of incomes in conformity with the principles of a sound population policy. Owing to the economic difficulties caused by the Versailles Treaty and the incompetency of previous governments, it has been impossible so far to provide the adjustment fund referred to. Its creation, however, is a vitally important necessity, which must overrule all other considerations, even though it may involve increased social charges for families with few children or no children at all. This necessity can now be explained to workers and employees far more convincingly than could have been done in the past; and there is no doubt that they will grasp its significance. If we succeed in convincing all classes of the vital importance of this task, they will continue to be content with the present modest level of the provision made against the vicissitudes of life, because, in doing so, they will help to attain the higher aims before us, viz., the maintenance of our national existence and the safeguarding of our national future.

The conviction must become universal that the problems in the domain of our population policy cannot be solved unless we have the courage to adjust the whole of our financial, social and economic policy to the principles already set forth. We can no longer carry on social policy in this country without, at the same time, combating unemployment and carrying on a healthy population policy. Unemployment, however, can only be definitely overcome if we succeed in finding a satisfactory solution of the problem concerning the position of women and in safeguarding the vital rights of the family.

The German nation has now realised, just before it was too late, that a breach with its past and a neglect of its racial ideals is bound to inflict grave injury upon everyone. Houston Stewart Chamberlain has somewhere referred to the nineteenth century as "the age of irreverence," thus foreseeing the development that took place during the past thirty years. A man's actions are not determined, in the last resort, by his education, his intelligence or his surroundings, but by the racial traits bequeathed to him by his remote ancestors. Just as a nation's past history can be a source of strength to it, the history of our family can be an inspiration to us throughout our lives. A study of it can teach us where our ancestors came from. What work they were doing, what was their worth or worthlessness, and what characteristics they may have passed on to us.

When every individual realises that he is only a link in the long chain that connects him with his ancestors and that he has the same obligations towards the future as they had, it will be time to dismiss our apprehensions regarding the continued existence of our people. Thus, it will always be necessary to cultivate the family sense. Women, especially, must again become the custodians of the family traditions. It is therefore very gratifying to see that the various women's organisations make it their special business to teach young girls to be conscious of their responsibilities, just as the corresponding men's organisations endeavour to foster the same spirit in men and youths.

The increased attention given by Germany to racial hygiene has resulted in a widening of the scope covered by the activities of the public health authorities. Numerous foreign scientists and also foreign nations are prepared to follow the lead thus given by us. It is not intended to replace the existing system of public hygienic services by a different one, but rather to supplement the one by the other. The work already done to combat disease will be continued as usual, in close collaboration with medical science. The introduction of a practical system of biological and racial culture, however, is certain to increase the public's appreciation of its duties towards the family and towards future generations, and will therefore raise the physical and intellectual standards of our people. Beyond that, it strengthens our desire for the preservation of peace.

For all these reasons we consider it our duty to direct the attention of the European nations, and of the white race in general, towards the dangers threatening our common civilisation from Russia in the east and from Africa - by way of large armies composed of races of non European stock specially trained by France in the south.

If there were another war, valuable national assets would be destroyed not only at the front, but also at home. Thus, racial hygiene and war (to quote Professor Ploetz) will always be irreconcilable enemies. The Chancellor wants peace not only for his own country's sake, but also because a European war would be the end of the white races and of white civilisation. Not only Central Europe, but France, Italy and Great Britain also, would perish, whilst Bolshevism would be the real victor.

I firmly believe that the recognition of this danger will bring the highly civilised nations closer together and will strengthen the feeling of solidarity.

SECTION THREE

NATIONAL SOCIALIST
RACIAL THOUGHT

Dr. Walter Gross

Head of the Reich Bureau for Enlightenment
on Population Policy and Racial Welfare

OF all the measures introduced in the new Germany those bearing on National Socialist racial policy caused the greatest stir internationally, for here was a State setting its feet upon paths hitherto almost untrodden and leading through untouched preserves, whose aims were in many respects liable to clash with established Liberal views. Relevant legislation served to corroborate and achieve these aims and it was no wonder, therefore, that - in the beginning at least - this particular phase of National Socialist reconstruction met with universal misunderstanding and prejudice. We are happy meanwhile to be able to discern that other nations have come to realise that Germany is, indeed, taking to new paths, but they are right ones and are necessary and, more than that, Germany is in many respects blazing a trail for others; mention need only be made of our law for the prevention of the transmission of hereditary diseases (Sterilisation Law) which has been followed in Norway, Sweden, Denmark and Finland by similar laws or draft proposals. However, no one will wholly understand or sympathise with our legislation who is not wholly familiar with the fundamental change in the philosophical conception of life which has come with National Socialism in the light of history.

Whereas formerly, and more especially under the powerful influence of Marxist teachings, the development and decline of States and civilisations was attributed to economic or purely political causes, we see today the determining role played by the human being in sustaining and shaping economy, the State, culture, politics, art and intellectual thought. We have come to feel that the protection and preservation of the people who, after all, are originally responsible for the achievements of the State and culture, is the chief factor in retaining these achievements; for good blood and the strength that comes from good blood is given a people only once and if allowed to degenerate cannot be regenerated as one would rebuild a city or restore devastated lands. Thus, wise statesmanship will place the preservation of the biological, that is, racial energy of its people before its political and economic concerns. The endless series of past empires and civilisations which have flourished and declined forcefully remind us how inexorable are the consequences of ignoring this truth.

History and the study of the science of population show that there are three biological stages which inevitably lead to the destruction of the vitality of a people and with it the destruction of the foundations of the State and culture as such. These three stages are:

- A decreasing population
- An increase of the hereditary unfit
- The promiscuous mingling of races

In these respects, Germany's position in 1933 was alarming. A declining birth-rate among the fitter inhabitants and unrestrained propagation among the hereditarily unfit, the mentally deficient, imbeciles and hereditary criminals, etc., had led, for instance, to a state of affairs in which the increase of the healthier section of the population in the past 70 years was only 50%, while the unhealthy and, in fact, those only fit to live in asylums, had multiplied ninefold in the same time, or 450%. The care of the latter costs the working population of Germany the not inconsiderable sum of 1 billion reichsmarks yearly, while the entire administrative costs of the Reich, Provinces and Communes amount to 713 million reichsmarks. It was, therefore, an act of self-preservation which caused the National Socialist State to promulgate the Law to prevent the transmission of hereditary disease. It was a measure taken in self-defence and much more besides. For a large portion of the hereditary unfit had brought children into the world in ignorance of the consequences of their own afflictions, and many - those still possessed of a sense of responsibility - were horrified at seeing the "sins of the fathers" visited upon their children. To this unfortunate category the National Socialist State lends a helping hand in freeing them from possible mental torment. Sterilisation relieves their conscience of the frightful burden of causing further pain and suffering to innocent beings.

It is frequently claimed abroad in circles hostile to Germany that the politically undesirable are hauled up for sterilisation. Anyone versed in German Law and the thoroughness and precautions attendant on the whole procedure knows full well the absurdity of such allegations and that no one can be sterilised simply on request or as a result of political pressure. The law for the prevention of the transmission of hereditary disease is only applicable in acknowledged cases of physical and mental deficiency such as congenital idiocy, schizophrenia, manic-depressive insanity, hereditary epilepsy, chronic St. Vitus dance, hereditary blindness, deafness and serious bodily defects; in addition, it applies to chronic inebriates. The procedure in regard to the act of sterilisation can take place upon application being lodged with the special Court of Heredity by the person concerned, his relatives, a local physician or such official persons as are connected with matters of public health. The competent Court, which is composed of an officiating judge, a medical officer and a doctor, decides whether sterilisation is called for or not. If the applicant or person under consideration does not agree with the decision of the Court, an appeal may be lodged with the Higher Court which has a similar composition as the Lower Court, although the individuals are never the same. The decision of the Court of Appeal is final. Even then the operation may be avoided by taking life-long sojourn - or at least for as long as the faculty of procreation exists - in a private home, provided such sojourn entails no costs for the Government. This clause was included in order that possible adherents of the Catholic faith who might have conscientious objections on the grounds of the Papal encyclical be given the opportunity of observing their religious tenets at all costs.

These measures of the National Socialist State, despite their broadmindedness, have been attacked mainly for political or dogmatic reasons. Such criticism is based on a number of objections which appear unfounded and extravagant. They may be summarised in three groups.

The first arises purely from the individualist standpoint which resents any intrusion into the life of the individual. According to its advocates, the individual has the right to be without children if he prefers or, despite obvious hereditary afflictions, procreate at will, or indeed, by transcending all frontiers and racial barriers, to contract marriage to his own taste. Fundamentally, that is, any restriction on the life of the individual demanded by the collective interests of the community is categorically rejected. Obviously, such an attitude must be deplored in every State since, if applied in all spheres, it would render communal and State institutions, both economic and cultural, impossible.

Civilisation is only possible through the individual becoming part of the whole and just as collective authority in the interests of all limits the egoism of the individual by, say, taxation laws or measures to combat epidemics, etc., it similarly has the right to implement such measures for the benefit of the community as are scientifically proved expedient in the way of population policy or eugenics. The need for such action prevailed in Germany.

The second set of objections is mainly based on humanitarian grounds. It is argued, for instance, that the act of sterilisation represents such a weighty sacrifice for the person concerned that society should only accept it if made voluntarily. But it is not humane that among civilised peoples the standard of living of that section of the population which is fit and able to work is lowered by burdening it with the excessive levies necessary for the maintenance of and keeping within its midst the hereditarily diseased who, despite these heavy costs, can never be healed of their ailments. After all, the healthy members of the race are also entitled to a share of compassion and humane considerations.

Nor is it justifiable to argue that sterilisation will not do away with the possible recurrence of similar cases. In arguing thus one might just as well refrain from putting out a fire because another might happen to break out elsewhere at some other time. Incidentally, sterilisation is and remains a humane duty to the individual. How great is the mental agony of a person suffering from some hereditary disease in the pitiful knowledge that not only he himself is incurable but that his children frequently begotten in ignorance of the complications of his own trouble, are doomed to a similar or worse fate. Timely sterilisation rids the hereditarily unfit of such mental torment.

Other objectors insist that the operation should only be performed with the consent of the individual. It is foolish, however, to want acquiescence from a human being who has no command over his morbid instincts or of one who is to be prevented from procreation for the very reason that he is suffering from some mental debility.

Everywhere in organised society, justice and morals are bound to interfere with personal liberty to a greater or lesser extent, even with that of the healthy individual. If an epidemic breaks out endangering the welfare of the community everyone, whether he wants to or not, must be vaccinated; similarly, just as the doctor takes preventive measures on this score, the specialist in the sphere of hereditary transmission, both medical and legal, backed by the knowledge of biological necessities must, if called upon, take upon his shoulders the responsibility which the individual patient is unable to bear.

A third and last group fears lest the suggestion of a biological stratification of society or the racial classification of humanity should lead to serious conflicts. As to this, it may be said that racial peculiarities are natural and any social or human system of differentiation will last only so long as it is in harmony with natural phenomena. Why, the very knowledge and acknowledgment of the social claims of the race, of racial hygiene, and its practical application, is calculated to limit, even prevent wars. For war, even if successful, signifies biologically an irretrievable loss of the best hereditary tendencies. Since National Socialist Germany frankly thinks along biological lines she wants nothing but peace. The National Socialist idea of State is the most peaceful conceivable, for it of all others sees its duty in the preservation of the pure racial continuity of its people.

Nothing but sheer want of sense could accuse the new Germany of hankering after war, for we are only too well aware what irreparable damage has been done and how heavy has been the toll taken of our people in the way of hereditary values through centuries of retrogressive selection, declining birth-rate and, finally, through the frightful decimation of the flower of our manhood in the War. If we need peace and quiet for the political and economic regeneration of our people tried almost beyond endurance, we need it doubly so to effect the reconstruction and vital racial aspirations of our population policy directed along biological lines, for nothing could be more disastrous than war with its ruthless destruction of the best and consequent indirect preferential selection of the less valuable.

Even a victorious war is biologically a loss. The true statesman is aware of this and will never take to the sword except as a last necessity. Here it becomes manifest that the national-racial principle - contrary to the aims maliciously attributed to it - is in itself the surest guarantee for a policy fundamentally peaceful.

Most open to misinterpretation are National Socialist views on the relations between the various races of the world. It has been questioned whether the fundamental racial principles of the new world theory must not breed condescension, even contempt of people of different race. Quite the contrary; these very principles offer the very best guarantee for mutual tolerance and for the peaceful co-operation of all.

We appreciate the fact that those of another race are different from us. This scientific truth is the basis, the justification and, at the same time, the obligation of every racial policy without which a restoration of Europe in our day is no longer practicable. Whether that other race is "better" or "worse" is not possible for us to judge. For this would demand that we transcend our own racial limitations for the duration of the verdict and take on a superhuman, even divine, attitude from which alone an "impersonal" verdict could be formed on the value or lack of such of the many living forms of inexhaustible Nature. But we of all people are too conscious of the inseparable ties of the blood and our own race to attempt to aspire to such an ultra-racial standpoint, even in the abstract.

History, science and life itself tell us in a thousand ways that the human beings inhabiting the earth are anything but alike; that, moreover, the greater races are not only physically but especially spiritually and intellectually different from each other. Yesterday one passed this fact by, and in attempting to unify political, economic, cultural and religious standards for all nations of the earth, one was sinning against Nature, violating the natural attributes of various racial and national groups for the sake of a false principle. Today we bow to the racial differences existing in the world. We want every type of being to find that form of self-expression most fitted to its own particular requirements.

The racial principles of National Socialism are, therefore, the surest guarantee for respecting the integrity of other nations. It is incompatible with our ideas to think of incorporating other nationalities in a Germany built up as a result of conquests, as they would always remain - because of their alien blood and spirit - a foreign body within the German State. Such foolhardy thoughts may be indulged in by a world which has as its goal economic power or purely territorial expansion of its frontiers, but never by a statesman thinking along organic, racial lines whose main care is the preservation of the greatness and along with it the essential unity of his people held together by the ties of blood relationship.

For this reason, we have nothing in common with chauvinism and imperialism because we would extend to other races peopling the earth the same privileges we claim for ourselves: the right to fashion our lives and our own particular world according to the requirements of our own nature.

And if National Socialism would wish to see the unrestricted mixing of blood avoided for the individual, there is nothing in this to suggest contempt. After all, we Germans ourselves, viewed ethnologically, are a mixture. The National Socialist demand is only that the claims of the blood and the laws of biology should be more closely observed in future.

Here again our standpoint is not so very far removed from that of other people with a sound mental outlook. The American Immigration Laws, for instance, are based on definite racial discrimination. The Europeans and the inhabitants of India, the Pacific Islands, etc., have instinctively held aloof from a mingling of the blood, and both sides genuinely regard any transgression as very bad form. Nevertheless, this natural attitude in no way detracts from the possibility of close co-operation and friendly intercourse. And, speaking on behalf of the new Germany, let me once more emphasise:

We do not wish our people to intermarry with those of alien race since through such mingling of the blood the best and characteristic qualities of both races are lost. But we will always have a ready welcome for any guests who wish to visit us whether of kindred or foreign civilisation, and our racial views only lead us to a fuller appreciation of their essential peculiarities in the same way as we would want our own peculiarities respected.

On the basis of this reasoning, the National Socialist State was bound to object to the imperialistic designs of the Jewish people on German soil. Thus it is purely an internal concern of the German people who could no longer tolerate the domination - a result of political errors in the past - of an alien race having neither sympathy nor understanding for them. During the political regimes of the past the Jews had managed to obtain an increasing hold on politics, art, culture and commerce. Since 1910, as many as 13 of them had immigrated every day into Germany from the East. Thus Berlin had :

Per Centage Jewish	Occupation
32.2 %	Chemists
47.9 %	Doctors
50.2 %	Lawyers
8.5 %	Newspaper Editors
14.2 %	Producers and Stage Managers
37.5 %	Dentists

No people on earth with a vestige of pride in itself and its national honour will be willing to put up with such domination of the key professions by members of a completely alien race. At the same time, the Jews were a determining factor in those political parties which were against any reconstruction on national lines. As to the so-called State Party, for instance, 28.6% of its parliamentary members were Jews, and in the Social Democratic Party the figure was 11.9% It is of some political significance that the founders of the German Communist Party, a branch of the Moscow Comintern, that destructive force, were Karl Liebknecht and Rosa Luxemburg, both Jews.

This predominance of alien influence foreign to the German nature in politics, science and things cultural, provided the objective for the law for the restoration of professionalism in the Civil Service and what has since come to be known as the Nuremberg Laws. The Jews in Germany constitute a group of aliens who can expect to enjoy the hospitality of the country just like the members of other races. But no Frenchman would wish to have his leading offices of State occupied by Englishmen, and no Englishman would want to see the key positions in the politics, art and culture of his country occupied by, say, Japanese.

Who then can reasonably object to the Germans removing the Jews from the prominent positions in their country? As to the higher percentage of crime which is an additional factor of importance in judging the Jewish question in Germany, it may be mentioned that the majority are immigrants from Eastern Europe, whose cultural and moral ideas could never be in harmony with those of the German people. The Nuremberg Laws, therefore, exclude members of the Jewish race from obtaining Reich citizenship. Persons of mixed parentage - some 300,000 in all - can become citizens of the Reich, but are excluded from holding office in the Civil Service, the Army and the medical and legal professions.

Exemptions are possible as provided for in the Laws. The regulation forbidding marriage between a Jew and a German and making illicit intercourse liable to punishment was designed primarily with a view to preventing the birth of further individuals of mixed blood whose fate is a sorry one everywhere in the world, because they are neither one thing nor the other. For those already in existence a distinction is made between those having two Jewish grandparents and those with only one. The former require the approval of the authorities for contracting marriage with someone of German or allied blood. The latter may not marry a Jew or a member of the former category.

They may only marry people of German blood and their children are exempt from the restrictive regulations (Army Laws and the Law for the restoration of professionalism in the Civil Service, etc.). In short, their children become full members of the German community.

These measures were necessary because we realised that a nation or a people can only preserve its culture and its intellectual individuality by keeping the blood pure. It has been said that "every race is a divine inspiration" - a shaft incidentally aimed at the racial policy. We would rejoin, however, "just because every race is a divine inspiration, the foremost task of civilisation is to keep that inspiration pure and reject the least contribution towards detracting from its purity."

SECTION FOUR

THE ADMINISTRATION OF JUSTICE

Dr. Franz Gurtner

Reich Minister of Justice

IT is sometimes said, even by critics usually endeavouring to be objective in their judgments, that National Socialism has abolished law in Germany and has substituted arbitrariness in its place. Those who hold that view must be completely ignorant of the principles maintained by National Socialism and of the conditions actually existing in Germany. The new German State is based upon the axiom that law is one of the main pillars supporting the solidarity of the nation and the political structure representing it. More than that, a conception of law deeply rooted in the nation's life and recognised as binding by every citizen is the foundation of the country's entire civilisation.

Seeing that law and justice are at the root of every activity carried on in the new Germany, it follows that the National Socialist State is a constitutional State in the best sense of the term. That term, however, must not be interpreted in accordance with the doctrine which demands that the interests of the individual must be regarded as the principal subject-matter of all legislation and that a comprehensive system of controls must be established to protect the individual against an excess of interference on the part of the State. That doctrine is no longer upheld in Germany. National Socialism looks upon the community of the nation as an organisation which has its own rights and duties and whose interests come before those of the individual.

When we speak of the nation, we do not confine ourselves to the generation to which we happen to belong, but extend that term so as to comprise the sum total of the generations that have preceded us and those that will succeed us. This view has found expression in the National Socialist doctrine asserting that "the needs of the commonwealth take precedence of those of the individual." It dominates National Socialist policy, and its natural corollary is that the rights of the individual must be subordinated to those of the community. The protection enjoyed by individuals is not based on the assumption that their particular rights are sacrosanct and inviolable, but rather on the fact that all of them are regarded as valuable members of the national community, and therefore deserve protection. The reason, therefore, why the National Socialist State can justly claim to be called a constitutional State is that its laws are intended to promote the interests of the community, that - in pursuance of the confidence that forms a connecting link between the rulers and the ruled - every citizen can rest assured that his claim to justice will be satisfied, and that everyone who loyally fulfils his duties towards the community can look forward to receiving an equal measure of loyalty from the organs of the State. The political and economic development of the past four years has convincingly shown that we are doing our utmost to provide a secure basis of existence for everyone. Everywhere, waste land is turned into productive soil. Millions of citizens who had been haunted by the spectre of unemployment for months and even years, have been supplied with work. Unceasing endeavours are made by the National Socialist Government to strengthen the defence forces of the country and thus to safeguard the life and work of every citizen.

The National Socialist ideas on justice differ fundamentally from those prevailing under the preceding regime. Their translation into practice is an arduous task, because it involves a twofold necessity. First, a large amount of new legislation has to be passed; and secondly, the persons who are to administer justice in conformity with the new spirit have to be educated for their work. Much has been done in both respects, but more remains to be done. Nevertheless, the achievements of the past three years sufficiently indicate the line that has been followed.

A correct appreciation of the changes already effected would be impossible if we were to ignore an event of truly historical importance. I refer to the unification of German law and German jurisprudence. For centuries, there had been no such thing as uniform German law. Each federal State had its own legal system, its own courts of law and its own legal authorities; and although an outward appearance of unity had gradually been established, to a limited extent, by certain acts of national legislation, the law continued to be administered in the name of the individual States, and not in that of the Reich. For many years, that state of things had been the subject of much regret on the part of many Germans, but a radical change proved unworkable because each State jealously guarded its special rights and privileges. National Socialism, among many other matters, stands for a unified Reich and for a uniform legal system. It does not allow obsolete privileges to block the road to progress and has therefore boldly abolished them. All the States have been made subordinate to the superior authority of the Reich. In that way, the separate judicial systems have been done away with, and all German courts now administer justice in the name of the Reich. The practical importance of this great change - the inauguration of which dates from April 2nd, 1935 - cannot be overestimated. The administration of justice and the enactment of new laws are now vested in one single hand, viz., in that of the Reich Minister of Justice. The experience gained by the courts in the course of their everyday work can now be made directly accessible to the superior authorities and can thus be utilised for purposes of legislation. Moreover, the uniform organisation of all juridical authorities throughout the country renders it possible to acquaint all of them with the intentions of the legislator without having recourse to roundabout methods. To the general public, the old system was a source of endless vexation and difficulty owing to its great diversity; but all these difficulties have now disappeared. It is indeed no exaggeration when we say that by unifying the administration of justice throughout the country, a century-old longing of the German people has been fulfilled.

It goes without saying that the legal position of the judges has not been affected in any way by this great change. In his speech to the Reichstag on March 23rd, 1933, the Leader and Chancellor solemnly affirmed their independent and irremovable status; and similar declarations have been repeatedly made since then. Such independence has always been an integral part of German thought and feeling and is inseparably connected with our views on a constitutional State. In National Socialist Germany, the office of judge is outside the domain of the authority wielded by the State and is thus different from all other offices held under the Government. This does not alter the fact, however, that the exercise of the judicial functions is now undergoing a change. Unlike the common law of England, German law is - for the most part - a form of "written" law. The judge is required to make his decision by reference to the particular paragraph of the code that deals with the case before him. In the past, this necessity often had as a result that the judgments given - although they conformed to the letter of the law - failed to pay adequate regard to the facts of real life. The National Socialist State does not intend to absolve judges from the necessity referred to, but expects from them that they will interpret the wording of the law in accordance with the underlying principles, and that they will apply these principles in such a manner as to do justice to the vital needs of the German people. To enable the judge to satisfy this demand, he must be closely and permanently associated with the spirit that pervades the new Germany and of which he is to be the living embodiment. Only then will he be in a position to give voice to the faith of the whole nation in the supremacy of the law. This, at least, is our ideal of what a judge should be. It is the aim before us in training young men for the office of judge. We have accordingly reorganised that training and trust that it will not only furnish students of law with the necessary professional knowledge, but will also familiarise them with the foundations of the nation's racial life, so that they can exercise their high office in the sense just indicated.

Another important factor in connection with the administration of justice in the National Socialist State is the lawyer. We expect of him that he looks upon it as his duty not only to represent the personal interests of his clients, but also those of the whole nation, so that true justice may be vindicated. German lawyers have fulfilled this expectation, and have gained the confidence of the nation and its courts to an extent formerly not always existing. The underground influence of unqualified advisers on legal matters has been largely checked by the National Socialist Government. Nobody is allowed to give legal advice in a professional capacity unless he is in possession of a Government licence; and such licence can only be obtained by those who have the necessary qualifications as laid down by law.

Criminal law and the methods of criminal procedure have undergone very considerable changes compared with the conditions existing before 1933.

It had become more and more customary during the post-war period to pay excessive attention to the personality of the criminal, to discover extenuating circumstances explaining his action, and to ignore the interests of the community and those of the injured. Consequently, a state of things had grown up in some parts of the country under which the infliction of the standard punishments prescribed by the law was almost the exception, whilst the application of extenuating circumstances or even a free pardon became almost the rule. In the prisons and penitentiaries, too, excessive mildness prevailed, and the life of the prisoners was made far too comfortable. The constant increase in convictions prior to 1933 proves that this system did not tend to add to the efficiency of the fight against the prevalence of crime. A knowledge of these conditions is necessary if we wish to adequately appreciate the work achieved by National Socialism. The Government desires to give effective protection to the community as well as to the individual against the activities of the criminal element and has taken suitable steps to ensure that chief attention shall be paid to the interests of the community when the penalties to be inflicted are fixed. It is considered unlikely that any system of education will produce satisfactory results in so far as adult criminals are concerned, and the sentences pronounced are therefore made sufficiently heavy to deter criminals from committing further crimes. In addition, due reparation is to be made for the moral injury done to the community by every act of crime.

Under the present system of executing the sentences, the deterrent influence of the punishment receives once more the recognition it deserves. As it is our aim to afford the largest possible measure of protection to the community, we have created special facilities for the judge that will enable him to inflict additional penalties upon those criminals who may be reasonably regarded as permanent dangers to the community. The judge is now in a position to order that habitual criminals shall be kept in custody after they have served their sentence. Persons who regularly misuse their trade or profession for the commission of crimes can be deprived of the right to exercise that trade or profession. Finally, persons who have proved to be habitual offenders against morality can be sterilised by order of the judge.

The methods of criminal procedure have been expedited as much as possible. Steps have also been taken to make it difficult or impossible for the accused to prolong the course of procedure for the purpose of adding to the difficulty of ascertaining the truth. No restrictions, however, have been placed upon the right of the accused to be represented by counsel. Thanks to these measures we have found it possible in many cases, e.g., offences against traffic regulations, acts of violence, etc., to make the punishment follow the crime without the least avoidable delay. I need not point out that this system has materially enhanced the respect for the law and for those who administer it and that it has increased the general feeling of security.

The process of transformation through which the German people are passing at the present juncture is one of historical significance. It is but natural that any attempts made to obstruct that process deserve particular attention. Special tribunals have therefore been created to deal with them. These, however, have no exceptional powers conferred upon them, but are ordinary courts like all others set up by our law. High treason and similar crimes go before the People's Tribunal, which is one of the high courts of the country. It is composed of professional as well as experienced lay judges, these latter having the same judicial powers as their professional colleagues. Like all other German courts, the People's Tribunal and the judges composing it are of independent status. The procedure to be applied is the same as that applied to all other criminal cases, and the accused has the right to make use of all the possibilities ordinarily available for his defence.

As regards its material aspect, too, criminal law has undergone a number of important modifications during the past three years, but space forbids their description in detail. I would like, however, to direct attention to a clause added to the criminal code by the Law passed June 28th, 1935, as it is of especial importance. It abolishes the maxim according to which no offence can be punished unless it is specifically mentioned in the existing code, and enables the judge to inflict punishment for acts which - although not thus specifically mentioned - are yet of such a nature as to demand punishment in pursuance of the general tenor of the law and in accordance with healthy national sentiment. Thus, the "written" law has ceased to be the sole source of our knowledge of right and wrong, although it will continue to be the principal source. The legislator realised the impossibility of making the provisions of "written" law so comprehensive as to cover all conditions actually met with, and thus adopted a principle with which the British people have been familiar from time immemorial, as only a small part of English law is "written." By far the greater part of it is derived from ancient usage and is known as "common law."

In our country, the question of right or wrong used to be exclusively decided in conformity with the wording of the law; but this formal view has now been replaced by the material one, according to which any act detrimental to the interests of the community or conflicting with them is liable to punishment. We believe that the respect for the law will become all the greater the more we absolve the judge from the necessity of taking the letter of the law for his guide and the more we enable him to base his decisions upon its living spirit.

I can only make brief reference to the innovations incorporated in our civil law and the procedure to be followed in civil cases. Although no fundamental changes can be recorded so far in these domains, certain defects have already been eliminated from them. Thus, the National

Socialist State has taken care to ensure that all unnecessary delay shall be avoided and that the claims of the parties are to be settled as speedily as possible. Certain obsolete formalities in connection with the swearing-in of the litigants have been abolished and a more elastic system - not unlike the method used in England - has been introduced instead. Special attention has also been paid to forced sales. Economic developments made it necessary to place restrictions upon the rigorous application of the rules governing such sales whenever it would ruin the economic existence of the debtor and damage the interests of the community. In every case, however, efforts are made to arrive at a fair adjustment of the conflicting interests of creditors and debtors.

Among the numerous laws promulgated during the past three years in the domains of civil and economic legislation there are a few that deserve special mention. Thus, the rights individual owners of real estate might have in respect of adjoining property, have suffered a certain curtailment in favour of institutions that are of particular importance to the community. As to patent legislation, the protection granted to the inventor has been extended and his professional honour has been specially recognised. On the other hand, his rights can be restricted (against payment of compensation) whenever this is necessary for the public good.

Marriage licences can be refused when it is evident that the parties have no real intention to contract marriage in the usual way, but merely desire to secure some external advantage that might be derived from marrying. Adoption is prohibited whenever it is merely intended to serve some trivial purpose, e.g., the right to a fine-sounding name, etc.

By way of conclusion, I should like to mention two instances aptly illustrating the responsibility which the law feels it owes to the new Germany. Thus, a standard form of lease agreement has been drawn up, with the collaboration of the Ministry of Justice, by the organisations representing landlords and tenants respectively. Its terms embody a fair adjustment of the interests of both sides and are not merely such as to serve exclusively those of the economically stronger party. The other instance concerns an arrangement which we call, "Legal Guidance for the People." Those administering the law are not only anxious to repair the damage done by breaking it, but also to prevent it from being broken at all, whenever this is possible. To that end, the experience gained by the courts from day to day is collected and made available to the whole people.

The foregoing account shows that - in the administration of the law as in other matters - the National Socialist Government is determined to protect the peaceful development of the German nation and to promote it to the best of its ability.

SECTION FIVE

THE PLACE OF WOMEN IN THE NEW GERMANY

Frau Gertrud Scholtz-Klink

Reich Women's Leader

WHEN National Socialism became the ruling power in Germany (1933), we women realized that it was our duty to contribute our share to the Leader's reconstruction programme side by side with men. We did not say much about it, but started work at once. Our first concern was to help all those mothers who had suffered great hardships during the War and the post- war period and all those other women who - as mothers - have now to adjust themselves to the demands of the new age.

Acting in accordance with the recognition of these facts, we first created the Reich Mothers' Service (Reichsmutterdienst), the functions of which are set forth in Article I of the regulations governing it:

> The training of mothers is animated by the spirit of national solidarity and by the conviction that they can be of very great service to the nation and the State. The object of such training is to develop the physical and intellectual efficiency of mothers, to make them appreciate the great duties incumbent upon them, to instruct them in the upbringing and education of their children, and to qualify them for their domestic and economic tasks.

In order to provide such training, several courses of instruction have been drawn up, each of which deals with one particular subject only, e.g., infant care, general hygiene, sick nursing at home, children's education, cooking, sewing, etc. These courses are fixtures in all towns with a population exceeding 50,000, whilst itinerant teachers conduct similar ones in the smaller towns and in the country. Every German woman over 18 can join them, irrespective of her religious, political or other views. The maximum number of members has been limited to 25 for each course, because the instruction given does not consist of theoretical lectures, but takes the form of practical teaching to working groups, where questions will be asked and answered. Since the establishment of the Reichsmutterdienst, i.e., between April 1st, 1934, and October 1st, 1937, some 1,179,000 married and unmarried women have been thus instructed in 56,400 courses, conducted by over 3,000 teachers of whom about 1,200 are employed full-time, whilst the remaining 2,300 (also possessing the necessary qualifications) act in an honorary capacity or in that of part-time instructresses.

Our next concern was with those millions of German women who, day after day, attend to their heavy duties in factories. We look upon it as most important to make them realise that they, too, are the representatives of their nation. They, too, must take pride in their work and must be able to say: "I have a useful duty to fulfil; and the work I do is an essential part of the work performed by the whole nation."

With this end in view, we have created the Women's Section of the German Labour Front (Frauenamt der Deutschen Arbeitsfront), which has now a membership of over 8,000,000. Foreign critics have frequently stated that German women have no chance of earning their livelihood by working in industrial or other undertakings. I therefore take this opportunity of emphasising that more than 11,500,000 women are employed in the various professions and occupations; the Women's Section of the German Labour Front attending to their interests. Moreover, we are of the opinion that a woman will always find it possible to secure paid employment provided that she is strong enough to do the work demanded of her. This applies to women workers of all categories, irrespective of whether the work is of the physical or intellectual kind. It is therefore the business of the Frauenamt to ensure that women are not employed in any capacity that might prove detrimental to their womanhood and to give them all the protection to which they are specifically entitled. In order to translate these ideas into practice, the Frauenamt has proceeded to appoint a "social industrial woman worker" (soziale PLACE OF WOMEN IN THE NEW GERMANY Betriebsarbeiterin) for every undertaking in which a considerable number of women are employed. The functions to be exercised by these Betriebsarbeiterinnen are of a general and a special kind. They have to see to it that all women employed in the same undertaking look upon their own interests as identical with those of the latter and that a proper spirit of comradeship grows up among them. They are assisted in their task by the works' leader and the confidential council, and they are in a position to gain the confidence of the other women workers because all of them are comrades of one another. They have to prevent strife, jealousy, and irresponsible talk from poisoning the social atmosphere of the works, to help those of their fellow-workers who may be oppressed by domestic worries, and to assist in rendering the conditions of work as dignified as possible. To that end, they have to furnish the works' leader with suggestions for any measures that may be required to adapt the processes of work - in conformity with the technical peculiarities of the undertaking - to the natural capacities of women. Finally, they have to assist in the transfer of women workers to other places of employment, in the task of making the aspect of the working premises as pleasing as possible, etc. This enumeration of their functions shows that they must not only be experienced social workers, but must also be familiar with the actual work. For this latter reason, they are required to devote several months to such work before they are appointed to the post of social workers. During that time they receive the same wages as the other women workers and are subject to the same regulations as they. Similar arrangements, although on a more modest scale, are made in connection with smaller works, i.e., those where the number of women workers is less than 200.

Special care is devoted by our organisation to married women workers with children and to those expecting to be confined. In this domain of social work we provide assistance, in conjunction with the National Socialist Welfare Organisation (N.S. Volkswohlfahrt), exceeding the standards set by the existing legislation. Such supplementary assistance consists of money, food, linen, etc.

I must not omit to add a few words in reference to the women students who spend part of their holidays for the benefit of those women workers - notably those who have large families - who are in need of a week's relaxation in addition to their regular holidays. The students generously attend to the factory work of these women during their absence; and as they demand no wages, the workers suffer no pecuniary loss whatever. In many instances, free quarters are provided for the students by the National Socialist Women's Organisation (N.S. Frauenschaft), whilst the Welfare Organisation grants special facilities to the women on holiday, such as additional food parcels, board and lodging in one of their mothers' hostels and so on. During the first few years of the operation of the scheme, the students relieved the workers to the extent of 57,700 days work. Large numbers of letters are received by us every day, in which workers and students alike tell us how grateful they are for their unforgettable experience. Works' leaders, too, continually inform us of the beneficial results achieved.

After completing the inauguration of the above schemes, we continued our work in a different direction, i.e., by organising ourselves. We have now co-ordinated the previously existing women's associations and thus created the German Women's Association (Deutsches Frauenwerk), which is sub-divided into sections along the lines laid down by the N.S. Frauenschaft.

The Deutsches Frauenwerk consists, apart from the Mothers' Service already mentioned, of the following sections: National and domestic economy; cultural and educational matters; assistance, and a foreign section. In addition, there are four large administrative departments, viz., general administration; finances; organisation and staff; the Press and propaganda matters, which the latter also deals with radio, films, and exhibitions.

In the section for national and domestic economy, women and girls are trained to apply the principles of national solidarity. They are taught that, in every household, the mother is responsible for the health of the whole family by providing good food and by generally exercising her duties with skill and efficiency.

The cultural and educational section makes the nation's cultural assets available to women; women artists are assisted in their work, and particular attention is paid to the achievements of women in the realm of science. The assistance section deals with the work done by female nurses, the Red Cross, and the air defence society. The foreign section establishes contact with women's associations abroad, supplies information to foreigners, exchanges experiences with foreign organisations, makes arrangements for seeing the institutions in connection with the work of the Deutsches Frauenwerk, etc.

All these groups are under the general direction of the N.S. Frauenschaft, which may therefore be regarded as the leading organisation, whilst the Deutsches Frauenwerk and the Frauenamt der Deutschen Arbeitsfront constitute the joint foundation for the work done by women throughout the country.

Foreigners have repeatedly asked me about the kind of compulsion exercised to make women take part in all this work. I wish to assure inquirers that we know of no compulsion whatever. Those who want to join us, must do so absolutely voluntarily; and I can only say that all of them are joyfully devoted to their work.

Let me conclude by quoting a remark which I made on the occasion of the Women's Congress held at the time of the Nuremberg party rally (1935): "All the work done by us as a matter of course, which is now so comprehensive that we cannot any longer describe it in detail, is only a means to an end. It is the expression of the determination of German women to assist in solving the great problems of our age. A spirit of comradeship animates all of us; and our devotion to our nation guides all our efforts."

SECTION SIX

EDUCATION IN THE THIRD REICH

Bernhard Rust

Reich and Prussian Minister of Science,
Education and Popular Enlightenment

THE nineteenth century witnessed so much educational progress in the domain of intellectual refinement that it may be justly described as the century of education. Germany took a leading part in this development, and her educational system was universally acknowledged to be particularly efficient. Many foreigners therefore availed themselves of the educational facilities Germany had to offer. If we now see that, despite these splendid achievements, the Third Reich has seen fit to make a radical change in the system of education, we may feel sure that it has been done for very good reasons. There is, indeed, twofold evidence to show that something was wrong with education. In the first place, the high level of popular enlightenment had failed to protect the German people against the poisonous effects of Marxist teaching and other false doctrines. Large masses of people had fallen victims to them, whilst other sections - more especially those of higher education - had been unable to take up an effective stand against the spread of the poison. If they had, the events of 1918 and the succeeding period of national disintegration and deterioration would have been prevented.

In the second place, a careful study of the situation shows that the German people are sound to the core and are gifted with just as much national sentiment as any other. Hence, the temporary lowering of their previous high standards could not have been the result of any innate inferiority, but the reason must be sought in a faulty system of education, which - notwithstanding its high intellectual achievements - tended to impair the healthy spirit of the nation, men's energies and their soundness of judgment, and to produce selfishness and a deficient sense of national solidarity. Besides, it was obvious that certain elements intending to secure private advantages for themselves by injuring the healthy forces of the nation had succeeded in achieving undue prominence in public life.

National Socialism was therefore compelled to ascertain and remove the causes that had brought about so unsatisfactory a condition, and to open up new resources capable of being used for a regeneration, the Fuhrer, in his book "Mein Kampf," having clearly indicated the road that had to be followed.

Two main causes had contributed towards the unsatisfactory results.

1. Although the intellectual capacities of young persons had been excellently trained and although they were thoroughly qualified for their vocations in after-life, the importance of knowledge for knowledge's sake had been over-estimated, whilst physical education and the training of the character and the will had been neglected. Metaphorically speaking, youth had been offered crystal-clear water to drink, but the health-giving mineral constituents contained in it had first been carefully removed. This interference was bound to do much harm to popular health.

2. Excessive importance had been attached to the individual as such, whilst it was almost forgotten that each individual is at the same time a member of a racial community, that it is only in that capacity that he can perfect his powers to their fullest extent, and that it is his duty to work for the good of that community. Such natural forms of the racial community as the family, the clan, the tribe, and the nation (natural because they are based on the ties of blood) either failed to receive the attention to which they are entitled, or they were disintegrated by an exaggerated individualism or superseded by artificial and super-national sham communities. Such a mental attitude enabled Jews and others animated by selfish motives or by international and anti-racial ideas to obtain a prominent influence upon all spheres of national life and access to high offices of State and to poison the healthy feelings of the nation by means of their educational policy.

It is the purpose of all education to prepare the rising generation for its functions in after-life as the true representatives of the nation and the State, both in a political and a cultural sense. Their training, therefore, must proceed along the lines just indicated. In conformity with the teaching of history and the laws of biological and racial science, it is necessary to train the faculties of the body, the character and the will just as much as the intellectual ones. The lost equilibrium must be restored; or rather, the harmonious co-existence of all these faculties must be maintained and developed instead of being destroyed. To be and to remain strong and healthy, has become the fundamental law governing Germany's youth, and it is the first and foremost duty of educationists to give effect to it. Such strength and health, however, is unthinkable without racial purity and the striving after a perfect racial type.

The attainment of high intellectual standards will certainly continue to be urged upon the young people; but they will be taught at the same time that their achievements must be of benefit to the national community to which they belong. As a consequence of the demand thus clearly formulated by the Nuremberg Laws, Jewish teachers and Jewish pupils have had to quit German schools, and schools of their own have been provided by and for them as far as possible. In this way, the natural race instincts of German boys and girls are preserved; and the young people are made aware of their duty to maintain their racial purity and to bequeath it to succeeding generations. As the mere teaching of these principles is not enough, it is constantly supplemented, in the National Socialist State, by opportunities for what may be called "community life." By this term we mean school journeys, school camps, school "homes" in rural neighbourhoods, and similar applications of the corporate principle to the life of schools and scholars.

History insists that every biological race deterioration coincides with the growth of big towns, that these latter exercise a paralysing effect upon community life, and that a nation's strength is rooted in its rural elements. Our National Socialist system of education pays due regard to these important considerations, and makes every effort to take the young people from the towns to the country, whilst impressing upon them the inseparable connection between racial strength and a healthy open-air life.

The systematic reform of Germany's educational system was started immediately after the coming-into-power of National Socialism, and received a great stimulus when, on May 1st, 1934, a National Department of Education was established.

The steps that had to be taken comprised the internal reorganisation of school teaching in accordance with the above principles, new methods for the training of teachers, and a re-modelling of the existing types of schools.

If these far-reaching changes were to materialise, teachers had first to be made capable of introducing them. This task has since been taken in hand by the Department in conjunction with the National Socialist Association of Teachers (N.S. Deutscher Lehrerbund). Numerous courses, camps and working communities have been arranged to provide the necessary instruction, which includes the teaching of the philosophy of National Socialism in addition to the strictly educational subjects. The uniform carrying-out of this work has been entrusted by the Department to the Central Institute for Education and Instruction (Zentralinstitut fur Erziehung und Unterricht). In the two training camps maintained by the Institute, prominent educationists - both men and women - are given such instruction for several weeks at a time; and on leaving the camps, they are commissioned to disseminate the newly-acquired knowledge among their colleagues through the medium of working communities. In addition, the various educational authorities frequently arrange for conferences for the same purpose, whilst special camps organised by the N.S. Lehrerbund provide instruction in the political aspects of National Socialism.

These arrangements are intended to enable the older generation of teachers to apply to their work the principles of National Socialism. The Government, of course, has also introduced fundamental alterations in the methods of training the younger teachers. Elementary teachers are required to attend one of the training colleges (Hochschulen fur Lehrerbildung), where they receive instruction in scientific and educational subjects and where life is based on the principles of comradeship. Attendance at these colleges - most of which are established outside the big towns - is also compulsory for teachers in intermediate and higher schools as a preliminary to their studies at other institutions where they receive the kind of special training they need. This arrangement ensures that a certain uniformity governs the training of teachers of all kinds. It goes without saying that the courses of study and the regulations for the examination of teachers, more particularly those in the higher schools, have been revised on similar lines.

The internal reorganisation of the educational system was introduced by several decrees dealing with fundamentals. As early as 1933, it was announced that all education had to be founded on the principles of biological and racial science, with which - in compliance with the Fuhrer's wish - all schoolchildren were to be made familiar. Detailed regulations were issued for giving practical effect to this announcement.

Much information on the educational policy of National Socialism may be gathered from a perusal of the so-called selection Decree (Ausleseerlass), which was issued by the Department in close collaboration with the Racial Policy Board (Rassenpolitisches Amt) of the National Socialist party. The decree names the conditions that have to be satisfied by the pupils of the higher schools at the time of their admission and in connection with their achievements. A strict control is to be exercised to ensure that all those who, after completing their studies, are likely to rise to leading positions in life, are racially sound, valuable and efficient. Attention is paid to the physical, ethical, intellectual and racial aspects, and is not confined - as hitherto - to the intellectual aspect only. The demands now made on young persons are: increased intellectual achievements; good physical health; a capacity for endurance; high ethical standards; a sense of community, and descent from pure German stock. A nation desiring to see these ideals realised must have for its guides persons that can be held up as models in all these respects. It does not follow that young persons not possessing good physical health are to be left outside or to be prevented from rising in life. On the contrary, the National Socialist State looks after their interests; and it must also be remembered that, whenever a question of physical unfitness arises, the medical practitioner has an important say in the matter.

Physical fitness is to be assured by the extended cultivation of gymnastic exercises and sports in accordance with the Regulations for Physical Culture in Boys' Schools (Richtlinien fur die Leibeserziehung in Jungenschulen). This matter has had the attention of the Government for several years past, a special section of the Department giving systematic instruction to teachers - especially head teachers - of all kinds of schools. The regular cultivation in the training camps already mentioned of early sports, bodily work, and marching exercise serves the same purpose.

A far-reaching change has also been introduced in the domain of intellectual education. In the past, there had been a tendency towards cramming into pupils' heads every new addition to learning, but restrictions are now to be imposed upon that tendency. It is not necessary to teach everything that is interesting or otherwise worth knowing. The selection of subjects will be guided by the answer to the question : What must boys and girls be taught so that they may become useful members of the national community and of the vocation or profession they may take up? It stands to reason that they must be made familiar with the civilisation of their country and with its origins, or - in other words - they must be taught subjects that have a direct bearing upon the life and history of the German people and that are of real use to them when they have grown up. To these must be added a knowledge of the benefits German civilisation has received from contact with other nations, the extent of this teaching being dependent upon the needs of the schools concerned in each instance.

The courses of study drawn up for all categories of schools are therefore founded on the principle that the fullest possible recognition must be accorded to the national aspect of education and to the practical requirements of life. Thus, the decree governing the teaching work done in the Grundschule (i.e., the lowest four grades of the Elementary School or Volksschule) provides that such work must start from and centre on a knowledge of the children's home district, that the pupils must acquire a solid knowledge of the rudiments of correct speaking, writing and arithmetic, and that due attention must be paid to the teaching of physical exercises, music, and manual training. Similar rules have been laid down for other schools, each according to its own type. The rural vocational schools, for instance, must concentrate upon the life and labour of the rural population, and the urban ones upon local handicrafts and industries, whilst the higher schools must group all their teaching around the so-called deutschkundliche Fächer (i.e., German, history, geography, the fine arts, and music). As regards elementary schools, the application of the above-mentioned principle has resulted in the compiling of a National Reader (Reichslesebuch) consisting of a nucleus compulsory for the whole country, which is supplemented by sections representative of the local literature of the different districts.

The introduction of National Socialist ideas into all schools has greatly stimulated their activities; and the uniform National Socialist outlook of the teachers sees to it that the German schools will not for a second time become the victims of that spirit of disunion which prevailed during a period when party strife and a lack of creative principles had their counterparts in education. The concentrated determination of the teaching profession and the systematic selection of the subjects taught ensure that German intellectual education will not only maintain, but even transcend its present high level. In the past, decisions regarding the internal affairs of each school were made by the whole teaching staff assembled in conference and were therefore subject to fluctuating majorities; but now that the National Socialist principle of leadership has been introduced, the conference has merely consultative functions, whilst the power to make decisions is restricted to the school leader who knows that his superiors, and the whole community, expect him to make his school a model of a German educational institution conducted on National Socialist principles.

It is also the duty of the school leader to maintain regular contact between his school and the progress of events, so that all questions of topical importance that affect our nation can receive attention as part of the teaching work. All the steps taken by the German people as represented by their vigorous National Socialist leaders, in order to preserve and strengthen its national existence and status, concern the schools too. This applies, for example, to aviation, air-raid protection, the self-sufficiency policy, the Four-Year Plan, etc. School children are to take an active interest in everything done by the nation and its rulers, so that they may realise that their own destinies are identical with those of the nation. This will enable them in later-life to render active assistance in moulding the nation's future.

The external structure of German education is as concentrated and systematic as its internal organisation. This explains, inter alia, why public schools are accorded preference to private ones. Although it is quite true that the National Socialist State attaches great importance to the vigorous initiative of the individual, it nevertheless demands that the special desires of the individual must adjust themselves to the requirements of the community. This applies more particularly to all matters capable of vitally affecting the life of the nation. The State must therefore claim that its own institutions are entitled to receive unconditional preference over those established by individuals or by organisations, more especially so whenever there is a danger that the latter kind cannot be unconditionally relied upon to follow the lead given by the State. In view of the importance of education, the State must therefore maintain that private schools and private teaching are justified only in those localities whose educational needs cannot be satisfied by public schools. Moreover, the denominational aspect being looked upon as a matter of secondary importance that must no longer be allowed to divide all Germans in their early youth and ever afterwards into two different camps, it has been the practice to impose restrictions upon private denominational schools wherever it is seen that efficient provision has been made for publicly conducted schools. This does not affect the continued existence of such private institutions as, for example, those of the Lietz Landschulheim type and others.

As regards children below school age (six years), provision has been made wherever necessary by the establishment of creches (for younger infants) and kindergartens (for the older ones). They are conducted by Government-trained teachers and are partly of a public and partly of a private character. Attendance at them is optional.

At the age of six, children enter the elementary schools (Volksschulen), which - generally speaking - are not organised on the co-educational principle. There they are taught, apart from general racial education, those theoretical and practical subjects which are required for all vocations. Special schools (Hilfsschulen) are provided for children whose mental faculties are below the normal. Another type of special schools (Sonderschulen) are provided for normally developed children suffering from serious physical disabilities (e.g., deaf-mutes, blind children, etc.). Specially-trained teachers are in charge of them while there. Attendance at the elementary schools is compulsory for eight years. Whenever the number of pupils is too small to justify a separate grade for each year, several grades may be combined, or boys and girls may be taught together.

Recognition of the fact that many boys and girls of healthy racial stock are rather out of place in the artificial and unhealthy atmosphere of our big towns, so that their valuable faculties cannot or but imperfectly develop there, has led me to introduce in 1934 a scheme I had long contemplated. I refer to what is called the Landjahr. The children spend nine months of the year in one of the Landjahr camps where specially suitable men and women teachers of youthful age are in charge of them. There, their physical health is to be promoted; they are to become familiar with every aspect of country life; their will-power is to be strengthened; they are to be politically educated, and to experience the blessings derived from an unselfish corporate life. Upon completing the Landjahr course, the children start upon their vocational training, or - if they prove especially gifted - they may be admitted to an Aufbauschule.

The four lower grades of the elementary schools are sometimes called the Grundschule, because they form the foundation for most of the higher schools. Children who are not going to join one of the latter, leave the elementary school at the age of 14. They are required to spend the next three years at a vocational school of the Berufsschule or Fachschule type. This part of the educational system is now also looked after by the Department of Education, having previously (up to 1934) been the domain of several other departments. The same as at the elementary schools, no fees are charged to pupils attending the Berufsschulen. These schools are not intended, as a rule, to furnish a general education, although their courses of studies include some subjects dealing with national politics. Their principal function is to supplement the work of training the young persons for some definite vocation. They are of many different types, according to the trades or industries domiciled in the localities concerned. Such schools have also been established for juvenile workers not apprenticed to an employer. The teaching work of the Berufsschulen not only acquaints pupils with the practical needs of their vocation, but also with its national political aspects. This is of particular importance to the agricultural type of Berufsschulen, because National Socialism has always stressed the great value of a healthy farming community. Thus, the former continuation schools (Fortbildungssehulen) have been superseded, except for a few special kinds, by the agricultural schools for boys and the rural economy schools for girls.

Attendance at a Fachschule is optional and implies exemption from attendance at a Berufsschule. The Fachschule supply a more extensive knowledge of the subjects taught than the Berufssehulen, and fees are payable by their pupils. Like the Berufsschulen, there are a great many different types of them, but all are supervised by the State. Their pupils, on leaving, may continue their studies at some höhere Fachschule, at which they may qualify themselves for a university career or for some leading position or appointment.

Attendance at the Berufsschulen and Fachschulen, therefore, coincides with the practical vocational work of the young people. The intermediate schools (mittlere Schulen) and higher schools (höhere Schulen), however, continue the education of their pupils for a few more years prior to their choice of a profession, and are therefore called schools of general education (allgemeinbildende Schulen). Those which admit candidates after they have attended the Grundschule for the customary four years are known as the grundstandige Form, and those whose pupils join them after spending six years at the elementary schools, are called the Aufbauform. Attendance at the Mittelschulen lasts six, or four years, according as they are of the grundstandige Form or of the Aufbauform. They are intended for boys and girls with a pronounced gift for practical work, and are differentiated to some extent on vocational or professional lines. The compulsory subjects taught by them are: the deutschkundige Facher, physical exercises, natural science, mathematics, and English. Besides these, French - but not Latin - is an optional language. Their leaving examination used to be described as the mittlere Reife. Pupils desirous of continuing their studies at a höhere Schule, must first pass an entrance examination for the latter. So far, Mittelschulen only exist in Prussia and a few other parts of Germany.

The höhere Schulen have had a varied development since the foundation of the first humanistisches Gymnasium about a century ago. There have always been two principal types of them: (I) the humanistische Schulen or Gymnasien, with Latin and Greek as the two chief foreign languages, and (2) the Realanstalten, where attention was specially concentrated upon modern languages, mathematics, and natural science. As a result of the competition between them, a large number of intermediate types were also established, so that the desired unity of final purpose became more and more hypothetical. This drawback was particularly manifest in connection with the order of teaching foreign languages, so that pupils whose parents had moved from one town to another were frequently unable to attend a school of the type they were accustomed to, which involved much loss of time and effort.

For these reasons the Department, after a careful study of the problem, decided to introduce a fundamental reorganisation of higher education at the Easter 1937 term, affecting boys' as well as girls' schools, both of the grundstandige Form and the Aufbauform. At the grundstandige höhere Schule attendance has been reduced from nine to eight years, by combining its lower and intermediary sections and dropping one of the six years formerly spent in them, whilst leaving the upper section's three years unchanged. This reduction of school time was necessary for reasons of population policy. There need be no apprehension lest the quality of the work done by the schools should suffer, because the uniform National Socialist attitude of the teachers and the compactness of the courses of study renders it possible to make the teaching far more intensive and to accelerate progress.

The teaching of boys and girls, though of identical value, proceeds along different roads, which is necessary for the reason that the respective spheres of men and women in after-life are likewise different. Henceforth, there will be practically two types of höhere Schulen for boys as well as for girls. For boys, there is the Oberschule and alongside the Gymnasium, and for girls there is also an Oberschule, which is split up (during the last three years of attendance) into a section for domestic economy and another for languages. Both categories are supplemented by an Oberschule in Aufbauform, which - in the case of girls - gives prominence to domestic economy. The Oberschule for boys has to be regarded as the principal type, as it is the one that must be provided in a district if there is one higher school only. Thus, the difficulties above referred to when parents change from one town to another can now be obviated much more easily. Apart from some exceptional cases, only one Gymnasium can be established in towns where more higher schools than one are needed.

With a view to meeting the various preferences and capacities of pupils, the upper section of the Oberschule is divided into two branches. In the language branch provision is made for a second modern language, whilst comparatively limited attention is given to natural science and mathematics. In the science and mathematics branch no second language is included, whilst the chief interest centres around natural science and mathematics. In the Gymnasium there is no analogous division.

The reduced number of Gymnasien is due to the fact that a knowledge of both ancient languages is not considered necessary for the majority of German boys and girls. This is borne out by the constant decline in the number of pupils attending the former Gymnasien.

The subjects common to all höhere Schulen and to the Mittelschulen are: the deutschkundliche Facher, physical exercises, natural science, and mathematics. The höhere Schulen, of course, provide more far-reaching instruction in them than the others; and no regard is paid to the pupil's future profession.

Foreign languages are taught on the following plan:

(a) Oberschule - English (1st grade), Latin (3rd grade), French or some other modern language (6th grade).

(b) Gymnasium - Latin (1st grade), Greek (3rd grade), English (6th grade).

The Oberschulen for girls give instruction in the same subjects as those for boys, except that they add some that are of special importance to women, whilst curtailing the teaching of foreign languages. Thus, in those specialising in languages, English is begun in the 1st grade, and French and Latin in the 6th, whilst in those where domestic economy is taught in the upper section, the only foreign language taught is English.

Apart from these grundstandige Schulen there are the Aufbauschulen for boys and girls. In those for boys, foreign language teaching is started in the 1st, 3rd and 4th grades respectively (corresponding to the 3rd, 5th and 6th grades of the grundstandige Oberschule).

The Aufbauschulen - which were first introduced by the reform scheme for the schools of Prussia in 1925 - have to fulfil a special purpose in connection with our population policy. In many parts of Germany there are few (if any) fairly large towns possessing grundstandige höhere Schulen. These parts are inhabited by a particularly robust type of population closely associated with the soil they cultivate. National Socialists look upon it as an important item to counteract the tendency among country people of migrating to the towns, but want them nevertheless to secure leading positions. For that reason extended facilities must be given them for acquiring a sound education.

The Aufbauschulen are intended to assist in this task. Accordingly, they are largely domiciled in rural districts, and Schulerheime are connected with them. The children in rural districts can now attend their local Volksschule for six years and have then an opportunity of continuing their studies for another six years until they possess the qualifications for university study. During the whole of that time they remain in direct connection with rural life. The Schulerheim is no longer a place where school children are merely housed and fed, but an educational institution. Whilst there, the children's corporate instincts can be encouraged by their close association with their comrades, thus laying the foundations for their sense of racial community.

Similar purposes are to be achieved by the National Political Courses of Instruction (Nationalpolitische Lehrgange) for the pupils of the higher schools and by the children's stay in the Landheime. In view of the increased demands on pupils due to the reorganisation of higher education, the Courses named have had to be temporarily discontinued notwithstanding the benefits already derived from them. All the more important, therefore, is the children's stay in the Landheime and Youth Hostels (Jugendherbergen). These facilities are open to pupils from all types of schools. They are an essential part of our educational system, because without them it would be impossible to master the great tasks that have still to be carried out if the young people are to take their proper share in shaping the country's future.

The leaving examination of all higher schools is called the Reifeprafung. After passing it, the young people are qualified for admission to any German university or other institution of university rank, and for entering a number of professions, including that of officers in the army.

The categories of higher schools have been increased in number since 1933 by the so-called Nationalpolitische Erziehungsanstalten. There are fifteen of them in Prussia and in some other parts of the country. Their educational purposes and their courses of study are the same as those of the other higher schools. They are, however, of the boarding-school type and work in close collaboration with the Hitler Youth. Their special aim is to give a good all-round training to boys who have already distinguished themselves for their intellectual capacities, their physical prowess and bodily skill, their strength of mind, and their loyalty towards their comrades. These institutions are also under the administration of the Department of Education. Early in 1937, the Reich Youth Leader - acting in co-operation with the Reich Organisation Leader - founded seven Adolf Hitler Schulen, whose specific purpose it is to train boys for the position of leaders in the National Socialist party. It is too early to state details regarding their work and their organisation, as they have only been in existence for a short time.

The third educational factor, in addition to the home and the school, is the Hitler Youth. It has been commissioned by the Fuhrer to train German boys - in close collaboration with the home and the school - for their great tasks in the future. The schools have to devote the major part of their time to intellectual education; and although, by that means and by other special arrangements, they do exercise an important influence in the direction named, they have but few opportunities for enabling their pupils to cultivate the corporate spirit beyond their own limits. This drawback is to be overcome by the Hitler Youth. The youth of all classes and all vocations is initiated by it in the practical working of a national community and is to be prepared for that achievement by physical, ethical and political training. Even though a certain overlapping was unavoidable during the early stages, it is evident by now that the collaboration of the three factors is becoming closer and closer.

Germany's former school system has done much. The new National Socialist school system will do more still and will make the young people racially sound, efficient and ready for sacrifices. They will regard their nation, their national existence and their national freedom as their greatest assets. They will be taught - in conformity with the wish of the Fuhrer - that the vital rights of other nations must be equally respected and that co-operation between all nations is both necessary and desirable. These aims are consciously fostered by the schools themselves and by special arrangements for the international exchange of students. The central organisation for such exchange is the Akademischer Austauschdienst, which works in close collaboration with the Department of Education, and whose activities receive a valuable stimulus from the successful efforts of the National Socialist party for international co-operation. Thus, the call addressed to German youth is: Love your German nation above everything, and be a good neighbour to all those nations that desire to live in peace with your own.

SECTION SEVEN

THE TRUTH ABOUT PROPAGANDA IN GERMANY

Dr. G. Kurt Johannsen

Managing Director of the Hanse Press.

PROPAGANDA is a word often pronounced with a certain intonation, and the word is associated with ideas like prejudice, exaggeration and but little discrimination in the selection of means and methods. In fact, propagandists have been thought of as cold-blooded and calculating creatures whose stock-in-trade is deception, not to say lies.

But such conclusions are unfair. It does not give consideration to the fact that every manifestation of human life has its positive and negative symptoms. Obstinacy may mean strength of character - or merely stubbornness; national feeling exists next to narrow-minded Chauvinism; real piety finds its counterpart in bigotry, and in hypocrisy. Both varieties grow in the same soil, and yet they are separated by a whole world. Only those who judge are often unable to differentiate between the real and the false. They do not notice the difference between the propagation of an idea and the yells of a cheap-jack. Like a boomerang, such an error returns to its sender. Remarks of an English paper that the general participation of the public in the Jubilee of the sovereign was a "mob" would be on the same level as referring abroad to demonstrations in National Socialist Germany as staged get up. There are critics everywhere who dissect and label every feeling, and attribute it to the lowest possible causes. They are only satisfied when they belittle in others what is, in most cases, missing in themselves.

In order to answer the question as to what propaganda really is, and what its meaning and importance are in present-day political life, we must begin in the past. But one does not need to start with the well-known and sometimes feared German thoroughness above; one may say that no historical revolution has taken place without preparation in the shape of propaganda. The propagandist is the herald and, at the same time, the believer in a great idea. The Puritans would have remained a harmless sect, cut off from the rest of the world, if they had not propagated their religious ideas in every city and village, influencing English life to this very day. What were their methods?

It is true that the Roundheads seemed plebeian and objectionable to Charles Stuart's Cavaliers. But this achievement, like every other great revolution, cannot be imagined unless an idea rouses the troubled souls, unless speakers lend the idea impulse, spread it to the smallest villages, into the drawing-rooms, and into the tap-rooms, into the lecture halls and into the workshops, explaining and interpreting the idea which has become a historical demand.

Propaganda? Dangerous demagogy? - These words are used by ministers who are no longer sure of themselves, and who try to keep a movement back with the usual police methods.

But the idea grows with the obstacles placed in its path. It can be obstructed and crushed to all appearance, and may, perhaps, disappear from the surface, but only to deepen below. It cannot be prevented, for it gives a period its true fulfilment, representing the real life in the nation, the old form having lost its meaning and breaking up when the time comes. This condition must be present, or it is merely a matter of a temporary symptom which is soon overcome. The Radicals who succeeded with their parliamentary reform in the early years of Queen Victoria's reign could not destroy the firm edifice of English Society. Nor did such men as General Boulanger in the Third French Republic, or Kapp in the early post-War period in Germany succeed. But who would wish to deny that National Socialism is the great revolutionary revival of the German people in all spheres of life.

The best bridge for understanding is comprehension of the historical development and the conditions of life of the other nation. In many countries the course of things taken in Germany is regarded with astonishment and, in some cases, with mixed feelings. A State broken by internal strife, which had become the political object of its neighbours after a lost war, and a people helpless in the hands of disputing parties and opposing groups, are now united, obeying one will. Let us leave out those who would prefer to see a weak Germany, for they are too shortsighted to see that a source of unrest does not make for good neighbours, although the Spanish example should have shown this clearly enough. But even those who have good intentions feel a kind of nervous anxiety when they consider New Germany. They see soldiers in numerous uniforms, men with Party badges; they hear the tramp of the marching columns of men belonging to the movement. There are mass demonstrations, pageants and national holidays, in which the whole people take part. Is that not frightful militarism? How about freedom? And, above all, is not everything just propaganda aiming at certain effects and working on a system of mass suggestion? We shall not fail to answer these questions. But first of all it seems best to glance at pre-War Germany, which was a land without propaganda.

The art of public speaking was, perhaps, never specially developed; in any case, it was completely neglected in the last century. While young people at college participate in debates, and gain practice in giving persuasive addresses, the most one learned in Germany was to give an address. The persuasive part, the development of the points in the speech, were unknown, with the result that public speeches had little effect. The academic lecture style was taken as a model. The speaker wished to instruct. No matter how clever he might be, and even though he avoided professorial boredom, it was hard for his listeners to follow him in the long run. A real speech was practically forbidden. To speak passionately and to carry the audience off its feet, so to speak, was called demagogy. Those speakers who were unable to gain a following called such speakers mob orators, or tub-thumpers. The polite speech thus became part of the regular programme, just like the reading of the minutes of a meeting or the resolution at its close. The hearers congratulated each other when the address was not too oily and pathetic, and, especially, when it was not too long.

In German political life there was in those days no Gladstone, no Joseph Chamberlain to arouse the people at election times. Even Bismarck, whose speeches in their clarity and depths of thought are perhaps better understood in our generation than in his own, had to cope with an ill-meaning Opposition in Parliament. Only a few thousands heard him there - never a whole people. Genius had no opportunity to make use of the power and magic of the spoken word.

The German governments made no attempt whatever to explain its intentions to the public, and to gain supporters. Its representatives were as "official" as possible, and the official organ, the Norddeutsche

Allgemeine, was so extremely boring that only those compelled by their professions ever read it. Was it any wonder that the Government lost the ability of speaking to the people, to the masses?

The Government performed its duties with painful conscientiousness; but how can one carry on a carefully planned policy when one knows in advance that all sections of the press are waiting for the first opportunity to attack the ministers, criticise them, and laugh at them? A clever member once said: "I do not know the Government's intentions, but I disapprove of them!" His unconscious humour, however, leaves a bitter flavour. The whole age is characterised by the picture of the old Chancellor, Prince Chlodwig zu Hohenlohe, who sat in the Reichstag with bent head, listening to the attacks made by the Social Democratic deputy Bebel, and unable to defend himself without notes and a prepared speech.

These are not trifles but matters of central importance. A Government must be listened to by the people at times of important decisions, the Leader must be able to count on his following, and the people must not just watch disinterestedly what is going on "up there," but know what the aims and objects are. It would not be necessary to refer so much to this point if it were not for the fact that the considerations of yesterday are the justification of today. We have learnt from what happened in the past. In the Great War it was shown that the German people could not stand the strain in the long run because those who governed could not strengthen their mental powers of resistance. The German people were exposed to great opposing propaganda. The Allies understood the methods of influencing nations, unlike the German statesmen. Not only the allied peoples, but also the neutrals, and finally the German people, too, experienced the effect of the vast propaganda apparatus built up on such a big scale. It is no longer the right time to subject the methods then employed to consideration; in fact, after the War persons from the former opponents' camp did so for themselves, but when in some countries reproachful references are made today to German propaganda, which, after all, is only directed towards the German people, it should not be quite forgotten that the pioneer performances in this field were on the other side. It is certain that Germany was not able to cope with this big-scale influencing of world opinion; her experts wrote pamphlets to oppose this propaganda, but they had no effect in the face of the clever attacks launched by the anti-German propagandists.

The second wave of propaganda began in Germany herself. When mentioning Germany as the country without propaganda, the absence of German enlightenment was meant. There was, however, international Marxist propaganda, which aimed at stirring up discontent. Those accustomed to the respectable forms of His Majesty's Opposition can hardly imagine the undermining propaganda of the "red" agitators. But one must admit that they knew how to talk to the masses, in their own language, and so the people went over to them. The class struggle phraseology was familiar to every workman. The simple slogans, which could be memorised without consideration, and referred to capitalists and militarism, spread to the lower middle classes. The idea of national unity, on the other hand, was a mere phantom to them. It was expounded with the aid of the threatening forefinger, and correspondingly scoffed at. In 1918 the home front in Germany was hollow; and when at the eleventh hour an attempt was made to establish contact with the masses, it was found that both parties were unable to understand each other. The words that might have formed the link could not be found. Repressions were too strong to enable words to be formed, while the hard faces, on the other hand, did not help matters. The German Empire was ruined in the course of this conflict. It could not make its ideas live in the hearts of the citizens any longer.

The post-War period is now regarded in Germany as an interlude. The turn of events began in August 1914. The dissolution which followed after the War also bore the germ of the new future in it.

The new idea arose from this chaos. It grew round the person of a man who did not belong by family, education or possessions to the class which usually controlled public life. Probably the secret of his success is due to just this fact. Adolf Hitler did not wish to start a new school of thought, as so many professors had done before him. Nor did he appeal to the educated, to lawyers, doctors and industrialists. He sought the German people. For this, his idea had to be simple, powerful, and generally comprehensible. But it also had to be comprehensive, could stop at no sphere of life, politics, culture or economy, and had to be sufficiently powerful to overcome the natural force of resistance.

How was the idea to be carried out? No society with a committee of people with well-known names was founded, nor was the publication of a thick volume or a journal the main thing. Other measures were resorted to. Nor was a mere vision enough; a group of men were collected, and they had to create the movement to fight against what was.

Power must be attained with the right means. National Socialism did not want a State based on the point of the bayonet, which, as Napoleon once said, is not a pleasant place for rulers. National Socialism wished to win the whole people. And the means of doing so was propaganda.

Now propaganda was rather difficult in Germany - the Germans regarded themselves as somewhat problematic. There were numerous theories and opinions regarding all vital questions. The nation was so divided that its uniform pulse could no longer be heard. What was needed was a common basis of thought and feeling, which first makes an amorphous mass into a nation. For this purpose, the art of simplifying matters was necessary, forming the essence of National Socialist propaganda. Without resorting to erudition, matters had to be freed from unnecessary ballast and brought back to their essentials. The appeal could not be made to the educated section of the community, but had to be directed to the mass of the people who alone regarded the word "nation" with distrust. States which have experienced the effects of international communism among their own workers will know how difficult this task is. And States which may have been lucky enough to have been spared this agitation up to now should be glad that they need not counter the effects of "red" agitation.

When the German people gave their Leader a mandate to guide their destiny in 1933, and this decision has been confirmed by overwhelming demonstrations again and again, so that National Socialism is entitled to keep criticism, which it has never fought shy of, within proper limits, Germany was on the brink of a communist revolution. She was in economic, social and other troubles of a worse nature than other countries have experienced, least of all the Allied states. In foreign affairs, Germany's position was so difficult that the whole discipline of the people was required to overcome each crisis. Can one demand in such times that every contemporary should, without any mandate from others, have the right to criticise this or that measure?

In quiet periods, public disputes as to opinion may even be stimulating, in times of trouble, they are dangerous, and a responsible State leadership cannot permit this. The German people decided clearly for National Socialism, and there is no further justification for continuing a campaign of press criticisms.

One sometimes hears the question as to why propaganda and people's enlightenment is necessary now that Germany has become National Socialist. With as much justification, one might assert that we are all in favour of understanding between the nations, and can, therefore, drop the subject. If this is done the idea is forced into the background, and people appear who are not so sure of the need for understanding as the silent believers in this idea.

National Socialism was victorious because it made the people politically active, bringing the burning questions of the day before the Man in the Street, making the results of his attitude clear to him, and persuading him to work for a principle, and not merely to think about his own business. It wishes to say the same as Baldwin did in his last important speech as Prime Minister when addressing the youth: "So I say take an interest in Government." The danger of the people losing interest in public life, or, if left to themselves, of lending their ears to false prophets and sensational rumours is too great. Rumours or false reports were never better described than in the prologue to Henry IV:

> I, from the orient to the drooping west,
> Making the wind my post-horse, still unfold
> The acts commenced on this ball of earth:
> Upon my tongues continual slanders ride,
> The which in every language I pronounce,
> Stuffing the ears of men with false reports.

Rumour can only be brought to an end by enlightenment. The object of this work of enlightenment is not, however, to talk at people until they agree with everything, or to keep everything they should not know from them. The German people, taken on an average, are much too well educated, too interested, and too thoughtful to allow themselves to be persuaded to accept something they do not want. It would be bad tactics, doomed to failure, if one were to speculate on the ignorance or limitations of the masses. If they are ignorant they should be enlightened. In this sense, propaganda is an educational work. It cannot be left to accident to decide what sources lead to the formation of the individual's conclusions, and on this account what is of importance in the life of the nation is to be brought to him. We do not only learn at school, after all, but also in life afterwards. But bad teachers in politics have often caused the greatest misfortunes. That is what the work of enlightenment of National Socialism wishes to prevent. People are to be instructed, and, especially they are not to be allowed to doze again, but to maintain an inner participation in the fate of the nation, and not to forget that each individual is a responsible link in the great community the German people represent.

Part II

How Germans Live - Labour

Section One

FINANCIAL POLICY

Fritz Reinhardt

Secretary of State in the National Ministry of Finance

I. THE MEASURES HITHERTO INTRODUCED
AND THE SUCCESS ACHIEVED

THE principal objects aimed at by the financial and fiscal policy of the new Reich are: (1) The reduction of unemployment. (2) The creation of the material conditions indispensable to the strengthening of the country's defence forces. (3) The adjustment of the rates of taxation to the principles underlying National Socialist population policy.

The reduction of unemployment is a sine qua non to the restoration of satisfactory conditions in the social, economic and financial domains, and without it the material conditions indispensable to the strengthening of our defence forces could not be created. The strengthening of our defence forces is essential to the maintenance of peace and to the protection of the nation's vital rights. The adjustment of taxes to the principles underlying National Socialist population policy is, in the main, a demand of social justice.

The principal measures hitherto applied to the struggle against unemployment have been the following:

(1) The placing of a charge on future revenue by the issuance of bills under the scheme for the provision of work, and by the granting of cash advances, interest certificates, loans, and tax facilities. (2) The granting of loans to couples intending to marry, and allowances in respect of children. (3) General exemption from taxation payments, and measures for the lowering and adjustment of taxes. (4) The

conversion of municipal issues, and measures for lowering the rates of interest and modifying the regulations governing credits. The immediate object intended to be attained by these measures, more especially by those enumerated under (1), (2) and (3), has been to stimulate the demands for goods and for services rendered. Whenever there is a rise in these demands, the following effects will be produced:

(a) Increased employment and therefore a decrease in public expenditure on unemployment benefits. (b) Increased turnovers, increased wage payments, and increased consumption, and therefore an increase in the yield of taxation. (c) A general improvement in the position of public finances.

The above measures have proved a complete success, as may be inferred from the following facts:

(1) Large-scale unemployment has ceased to exist. When Herr Hitler assumed office, the number of registered unemployed was just over 6,000,000. The present number is in the neighbourhood of 1,000,000; but even that figure is not a correct index of the actual amount of unemployment. It happens in every national economy that a certain percentage of employed persons constantly transfer their services from one place of employment to another and thus become temporarily unemployed. These persons, therefore, are not a charge on the public funds. A sufficient number of them must always be immediately available in order to satisfy any sudden demand for their labour. It is estimated that their present number amounts to some 500,000. The remaining 500,000 unemployed are either totally or partly unemployable. There are several trades in which an actual shortage of labour has already made itself felt, and it has thus become necessary to make use, in some instances, of persons only partly suitable for the work concerned. The permanent unemployment of fully employable workers has been eradicated in Germany and will never recur to the extent reached in the past. In 1932, there were about 26,000,000 unemployed throughout the world. At present the figure stands at about 19,000,000, a decrease of 7,000,000. Out of this decrease, 5,000,000 persons fall to the share of Germany. During the same period in which the rest of the world succeeded in reducing the number of its unemployed from 30,000,000 to 18,000,000, i.e., by 2,000,000, National Socialist Germany was able to provide work for 5,000,000 of her unemployed population. When National Socialism came into power, mass unemployment was higher in Germany than anywhere else, the number of unemployed being 94 per 1,000.

Today, Germany no longer ranks among the countries in which mass unemployment exists. The above figures prove that Germany's fight against the scourge of unemployment has actually been a complete success. Without the elimination of the exaggerated party system by the Hitler Government, and without the resulting substitution of National Socialist discipline for the Liberalistic absence of systematic efforts, such success would have been unthinkable.

(2) The general index of industrial production was three times as high in 1936 as it was in 1932. As regards the production of goods for consumption, too, the rise in the index figure is taking place at an increasing rate.

(3) The proceeds derived from the sale of agricultural products and from the retail sale of commodities generally have considerably increased.

(4) In 1936, the money paid by way of wages and salaries exceeded by 9,000,000,000 reichsmarks the corresponding amount paid in 1932. During the same period, the total national income went up by 17,000,000,000 reichsmarks. Everything indicates that the upward movement will continue for a long time to come. In 1937 the national income will amount to 68,500,000,000 reichsmarks, or 50% more than it was in 1932.

(5) Between 1933 and July 31st, 1937, savings-bank deposits increased by some 5,000,000,000 reichsmarks, or 40%, and the deposits with agricultural co-operative societies by some 400,000,000 reichsmarks, or 25%

(6) There has been a considerable increase in social-insurance contributions. The net assets of the social-insurance institutions increased by 1,000,000,000 reichsmarks.

(7) The number of bankruptcies and composition proceedings is now one-eighth of what it was in 1932.

(8) The expenditure of public money on unemployment benefit decreased from 2,800,000,000 reichsmarks in 1932 to 1,000,000,000 reichsmarks in 1936.

(9) The yield of National taxes, notwithstanding various reductions, remissions, etc., underwent the following development:

Year	National Tax Income
1932	6,600,000,000 reichsmarks.
1933	6,800,000,000 " "
1934	8,200,000,000 " "
1935	9,600,000,000 " "
1936	11,500,000,000 " "
1937	14,000,000,000 (Estimated)

The figure for 1937 was more than twice as large as that for 1932, and there is every probability that the upward movement has not yet come to an end and that it will not do so in 1938 either. The turnover tax and the general income tax, more particularly, are constantly yielding larger amounts.

(10) Thanks to the drop in the number of unemployed and to the resulting increase in economic activity, it has been possible to restore healthy conditions in the field of municipal finance. Municipal budgets are again balanced. Many municipalities have already earned budgetary surpluses and are now able to accumulate reserves. The share of the municipalities in the yield of national taxation has been reduced in favour of the Reich, because their own tax yield has increased. The conversion of municipal indebtedness in 1933-4 and the lowering of the rates of interest have contributed towards the restoration of sound financial conditions.

II. THE CHARGE ON FUTURE REVENUE

It has been found that the placing of a charge on future revenue has had no adverse consequences. The financial and fiscal measures thus introduced have resulted in a very considerable economic revival, which, in turn, has so greatly augmented the yield of taxation that the policy adopted has been an unqualified success.

Thanks to the steps taken, additional economic assets have been created which are of lasting value and will enable the body economic largely to increase its productive efficiency. In addition, existing economic assets have been modernised or otherwise improved in value. From the very start of the National Socialist revolution, the party had proclaimed that it was its aim to prevent economic assets from deteriorating in value, to create additional ones, and to increase the remunerativeness of all of them for the benefit of the nation as a whole.

The charges placed on future revenue are partly of short and partly of medium currency; but a certain percentage is now converted into long-term loans issued by the Reich. The object of the conversion is to place at the disposal of the Government, within the framework of the ordinary budget, the funds that will be required to finance the strengthening of the country's defence forces and other important projects.

The short and medium-term indebtedness and the provision of the money needed for the redemption of the long-term loans and for the payment of interest on them are more than covered by the additional yield of taxation. In view of the extent and the productive efficiency of Germany's national economy, the amount of long-term loans issued so far can only be described as small. The continued financing of the important projects named can be effected in the same manner as hitherto provided that the amounts which cannot yet be provided by the budget can be raised in the capital market and that the service of the long-term issues can be maintained by means of the increased taxation yield. Everything will be done, now and in future, to preserve the balance of the current budget and to prevent the accumulation of short and medium-term indebtedness. The extent of such indebtedness will never exceed the limits set by the rate at which the yield of taxation continues to increase or by the possibility of converting it into long-term loans.

III. GRANTS OF LOANS TO COUPLES INTENDING TO MARRY AND CHILDREN'S ALLOWANCES

The principal measure introduced to combat unemployment was the Act passed on June 1st, 1933, Section VIII of which provided for the granting of loans to couples intending to marry. This provision has been in force since August 1st, 1933. In order to qualify for such a loan, the prospective wife must have been in some sort of paid employment for nine months out of the two years immediately preceding the marriage. Prior to October 1st, 1937, the prospective wife was also required to give up her paid employment (if any), but this undertaking is now no longer insisted upon. Women already married are permitted to take up paid employment for the duration of the second Four Year Plan.

Between August 1933 and December 1936, we granted 650,000 such loans, the average amount of each being 600 reichsmarks. We shall continue to grant from 15,000 to 20,000 similar loans each month until there are no longer any candidates for them.

The effects so far produced by this policy may be summarised as follows:

(1) The labour market has been relieved to the extent of 650,000 persons. Assuming that, out of the 650,000 recipients of the grants, about 150,000 young couples would have married in any case, the fact still remains that some 500,000 more marriages were concluded during those three years and 500,000 more households were established than would have been the case without the loans.

(2) The labour market has been relieved by at least another 150,000 persons owing to increased employment in the furniture industry, the industries turning out household requisites, and similar ones.

(3) An expenditure of about 400,000,000 reichsmarks has been saved per annum in respect of unemployment relief.

(4) The major part of the sum of about 400,000,000 reichsmarks hitherto paid by way of grants has been spent on purchases, thus increasing - directly or indirectly - industrial output, and causing a corresponding increase in the tax yield.

(5) The number of marriages has considerably increased and the birth-rate has gone up.

No interest is payable on the loans. They are to be repaid at the rate of 3% per month so long as the wife is in paid employment, and at the rate of 1% per month thereafter, but a reduction of 25% is made from the total amount in respect of each child (excluding still-born children). If desired, the monthly payments of 1% (or 3%) may be deferred for a period of twelve months after the birth of each child. Applications to that effect are regularly granted by the Revenue Offices. When payment has to be resumed after the lapse of that period, the monthly amount on which it is calculated is no longer the sum originally advanced, but only that part of it which is still left after deducting the allowance made in respect of the child. The object aimed at by these provisions is to enable the young couples to spread the repayment instalments over a longer term and to obtain larger reductions consequent upon the birth of more children.

Up to the present, more than 450,000 reductions have been thus granted, corresponding to an equal number of children born. Their value exceeds already the sum of 65,000,000 reichsmarks, and the total amount in respect of which repayment is deferred exceeds 25,000,000 reichsmarks.

The payment of the grants will be continued, as already stated, so long as there are any candidates for them, and that presumably will always be the case. This measure will therefore constitute a permanent feature of the National Socialist State. It has originated from the desire to fight unemployment and to improve the social, economic and financial position of the country. Beyond that, it is inspired by the conviction that proper steps have to be taken to safeguard the continued existence of the German people.

The funds required by the Government to grant these loans are obtained by raising the rates of income tax payable by unmarried persons.

The proceeds derived from the repayment of the loans are used in the form of allowances paid to poor persons with a large number of children.

Between October 1935 and December 1936, nearly 300,000 families received such allowances, the average amount in each case being 370 reichsmarks. Applications are only considered if they are made by persons whose household includes not less than four children below 16. In addition, applicants must prove that their income does not exceed the limit fixed for the purpose of these allowances.

Since August 1936, recurring allowances have been paid besides the non-recurring ones. They are restricted to families with a large number of children and amount to 10 reichsmarks per month in respect of each child above 16 except the first four. Applicants must be in receipt of monthly incomes not exceeding 200 (prior to October 1937, 185) reichsmarks gross. If, for instance, the weekly wages of a worker are 40 reichsmarks and if he has seven children below 16, the sum of 30 reichsmarks per month is paid to him by the Revenue Office so long as the above conditions remain.

Children's allowances differ from wages and salaries in that they are exempted from taxes and social insurance payments. Thus, in the case just cited, the purchasing capacity of the family concerned has gone up by nearly 20% since August 1936. At present, recurring allowances are paid in respect of about 400,000 children.

No other financial aid from the public funds to which the persons concerned may be entitled, such as unemployment relief, etc., is in any way curtailed or discontinued on the ground that they are in receipt of recurring children's allowances. These latter are intended to improve the social position of families with a large number of children.

Children's allowances are not regarded as charity payments, but as the necessary outcome of a policy whose aim it is to alleviate social inequalities. The justification for granting them lies in the fact that persons with a large number of children have to pay larger amounts in respect of turnover tax, taxes on consumption, and inland revenue than others, and it is these amounts which are refunded to them. In like manner, the allowances compensate them - either wholly or partly - for the amount paid by them in respect of social insurance, and (when the number of children exceeds six) for part of their rent. Thus, the allowance made for the fifth child in a family is equivalent to exemption from the taxes and duties named, that made for the sixth and seventh child to exemption from social insurance payments and part of the rent, and that made for any additional child to exemption from a further part of the rent. It is intended that the facilities thus accorded shall be applied to the improvement of the children's standard of living.

Recurring allowances in respect of children and the measure described in Section IV of this article are the first fruits of a policy aiming at an adjustment of family burdens. The system of allowances will be extended as the necessary funds become available, the ultimate aim being to create a national fund large enough to make it possible to pay them to all persons working for their living irrespective of the nature of their work. The first step in this direction was taken in October 1937, when the number of persons entitled to benefit from them was enlarged by the inclusion of handicraftsmen, small tradesmen, etc., whose annual income does not exceed 2,100 reichsmarks, whilst the income limit will be gradually increased in subsequent years.

All these measures naturally tend to increase the purchasing capacity and therefore the standards of living of the persons concerned. Thus, certain principles underlying the country's economic, social and population policy have been uniformly applied to serve a practical purpose.

IV. GENERAL TAX EXEMPTIONS, REDUCTIONS AND ADJUSTMENTS

The chief measures here concerned are the following:

(1) Exemption from the motorcar tax in respect of all passenger cars licensed subsequent to March 31st, 1933. The effect has been a considerable rise in the demand for passenger cars.

(2) Reduction of the turnover tax and real estate tax (the former by 50%) payable by farmers, the former having become effective as from October 1st, 1933, and the latter as from April 1st, 1934. The effect has been an increase in agricultural production.

(3) Lowering of the rate of contributions in respect of unemployment assistance, effective April 1st, 1934, and January 1st, 1935. The effect has been an improvement in the purchasing capacity of wage earners.

(4) Lowering of the tax on inhabited house property, effective April 1st, 1936. The effect has been to make it easier for house-owners to spend money on the upkeep and repair of their property.

V. THE LEGISLATION GOVERNING TAX REFORM

The Acts providing for the reform of the taxation laws, passed October 16th, 1934, represent another aspect of the legislation intended to stimulate the demand for commodities and services and to raise the nation's purchasing capacity.

They provide, among other matters, that enhanced regard is to be paid to the family status of income-tax payers, that the family status is also to be taken into account when assessing the poll tax and the tax on assets, that the tax-free income is to be raised in respect of the poll tax, and that certain exemptions are to be introduced in favour of children and grandchildren in connection with the legacy duties.

Married wage-earners are completely exempt from income tax when their monthly income does not exceed the following amounts, and when the number of their children is as stated: 260 reichsmarks - four children; 351 reichsmarks - five children; 793 reichsmarks - six children; 910 reichsmarks - seven children; 1,027 reichsmarks - eight children, and so on. If their income exceeds these amounts, the tax then payable is extremely low. In the case of a married man with six children and an income of 800 reichsmarks, for example, it is as low as 1.04 reichsmarks per month.

As regards the poll tax, no regard was paid in previous years to the family status; but this is no longer the case now. The change became effective on January 1st, 1935. Before that date, a married workman with four children and an income of 50 reichsmarks a week had to pay (in Berlin) 42 reichsmarks per annum by way of poll tax. Now, however, he is completely exempt from that tax, thanks to the provision by which he is entitled to a reduction in respect of every child except the first. As, in addition, the tax-free income (in so far as the poll tax is concerned) has also been materially increased, the number of persons liable to that tax has correspondingly decreased.

As regards the tax on assets, a change was made (effective in 1936) by which 10,000 reichsmarks is exempt from it in respect of the husband, the wife, and each child under age. If, for instance, a married man with three children owns capital to the value of 40,000 reichsmarks he has no tax whatever to pay on it, whilst he had to pay 200 reichsmarks per annum before the change was introduced.

Since January 1st, 1935, exemptions have also been in force in respect of legacy duty, amounting to 30,000 reichsmarks in the case of each child and 10,000 reichsmarks in the case of each grandchild. Prior to 1935, a child inheriting 25,000 reichsmarks from his or her father, had part of it deducted therefrom on account of the duty; now, however, no duty whatever is payable on such a legacy.

We have already begun to adjust our fiscal system to National Socialist principles. The greater regard now paid to the family status is not only due to reasons in the domains of social and population policy, but is also prompted by the conviction that such a policy is bound to increase the purchasing capacity of the families affected by it.

VI. THE REFORM OF THE LEGISLATION GOVERNING TAXES ON INDUSTRY AND REAL ESTATE

The reform of fiscal legislation introduced on October 16th, 1934, constituted, in effect, an important step forward in the direction of simplification. The same remark holds good for the further reform introduced on December 1st, 1936, and made applicable to the tax on industry and to that on real estate, which, until recently, were levied by the federal States, the municipalities, and the municipal federations.

Although these two taxes were payable throughout the country, there was no uniform legislation concerning them. Each of the sixteen federal States had its own rules and regulations, so that there were thirty-two different laws governing them.

The Act that came into force on December 1st, 1936, has simplified all this. The previously existing thirty-two laws have been abolished, and two new ones - valid throughout the country - have taken their place, one dealing with the tax on industry and one with that on real estate.

A notable feature of the new legislation is that the two taxes here concerned have been converted into municipal taxes pure and simple, so that the proceeds derived from them will no longer flow into the coffers of the federal States. This change will make it necessary to arrive at a new financial adjustment between the Reich, the States, the municipal federations, and the municipalities.

When the simplifications and alterations introduced by the new Act have become practically effective, the time will have arrived for the structural reorganisation of the Reich and for the constitutional changes necessitated thereby.

VII. IMPROVED METHODS OF ENSURING THE PAYMENT OF TAXES

Although, thanks to the continued economic improvement, the tax yield is always rising, regulations have been issued for the purpose of ensuring the due payment of all taxes. Their effect has been - apart from a not inconsiderable rise in the tax yield - a better application of the principle of equal justice for all. Since the substitution of the National Socialist regime for that based upon a multiplicity of political parties, there has been a marked improvement in what might be called" fiscal honesty" and in every taxpayer's willingness to "render unto Csesar" what is due to him, and to comply with the date limits set for payment.

VIII. GERMANY'S FINANCIAL STATUS IS THOROUGHLY SOUND

Unemployment has practically disappeared in Germany. There is great activity in trade and industry. The public budgets have been balanced. The proceeds derived from taxation are sufficient to ensure that the capital and interest service of the loans issued will always be promptly effected and that, in addition, funds will be available for the capital and interest service of further issues should these be required.

We have no intention of being satisfied with the successes already achieved. Whilst continuing to finance the great projects and the other tasks entrusted to the German people by the Leader and to translate into practice the principles of National Socialism in the domain of its population policy, we shall also continue to make social, economic and financial progress. Our financial status is thoroughly sound; and all the financial conditions indispensable to the strengthening of our national defences, to the carrying-out of the Four Year Plan, and to the successful working of every other measure intended to safeguard our vital rights, have been provided.

SECTION TWO

THE NATIONAL FOOD ESTATE

R. Walther Darre

Reich Minister of Food and Agriculture, Reich Farmers'
Leader, Reichsleiter of the National Socialist Party

WHEN the National Socialist party acquired power on January 30th, 1933, German agriculture was on the brink of ruin. Some 12,000,000,000 reichsmarks of new debt had been contracted by farmers between 1924 (when the currency was stabilised) and 1932. The area covered by the farmsteads sold by auction during that period was about equal to that of Thuringia. The proceeds derived from the sale of farm produce decreased from some 10,000,000,000 reichsmarks in 1928-9 to 6,400,000,000 reichsmarks in 1932/3 - an amount insufficient to recover the cost of production. On the other hand, farmers had to pay high rates of taxes and interest and heavy social charges. As early as 1930, the National Socialist party directed public attention to the desperate state of the farming industry and asked that the country's agricultural policy should pay increased attention to these matters, more especially by creating new legislation dealing with farm property, by regulating markets and by setting up a corporate system of self administration. These demands have now been satisfied under the National Socialist regime. Some 700,000 hereditary farms (Erbhofe) have been created and about 40% of the soil used for agricultural purposes has thus been liberated from the arbitrary interference of professional speculators in real estate. The law enacted to that end has strengthened the farmer's connection with the soil he tills and has secured his rights of possession. Besides, the charges on farm property have been reduced to a reasonable level, partly by lowering the rates of interest and facilitating the repayment of debts and partly by granting tax abatement.

The National Food Estate (Reichsnahrstand) was set up by the Act passed on September 13th, 1933. It is the sole organisation in the country embracing all persons associated in some way with farming or with the production and distribution of human food. The formerly existing organisations whose objects were similar have either been incorporated with the National Food Estate (N.F.E.) or have been dissolved. Those now incorporated with it include, among others, the Chambers of Agriculture, the Council of Agriculture, the National Farmers' Association, the German Agricultural Federation, etc. The highly developed system of co-operative societies was likewise made subject to the administration of the N.F.E.

Membership of the N.F.E. includes all the owners, lessors and lessees of agricultural land, together with their families, employees and workmen. The term "agriculture" is understood to comprise horticulture, viniculture, and fishery as well. Membership further includes, as has been said, all those connected with the production and distribution of food, e.g., the producers of foodstuffs, millers, bakers, butchers, provision dealers, etc. The extension of membership to so many trades was necessary because, without it, the market organisation could not be controlled to the extent considered desirable in the national interests. Organisations have been created for all the markets here concerned, such as those for cereals, cattle, dairy products, sugar, potatoes, eggs, beer, fish, fruit, vegetables, wine, and others. Each of these separate market organisations is composed of all persons connected with its particular trade, thus - for instance - that for cereals consists of all the growers, grain dealers, grain associations, mills, mill-produce dealers, and bakers. The market organisations are partly regional and partly national, i.e., those set up for each part of Germany (the regional ones) are subordinated to one competent for the country as a whole (the national one). Thus, for example, the twenty regional organisations for the grain trade are combined to form the national organisation for that trade, and so on.

National Socialists have all along realised the importance of farmers as a class and that of farming as an industry. Notwithstanding the industrialisation of Germany, agriculture still absorbs almost 30 per cent of all those who work for their living. The greater part of the country's food is produced by the intensive cultivation of the soil, even though there are large districts where the latter is of relatively poor quality. The promotion of farming and food production is therefore one of the most essential objectives at which German agricultural policy must be aimed. The scope of that policy extends, in the first place, to the tillers of the soil, to their families and children, to the preservation of rural traditions and modes of thinking, and to the farmers' views on honour and the interests of his vocation. The N.F.E., therefore, looks upon it as its special function to establish social harmony between employers and employees, to provide the ambitious and efficient farm labourer with facilities for advancement, to strengthen the ties that connect him with the soil he tills, and to accord preference to him when creating new farmsteads and new homesteads. Particular attention is also directed towards the improvement of the conditions of labour, to the housing problem, etc. The educational system is promoted by the establishment of vocational schools for farmers and in other ways. The feeling of solidarity among villagers is encouraged, and it is also intended to cultivate that feeling on a nation-wide basis. Visible expression is given to the last-named object by the National Farmers' Congress (Reichsbauerntag) which is convened at Goslar once a year in the late autumn.

The second specific aim of the country's agricultural policy is concerned with the farm as such, more especially with measures likely to increase and improve the output in one form or another (production, stockbreeding, supply of high-grade seeds, soil improvement, etc.). These important tasks can be carried out most conveniently by the close collaboration of the N.F.E. with the competent Government departments. Other matters here concerned are: advice on agricultural matters, vocational instruction, the machinery supply, and the holding of agricultural shows. In this latter respect notable progress has been achieved in recent years; and the National Food Estate's annual show always provides excellent opportunities for studying the work already achieved.

Finally, the N.F.E. is entrusted with the control of the agricultural produce markets. Reference has already been made to the organisations established for that purpose, it being the special task of the N.F.E. to ensure their harmonious co-operation and their conduct along uniform principles.

Co-operation between the N.F.E. and the Government departments is very close. Thanks to the valuable work done by the members of the National Labour Service, large districts in the Ems country, along the shores of the North Sea and elsewhere have been opened up for cultivation. The N.F.E. is also connected with such matters as the regional planning of the Reich, the provision of land for public purposes, the creation of national reservations, afforestation schemes, etc.

The N.F.E. comprises 20 regional organisations, divided into about 500 district organisations, which in turn, are subdivided into a large number of local groups. The "leader" of the National Food Estate is R. Walther Darre, who is also the Reich Farmers' Leader. Each regional organisation is presided over by a Regional Farmers' Leader, each district organisation by a District Farmers' Leader, and each local organisation by a Local Farmers' Leader.

The administrative organs of the N.F.E. comprise one central office domiciled in Berlin and 20 regional offices domiciled in the various regional districts. Each administrative office is divided into three departments, one each for the three special functions of the N.F.E. already described (i.e., the human element, the vocational element, and the control of the markets). The N.F.E. is not a department of the Government, even though its Leader is at the same time the National Minister of Food and Agriculture. The ideal of self-administration is realised by the arrangement under which the regional and subregional "leaders" assist in an honorary capacity in carrying out the functions of the N.F.E.

Particular interest - not only in Germany, but also elsewhere - is taken in the market control set up by the N.F.E., which is more consistently carried out than any corresponding system introduced in other parts of the world. The successes achieved prove that the fundamental principles underlying the German system are sound. According to the calculations of the Institute for the Study of the Business Cycle, the proceeds derived from the sale of agricultural produce increased in value from 6,400,000,000 to 8,800,000,000 reichsmarks during the three years that have passed since the introduction of the control system, whilst the prices payable by consumers did not undergo a rise in any way comparable to the benefit obtained by the producers.

The special features of the market control system have originated from the following facts:

Germany has neither the size and the natural resources of such a country as the United States, nor does she possess an overseas empire, as does, for instance, Great Britain. Although she has become largely industrialised, she has not abandoned her agricultural basis. Her soil is none too rich, and has nevertheless to support a population numbering about 360 to the square mile. Regional differences, especially between the chief centres of food production and food consumption, are very considerable. The number of small and medium-sized agricultural undertakings is also very large, which adds to the difficulty of organising them. Thus, neither the market policy of the overseas countries with their surplus production nor that of the countries relying upon measures for the protection of the price-level could be adopted. It would have been a mistake to give one-sided assistance to the farmer, whilst leaving the position of the consumer as it was. The method that had to be applied was that of guiding and supervising imports and of regulating the accumulation of stores containing such foodstuffs as cannot be produced at home. Moreover, regard had to be paid to the special social structure of Germany; and this could only be done by making the market organisation very comprehensive.

The introduction of that organisation presented some considerable difficulties. The various markets were in a condition bordering on chaos. In almost all of them the speculative character of the wholesale trade tended to augment the lack of proper organisation. The uncontrolled influence of the prices ruling in the world's markets reduced those obtainable at home to a ruinous level and made production unremunerative. The unscrupulous competition among dealers led to widespread insolvency, the consequences of which were most disastrous to the farmer. Unfair business methods and an excessive number of middlemen helped to aggravate the position still further, more particularly in the "upgrading" industries.

The first step towards the restoration of healthy conditions was the reorganisation of the milk market by the National Commissioner for the Milk Trade. The experience thus gained was subsequently utilised when the final regulations were drawn up. It goes without saying that, in doing so, due regard was paid, to the peculiarities of the local markets and of the individual dairy products. The terms of delivery as between the farmers, the dairies and the retail trade were defined. Prices and price margins corresponding to the work done by each section and to the purchasing capacity of the consumers were fixed, and excessive margins were reduced. Unremunerative undertakings were shut down against payment of compensation, and undertakings essentially necessary to the country's economic interests were encouraged. Special importance was attached to the production of high-class goods and to standardisation. The recent N.F.E. Show held at Frankfort has furnished convincing evidence of the high degree of efficiency attained by these methods. Prices have now been stabilised, both as regards the farmer and the consumer. What was considered impossible a short while ago has been achieved - the price of butter has, for instance, remained unchanged for two years and a half, and the same remark applies to most of the other kinds of agricultural produce. The interference of speculators and vested interests has been eliminated, notably in the grain trade. Prices no longer fall to pieces when the harvest has been particularly abundant. Neither the quality nor the extent of each farmer's production is subject to any control. He can produce what he likes and as much as he likes. The market regulations will always enable him to sell at adequate prices those commodities for which there is a general demand. The number of middlemen in the process of distribution has been reduced to a minimum. During the preceding economic era, production was rationalised. Today it has become necessary to organise the distribution, and therefore the supply, of the goods in accordance with the dictates of common sense, without restricting production in any way. This makes it possible to effect enormous savings, which can then be utilised for the benefit of the producer or the consumer. The increase in the yield of agricultural production is mainly due to such savings.

The "leaders" of the market associations, assisted by a committee representing the economic interests involved, are held responsible for the proper application of the market regulations which, after all, are merely the outcome of considerations governed by common-sense principles. They are intended to serve, and they do serve, the national interests as well as those of the economic groups affected, more especially those of the producers and consumers. The dealers are required to be reliable, to have an expert knowledge of their trade, and to be financially sound. These various requirements are ensured by a system of licensing. The erection of new undertakings and the enlargement of existing ones is subject to the consent of the market associations, so that the interests of the nation as a whole can be properly protected. In this way, misplaced investments are prevented, and the remunerativeness of the undertakings that are of vital importance to the country is promoted. Considerable value must be ascribed to the system of "compensatory contributions", the origin of which dates back to a time not so very long ago. Deductions were then made from the prices of milk used for drinking purposes, and these amounts were utilised to increase the prices of milk used for manufacturing purposes. The system has proved eminently successful, as it is now possible to induce the producers of milk in remote districts greatly to augment the volume of their production thanks to the millions of reichsmarks diverted towards that end. It should be noted that the money employed for this purpose is not contributed by the taxpayer, but by the industry concerned. In some instances, the system has been used for the introduction of methods tending to cheapen production.

The application of uniform principles to the whole domain of food production and food consumption has provided the agricultural policy of the National Socialist Government with a degree of efficiency hitherto regarded as impossible. This is acknowledged over and over again by the visitors from abroad who have made it a point to study conditions on the spot, no matter whether they have come to investigate the principles underlying the system of market control, the promotion of farming efficiency, the preservation of cultural traditions, or matters of vocational organisation. The discussion of the agricultural problems confronting individual countries, the solution of which is taken in hand everywhere, can be made very fruitful. It enables members of the various European nations to realise the fact that all of them have to work shoulder to shoulder in a common task and makes them anxious to contribute their own share for the benefit of all.

SECTION THREE

SOCIAL POLICY IN THE NEW GERMANY

Dr. Robert Ley

Leader of the National Labour Front

INTRODUCTION

THE great importance of social policy to the working population of Germany cannot be properly appreciated without some knowledge of the changes that have come over the country's economic structure during the last fifty years or so. In the 'eighties of the past century, that structure was relatively balanced; but since then the process of industrialisation has made enormous headway. Large parts of the population are now concentrated in the big towns and in the industrial districts, whilst - on the other hand - extensive agricultural regions are but sparsely populated.

The percentage of persons engaged in agricultural pursuits went down from 42 in 1882 to 21 in 1933. During the same period, the percentage of persons employed in industry, including handicrafts, rose from 36.9 to 38.8, and that of persons engaged in commerce and traffic, from 9.6 to 16.9. In 1882, about 14,700,000 persons were absorbed by industry, as compared with some 25,300,000 in 1933. The number of persons engaged in commerce and traffic rose from 3,800,000 in 1882 to 10,400,000 in 1925 and to about 11,000,000 in 1933, nearly three times as much as in 1882. This great structural transformation was accompanied by internal migration on a considerable scale, with the result that, for instance, the density of the population in such industrial areas as the State of Saxony and the Prussian provinces of the Rhineland and Westphalia is now 346.8, 318.3 and 249.3 per square kilometre respectively, whilst it is as low as 38 and 43 respectively in such agricultural areas as Mecklenburg - Strelitz and Grenzmark Posen - Westpreussen.

Another factor that has materially affected the position is the increased concentration in industry, commerce and traffic. Whilst the percentage of persons operating a business of their own decreased from 46 to 19 during the past fifty years, that of workers and other kinds of employees increased from 55 to 76. The workers soon discovered that, as individuals, they were unable to obtain a proper share in fixing the conditions of labour, and therefore created their own organisations - an example followed shortly afterwards by the employers. Under the influence of the 'class' principle, these organisations gradually developed into mutually antagonistic forces; and in many instances, they regarded it as their principal task to fight one another. It is quite true that the Government, especially after the close of the War, became conscious of its duty to intervene in all serious labour disputes; but it continued to adhere to the Liberalistic dogma that the conditions of labour must be fixed - generally speaking - by the interested parties themselves. However, neither the organisations of the workers nor those of the employers proved capable of accomplishing this task in a satisfactory manner, so that strikes and lock outs followed upon one another in rapid succession. The social tension thus resulting was bound to develop into a grave internal crisis at some moment or other.

Germany found herself in the midst of such a crisis when Herr Hitler took over the Government of the country. Labour disputes had become a chronic feature. The Government's arbitration boards were either too weak or too much under the influence of the politicians to bring order into the growing chaos. The trades unions that were swayed by Marxist teaching did not want social peace. They calculated that their chances of acquiring political power would improve with the growing dissatisfaction of the workers.

One of the first necessities with which the Hitler Government found itself faced was that of dissolving the organisations that kept alive the antagonism between employers and employees. They were replaced by the German Labour Front - a body comprising employers as well as employees. At the same time, preparations were made for the creation of an entirely new system of social order based on the following National Socialist principles: the solidarity of all persons working for their living; the idea of leadership; the recognition of the factory, etc., as a bond of union, and the ethical conceptions of honour and loyalty. All this preliminary work crystallised in the passing of the Act governing the regulation of national labour (January 20th, 1934).

THE NATIONAL LABOUR LAW

That Act has been correctly described as the Magna Carta of Germany's social policy. The National Socialist principle of the solidarity of all persons working for their living finds its chief expression in its application to the individual works or factories. They are the nuclei of all social and economic life. The object aimed at is clearly set forth in Article 1 of the Act, according to which employers and employees are required "to collaborate with one another in order to promote the objects for which the undertaking has been founded and for the common benefit of the people and the State." The same principle of solidarity is given expression in Article 2, where it says that the employer - described as the "leader" of the undertaking - is required to promote the welfare of the employees, whilst the latter are asked to show that spirit of loyalty towards the employer which is founded upon their joint interest in the undertaking.

On the basis of this mutual loyalty it became then possible to extend the National Socialist principle of leadership to the economic and social sphere, more particularly so because the employees are protected from any misuse of the powers thus conferred upon the employer by the Government appointed trustees of labour. These latter are the Government's representatives in the domain of labour. Their principal task is to preserve social and economic peace. They have to supervise the confidential councils (see below) and to settle any disputes that may arise. If it is found impossible to elect the members of the confidential councils in the ordinary way, the trustee of labour may make use of his power to appoint them himself. Such members as prove unsuitable for their task, either because of incapacity or on personal grounds, can be removed from the councils at his behest. He is entitled - either at the request of the confidential council or at his own initiative - to modify the works' regulations or to draw up such regulations himself and to issue them with binding force if, contrary to the provisions of the law, no regulations have been drawn up by those required to do so or if the existing regulations fail to comply with the legal requirements. He is empowered in certain cases to issue wages regulations (to take the place of the wages agreements customary until 1933), and the works regulations have then to be adjusted to them. He is also authorised to issue guiding lines governing individual employment agreements, to which the works leader is required to adhere. Finally, he acts as prosecutor in connection with cases brought before the courts of social honour, and has to be consulted before any works are shut down and before any large numbers of workers are given notice. In special instances, additional functions can be transferred to him by the Minister of Labour or the Minister of National Economy. The trustee can only carry out his numerous tasks on condition that he maintains close contact with all those who are engaged in economic pursuits. The law has therefore empowered him to make use of experts who are specially sworn in and who have to "promise" that they will exercise their functions to the best of their ability and knowledge, that they will not unduly promote the interests of any one party, and that they will devote themselves exclusively to the welfare of the community."

Another instrument of which the trustees make use in the interests of the maintenance of social peace is the so-called confidential council already referred to. Confidential councils have to be set up in all works where more than twenty persons are employed. The members are elected by the employees. It is their special duty "to deepen the confidence that must exist in the works community." The chief difference between them and the works councils created under the provisions of the Act of 1920 is that they are intended to remove the antagonism between employers and employees consciously fostered by the Act just referred to, in which it was provided that the works councils had "to represent the special interests of the employees as opposed to those of the employers." Thus, the representative body of the employees is no longer an organ of class warfare, but one serving the interests of the community. Seeing that all members of the confidential councils must belong to the German Labour Front, it is evident that a close connection exists between the two organisations.

Although the new Act explicitly states that each undertaking has to settle its own affairs itself, it does not follow that there is a complete absence of regulations applicable to all of them in a general way. Thus, for instance, the wages regulations issued by the trustees of labour are of a compulsory character. Since May 1st, 1934, some 2,100 sets of such regulations have been issued - a circumstance which proves that the National Socialist Government is well aware of the dangers that might result from too individual a system of labour conditions during the period of transition.

It is in conformity with the spirit pervading Germany's new social legislation that additional protection is now accorded to employees against unjust dismissals. Every employee who has been connected with an undertaking for not less than one year is entitled to appeal to the Labour Courts if, in his opinion, the notice of dismissal sent to him is unjust and is not prompted by the necessities of the undertaking.

If the court orders the employer to withdraw the notice and if he refuses to do so, he is required to pay compensation to the employee concerned. Normally, the sum thus payable must not exceed one-half of the income earned by the employee during the year immediately preceding his dismissal. If, however, "it is obvious that the dismissal is due to the high-handed action of the employer, that the reasons given for it are of a trivial nature, or that the power vested in the employer has been grossly abused," the court may order the employer to pay compensation equal to the amount earned by the employee during the whole year. Whenever it is intended to dismiss a large number of employees, the trustees of labour are entitled to postpone the date at which the notices become effective by a period up to two months.

It follows from the foregoing brief outline of Germany's new labour legislation that there can be no question of "the creation of a new kind of white slavery," as had been asserted by hostile critics abroad during the first few years after Herr Hitler's assumption of government. The truth, indeed, is that the liberty promised to the German workers by the preceding regimes but never really granted has now become a reality. The worker has been made a partner of the works community on a footing of equality. He has received increased protection from dismissal, and his social honour is safeguarded by a special code which has no equal anywhere. The stigma of proletarianism has been removed from him. It is self-evident, of course, that there can be no fruitful collaboration between the employer and his employees unless all are animated by the National Socialist spirit of solidarity. To cultivate that spirit is the special task allotted to the German Labour Front. The tribunals of social honour see to it that decency, comradeship and loyalty are more than mere words when applied to the private intercourse between all members of the works. Anyone whose actions conflict with the essence of the spirit of solidarity or with the duties incumbent upon him as part of the works community, has to face severe penalties, such as his removal from the undertaking at which he was employed or his disqualification from the office of a works' leader or for membership of the confidential council, all of which are equivalent to his elimination from the social sphere. Such penalties have already been inflicted in a number of instances and have been given full publicity.

THE GERMAN LABOUR FRONT

The legal foundation upon which the German Labour Front rests is a decree issued by Herr Hitler under date of October 24th, 1934. In Article 2 it is stated that the establishment of nation-wide solidarity of all persons engaged in economic activities is to be its chief purpose. In other words, the German Labour Front (G.L.F) is required to make the conviction prevail in all undertakings that - in the economic as well as in the political sphere - success depends upon the closest possible collaboration of all. Another object for which it has been founded is to maintain industrial peace, and to do so in co-operation with the trustees of labour. In order to achieve this object, the works' leaders must have a profound understanding of the just demands of the employees and vice versa. To this end, a special agreement was concluded in March, 1935, between Dr. Schacht, the Minister of National Economy, and Dr. Ley, the head of the G.L.F., for the creation of social self administering bodies, viz., the local labour committees, the regional councils of labour and economy, the National Council of Labour, and the National Economic Council. Their function is to attend to economic and social questions transcending the scope of the individual undertakings and to give due prominence to the spirit of solidarity in solving them.

The G.L.F. is organised in a twofold way - first, in conformity with the organisation of the National Socialist party, and second, in conformity with that of the country's national economy. On the occasion of the Nuremberg party rally (September 1936), Dr. Ley gave a detailed account of the practical work already done by the G.L.F. He showed that, among other matters, some 38,000 homesteads had already been created by that organisation, whilst an additional 65,000 were in course of erection and an additional 80,000 were contemplated. Not less than 234,000,000 reichsmarks was paid by way of benefits in the course of three years; and 2,500,000 persons attended the educational courses that were held in more than 400 training centres. More than 1,000,000 youths and young girls have so far taken part in the national vocational contests.

Special mention should be made of a sub-organisation of the G.L.F.-styled "Strength through Joy" - which is mainly concerned with holiday and leisure-time arrangements. Thanks to this branch of the G.L.F., Germany's social policy has been extended to the cultural sphere.

The great popularity of the arrangements made by the " Strength through Joy" organisation is proved by the large number of participants in them. The section for travelling and hiking is perhaps the most popular one, its membership having trebled in the course of the past three years. Its pleasure cruises to foreign countries have attracted great attention, both at home and abroad. They have enabled German workers to visit Norway, Finland, Great Britain, Lisbon, Madeira, the Azores and the Baltic countries; and even though personal contact with the inhabitants of those parts has necessarily been but brief and cursory, it has been sufficiently effective in showing up the preposterousness of many an anti-German prejudice.

Equally valuable results have been attained by the tours within Germany. Whatever regional antagonisms may still have divided Germans, they have been dispelled by numerous opportunities thus afforded for obtaining a better knowledge of one another. Ethically and morally too, division into North and South has vanished. In 1934, the number of persons taking part in these travelling and hiking arrangements amounted to some 2,000,000; but by the end of 1936, it had gone up to more than 6,000,000, whilst several more millions will be added during the current year. The ultimate object is to enable 14,000,000 persons of small means to benefit from these arrangements every year. The cost is so low that 16 reichsmarks will pay for one week's seaside holiday this year.

Other sections of the" Strength through Joy" organisation deal with sporting, artistic and educational matters, all of which tend to promote the spirit of national solidarity. On the occasion of the third annual meeting (November 27th, 1936), the management was in the proud position to announce that 52,700,000 persons had attended the 142,000 entertainments organised by the entertainment section during the preceding couple of years. During the first eleven months of 1936, the number of persons attending the stage performances of the theatres co-operating with the organisation amounted to 4,850,000.

Nearly 17,000,000 persons attended the variety entertainments arranged for the evening hours. Millions of German citizens have thus been enabled to derive pleasure and enjoyment on a scale which would have been unattainable by them without the aid of the organisation. Foreign critics have often pointed out the relatively low level of the wages paid in Germany and have commented on the fact that there has been no appreciable rise in that level notwithstanding the enhanced activity in the economic field during the past three years. They forget, however, that the real purchasing power of the masses has considerably increased, as the German workers are now in a position to benefit from the manifold facilities offered by the G.L.F. and its affiliated organisations.

Another special section is that attending to the aesthetic aspects of work. Its activities extend to the provision of up-to-date swimming baths, washing and dressing rooms, canteens, green spaces, etc., in connection with factories and other undertakings, to the improvement of the dwelling accommodation on river-craft, to the creation of model villages, and to the elimination of everything that detracts from the outward appearance of the workers' homesteads. More than 500,000,000 reichsmarks has already been spent on these objects at the instance of that section and with its collaboration. As regards their pleasant appearance, the access to them of light and air, and their tasteful design, the German factory buildings are second to none.

A few remarks must be added on the subject of sports. The "Strength through Joy" organisation has taken a remarkable interest in furthering them. Even when it is remembered that physical education is one of the main planks of the reconstruction programme of modern Germany, the fact that 6,000,000 persons took part last year in the sporting arrangements made by that organisation is an achievement of no mean significance. The number of sports instructors went up from 1,300 at the end of 1935 to 2,800 a twelvemonth later. The report presented to the annual meeting held on November 27th, 1936, rightly speaks of a cultural achievement and contains the following passage:

Three years ago we began to arouse and mobilise the intellectual and ethical capabilities inherent in the German workman by enabling him to realise the beauty and grandeur of life in nature, art and the company of those of his fellows who share his own views. In doing so, we have broken with a social convention that had been valid for decades and have removed the antagonism between work and culture.

The report shows that the objects aimed at have already been attained to a considerable extent.

REORGANISATION OF PUBLIC WELFARE WORK

The scope of this article does not allow us to give an account of all the branches of social policy. We therefore limit ourselves to a description of those especially characteristic of the attitude of the Third Reich towards these matters, and now turn to the National Socialist achievements in connection with public welfare work, the most important of which is the Winter Relief Scheme - an organisation well known abroad. It is conceived as a comprehensive effort on the part of the whole German people. Within its framework, the various organisations of the National Socialist party, the independent private associations, the Roman Catholic "Caritas," the Home Mission, the Protestant Church, the Red Cross, the Salvation Army, and others, harmoniously collaborate with one another. Even very small religious groups, such as the Adventists, are represented among them. For reasons of convenience the Jewish organisations have alone been left outside the scheme; but this does not mean that the charity work carried on for the benefit of necessitous Jews is in any way inferior to that carried on for the rest of the population. Any allegations of a contrary nature that are made by anti-German writers are pure inventions.

During the winter months of 1933/4, some 17,000,000 persons were looked after by the Scheme. Thanks to the improved economic conditions and the decrease in the number of unemployed, the figure went down to 13,800,000 in 1934/5, and to 12,900,000 in 1935/6. Among the beneficiaries were 69,336 foreigners. Although the number of persons looked after has gone down year after year, the aggregate amount collected has continually gone up, as may be seen from the following figures: 1933/4 - 350,000,000 reichsmarks; 1934/5 - 360,500,000 reichsmarks; 1935/6 - 372,000,000 reichsmarks. Hence, individual benefits could be correspondingly increased. A comparison with the results achieved by the Winter Relief Schemes of 1931/2 and 1932/3 when the total collections amounted to 97,000,000 reichsmarks and 91,000,000 reichsmarks respectively, clearly shows the great change that came over the attitude of the German people in this respect since the taking-over of the Government by Herr Hitler. Not less than 52,903,070 (metric) hundredweight of coal was distributed in 1933/4, or nearly fifty times as much as in 1931/2.

The methods adopted under the scheme present a good deal of variety. Once a month, every household, etc., limits its principal meal to a so-called "one-dish dinner," the money thus saved being passed on to the organisers of the scheme. Additional funds are obtained by street collections on the part of members of the party organisations, the various vocational groups, etc., and people are also asked to subscribe fixed amounts at regular or irregular intervals. The Fuhrer's motto: "No one shall go hungry, and no one shall feel cold," guides the activities conducted under the scheme. The circle of beneficiaries includes persons out of work or doing part-time work only, those receiving assistance from the public welfare authorities, those in receipt of small annuities, etc., so that the surprise sometimes expressed by foreign critics at the alleged disproportion between the small number of unemployed and the large number of persons benefiting from the Winter Relief Scheme is easily explained.

The cost incurred under the Scheme works out at 1.7% of the total value of the collections, this low percentage being due to the large number of unpaid collectors, of whom there were 1,234,000 in the winter months of 1935/6.

Next in importance to the Winter Relief Scheme is the "Mother and Child" organisation. Its object is to improve the racial biological standards of family health. The methods adopted to that end are threefold: First, assistance is given to healthy families in economic distress (money, deliveries in kind, opportunities for work, facilities in connection with dwelling accommodation); secondly, assistance is given to mothers and children just before and after the birth of the latter by sending them to suitable recreation homes; thirdly, numerous kindergartens are provided in the towns and in the country. The funds required for these measures are mainly derived from the contributions paid by the members of the National Socialist Welfare Organisation - the leading organisation of its kind in modern Germany, with a staff of 21,935 helpers in 1936. Some 1,098,000 children below school age were looked after in the kindergartens. More than 3,000,000 persons made use in 1935 of the facilities for advice placed at their disposal. Economic assistance was given, in 1935, to 1,180,000 families comprising 4,760,000 persons. The total sum of money spent on economic relief up to September 1936 amounted to 38,600,000 reichsmarks.

It should be noted that the various schemes here described are of a voluntary character, that they are financed by the people, and that they are supplementary to the enormous achievements of the National Socialist State in respect of social insurance, war veterans' relief, national relief, publicly financed charitable institutions, and labour exchange, most of which - as has been said before - have to be left outside the scope of the present account.

HOMESTEADS FOR WORKERS

There is room, however, for some remarks on two publicly conducted activities, viz., the homestead scheme, and the work done by the labour exchanges.

Everybody who has travelled through Germany in recent years must have noted the numerous pleasant looking dwelling houses (and colonies of them) on the outskirts of large towns, each of them surrounded by a small garden. These homesteads are financed with the aid of the Government. Their present number is about 140,000; but an additional 60,000 or 70,000 will be built in the course of the present year, so that there will soon be some 200,000 in all parts of the country. Even this, however, only marks the beginnings of a far larger scheme, as it is intended to raise their number to several millions within the next few years. National Socialists are firm believers in the "back-to-the-land" movement and hold that something must be done to stop the excessive congregation of human material in towns and industrial districts. Besides, the homestead scheme is of considerable economic value. On an average, 400 reichsmarks' worth of supplementary foodstuffs is produced by each homestead per annum.

At its inception, the scheme was intended to be mainly a charitable measure. This was expressly stated in President Hindenburg's decree issued October 6th, 1931, relative to "surburban homesteads."

Preference was to be given to big towns and industrial districts where unemployment was particularly severe. The National Socialist Government has abandoned that conception. The homesteads now created are chiefly intended for persons in full employment, and preference is given to small and medium-sized municipalities and to country areas. The object aimed at is to assist in creating a working population more or less permanently settled on the land occupied by it and enjoying a fair measure of economic security. Although on principle every German citizen possessed of small means only is entitled to benefit from the scheme, provided that he is honest, healthy and nationally and politically dependable, it has become more and more customary in recent years to confine the scheme to workmen. Last autumn, for example, the public funds provided for its working were exclusively assigned to the erection of workmen's homesteads.

Private funds are being increasingly used to finance the scheme. At first, practically the whole cost of each homestead was covered by loans obtained from the Government. Today, however, the funds required are largely raised in the private capital market. From 15 to 20% of the cost has to be found by the worker himself. Public funds are now only granted to finance the "peaks" of the invested money. As a rule, no loans exceeding 1,500 reichsmarks are granted per homestead, although in exceptional instances an additional 300 reichsmarks and a Government guarantee of second mortgages are also obtainable. The size of each homestead together with the ground it occupies must be large enough to include 1,000 square metres of usable land.

Not every German worker is either able or willing to acquire a homestead of his own. Moreover, there is still considerable lack of dwelling accommodation in the towns, notwithstanding the increased building activity since 1933. It has therefore become necessary to use public funds for the erection of workmen's flats as well. The money thus made available helps to finance buildings of this kind, the flats being let to workmen at reasonable rents. The "barracks" type is avoided, most of the buildings concerned being relatively small and only rising to the height of a few storeys. Since the early part of 1935, about 100,000 such "people's dwellings" have been provided.

LABOUR EXCHANGES

The distribution of labour in modern Germany is regulated by the Government in a systematic manner. The "totalitarian" principle, which governs all the activities of the Third Reich, has thus impressed its stamp upon this domain also.

The public authority dealing with these matters is the Government Board for Labour Exchanges and Unemployment Insurance. Its name sufficiently indicates its twofold purpose. By the collaboration of all the competent bodies it has become possible to reduce the number of unemployed from 6,014,000 in January 1933 to about 1,100,000 in August 1936. Seeing that at most 50% of the latter can be regarded as still employable, it follows that mass unemployment has ceased to exist in Germany.

One of the aims in view - in so far as the distribution of labour is concerned - is the application to it of the National Socialist views on population policy and vocational policy. This means that, as a first necessity, the influx of workmen from the rural districts to the industrial centres must be reversed, and, in addition, that preferential treatment must be accorded to older workmen and to married men with children. The first-named purpose is achieved by an Act passed May 15th, 1934 by which the President of the Board referred to above is empowered to rule that his consent must be obtained before non-local workmen and other employees are permitted to look for employment in districts where unemployment is high. The prohibitions thus enforced in regard to Berlin, Hamburg, Bremen, and the Saar have achieved the desired object. In Berlin, for example, unemployment was reduced by two-thirds within a couple of years. It was therefore possible to cancel some of these prohibitions (viz., those affecting Bremen, the Saar, and, to some extent, Berlin) by a decree which became effective in December 1936.

A decree issued May 11th, 1934, prohibited the admission of agricultural labourers to certain industries, to the post office and railway services, etc. By the decree issued on February 26th, 1935, the President of the Board was further empowered to withdraw agricultural labourers from non- agricultural vocations and thus enable them to return to their original occupations.

Further assistance to agriculture was provided by the arrangements enabling young men and women volunteers to place their services at the disposal of farmers for periods of six months or more. On an average, some 100,000 young persons volunteered to do so during the period 1933-5. They are given free board and lodging by their employers, and also receive a monetary remuneration out of the funds controlled by the Board. Many of them have continued to stay with the farmers after the expiration of their original term of six months. Now that this measure has served its purpose well, the relevant decrees issued by the President of the Board have also been withdrawn, effective December 1st, 1936.

Other regulations concern the exchange of younger for older employees. It had been found that the decline of unemployment since Herr Hitler took up office mainly benefited the younger unemployed (between the ages of 18 and 25). In that category, unemployment decreased by two-thirds, whilst the decrease was only half as much in the age group from 40 to 60. Such a development conflicts with the principles of National Socialist family policy. By a decree issued August 10th; 1934, the President of the Board was accordingly authorised to make arrangements for the interchange of younger and older employees. This measure affected some 130,000 employees during the period October 1934 to October 1935. It was also provided that the consent of the competent local Labour Exchange had to be obtained before persons below 25 were given employment. That interchange has now come to an end, and - in view of the progressive shortage of labour - the consent just referred to is hardly ever refused.

Another measure intended to facilitate the most suitable distribution of the available labour is the introduction of the so-called "employment book." This was made compulsory by the Act passed February 26th, 1935 The book contains exact particulars regarding the owner's age, whether married or unmarried, his vocational training, his qualifications for employment, and similar matters. By now, some 20,600,000 workers and other employees have been supplied with such books.

It will be gathered from the foregoing account that the distribution of labour in Germany is not subject to hard and fast rules, but is governed by the conditions that prevail at the time concerned. Restrictions in connection with the search for work, etc., are only imposed in so far as the primary interests of the State and those of the body economic make it necessary.

This remark also applies to the rules governing the distribution of labour under the Four Year Plan as drawn up towards the close of 1936 by General Goring, Herr Hitler's commissioner responsible for the working of the plan. Owing to the decrease of unemployment, the number of available trained workers has progressively declined, more especially in such key industries as the building trade and the iron and non-ferrous metals industry. The number of unemployed bricklayers went down from 162,000 in 1933 to 8,000 in 1936, and that of unemployed locksmiths and engine-fitters from 262,000 to 31,000. There was a risk that serious inconvenience might arise in those two industries if nothing was done to improve the position; and as the conditions in other industries tended to change in the same manner, it was considered wise to make timely arrangements for a supply of trained apprentices before it was too late. Accordingly, General Goring decided to introduce a series of measures which were announced on November 7th, 1936. The first of them deals with the two key industries just referred to. On the strength of the reports received by the President of the Board for Labour Exchanges from works employing ten or more persons, he is authorised to demand that the works concerned shall add to the number of their apprentices. It may be assumed that he will but rarely avail himself of this authority, because the reports already received show that employers have spontaneously complied to a far-reaching extent with their duties in connection with the training of apprentices. Here, too, the initiative of the Government commissioner is therefore of a subsidiary nature only. In exceptional cases - i.e., when the works are unable, for special reasons, to increase the number of apprentices - they may be asked to pay a sum of money by way of compensation. At present, these rules are only applicable to the two key industries named; but it may be taken for granted that they will be applied to other industries as well if the need for doing so should arise.

The second and third of the measures introduced by the commissioner for the Four-Year Plan are intended to ensure that there is always a sufficient supply of workers in the metal-working industry and in the building trade. Whenever it is desired to employ ten or more additional metal workers, the consent of the Labour Exchange must first be obtained, which will only be given after carefully considering the primary interests of the State and the body economic. Moreover, it has been provided that trained workers employed in work not really suitable for them in view of their past training may be transferred by the Labour Exchanges - if necessary, without formal notice - to other work for which their skill and knowledge makes them more suitable. A further rule serving the same purpose-i.e., that of making more rational use of the available labour - makes it compulsory to inform the authorities beforehand of any large piece of work which it is intended to take in hand. Lastly, there is a rule by which preference is to be given to older workers when vacancies have to be filled up. That rule is in the nature of an appeal to the works' leaders, reminding them of their moral duty in this respect. If they fail to respond to it, compulsion will be used by the Government.

There can be no doubt that the Four Year Plan makes additional demands upon the workers. It is an important aim of Germany's economic policy to maintain the existing equilibrium of wages and prices; and for that reason, no wage increases are possible. General Goring, however, acting as the Fuhrer's Commissioner for the Four Year Plan, has issued a decree dated December 3rd, 1937, which provides that payment in full is to be made for the following public holidays: New Year's Day, Easter Monday, Whit-Monday, Christmas Day, and Boxing Day, although, of course, no work is done on these days.

Germany's social policy is thus a healthy combination of freedom and compulsion. No other policy would enable the country's predominantly industrial population to preserve its continued existence on the relatively limited space within which it is confined. Beyond that, the new social order pays due regard to such specifically German character traits as a sense of honour, loyalty, comradeship, fairness, collaboration, and a pronounced love of nature. All these characteristics were temporarily submerged owing to the soulless mechanisation typical of some aspects of modern civilisation. No correct appreciation of Germany's new social order would be complete if it confined itself to a study of the institutional innovations. The spirit that has created the new forms and that finds its expression in them is far more important than these can ever be.

There is probably no country - except Russia - in which international Marxism has done more serious damage than in Germany. The German people have a natural liking for abstract speculation - a circumstance which made it easy for the spokesmen of the various Internationals to poison the minds of nearly one-half of the German population by their anti-national propaganda. In the end, a widespread conviction had grown up that the national interests were the special prerogative of the capitalists and that the workers' only hope of salvation was the world revolution.

Today we find it difficult to realise the depth of the antagonisms that divided the German nation prior to 1933. In some other countries there is undoubtedly a greater cleavage, at least outwardly, between the various social groups than exists in Germany; but in our country things had gone so far that, although the vital needs and the life habits of all its inhabitants are very much the same, the various sections were unable to understand one another, as the political views they held were so fundamentally different. They were, indeed, quite ready to fly at each other's throats and looked upon one another as enemies rather than as fellow-citizens. The tension between the workers and the middle classes, and between the different vocational groups had become so great that civil war - always latent - threatened to break out openly at any moment. Since then, however, a complete transformation has taken place. The workmen, the handicraftsmen, the farmers, the average citizens - none of them resemble their former selves. Naturally, there are still a few who cannot or will not detach themselves from the past, but their existence is made negligible by the fact that the broad masses of the people have changed their political outlook within a remarkably brief space of time. Consider, for instance, the workman.

Accompany me on a stroll through the factories of the country, and you will discover that the spirit that prevails in them has changed.

Germany has been re-born. The Leader told us on the occasion of one of the party rallies - and he has often repeated it - that he regards this fundamental transformation as the most wonderful achievement of our time. Where there was hopelessness and despair, there is now faith, a joyful outlook on life, and renewed hope. Formerly, there was mutual enmity, jealousy, envy, and hatred, but today everybody tries to make himself useful to his fellows, to be their loyal comrade, and to render them some small service whenever he can.

I have always stated in my numerous speeches and addresses that it would be wrong to assert that all our troubles had vanished, and that everybody could now look at things through rose-coloured spectacles. The truth is that our troubles are still great and that they will remain so. The sacrifices demanded of each individual are perhaps greater than before; and the work many of us are expected to perform is certainly much more difficult now than in the past. We have not reached that state of supreme bliss that may result from the absence of all worries, anxieties, and oppressive burdens. And yet, people have taken a new delight in life, in mutual collaboration, and in everything that makes a nation what it is.

Formerly, every citizen who was a little better off than his neighbour, or earned more than he, or exceeded him in skill and efficiency, was treated with spiteful jealousy. Certain quarters made it their business to exploit that antagonism for the furtherance of their political ends, and the vitiated atmosphere thus created, was like a blight affecting the whole nation. That does not mean that optimism, hopefulness and a sound faith in the future had completely died out. But these characteristics were confined to individuals, and when the latter came together in mass meetings or created a political party, their place was immediately taken by discontent, strife, and a lack of mutual trust.

Now, however, that disunited people has been given a new leadership. Critics may fail to understand what I mean by this and may ask: "Were there no leaders in the past?" There have certainly been States, and political, social, and economic regimes since the dawn of history; but true leadership is something absolutely new and unique. This nation has passed through every form of political organisation. It has had its emperors, kings, princely rulers, and republics. It has tried all kinds of economic organisations. Vocations, class divisions and class distinctions have come and gone. But a genuine leadership has never existed during the past two thousand years; and the individual citizen has never felt that there is someone at the head of affairs who takes a personal interest in him, that his own troubles are also the troubles of his leaders, and that people occupying responsible positions look after him.

Those who make a total claim to the soul of a people must not content themselves with advocating their principles, but must also possess a gift for organisation. It is not sufficient that everybody is theoretically convinced of the truth of those principles. The point that really matters is that the idea proclaimed must continue to remain a living force and must be translated into actual practice. For this reason, National Socialism has created an organisation that is truly all-comprehensive. Foreigners may find it strange that almost all Germans belong to some organisation or other and that a good many of them wear a uniform or are known by some designation of their status. This, however, is not so strange as it looks. The object of that great organisation is to make every German realise that he is personally called upon to do his share in the governance of the country within the sphere allotted to him, and that he is not merely governed from above. National Socialism does not wish to rely for support upon a small number of ruling elements, but desires to be always representative of the will of the whole nation. That means that the National Socialist movement must maintain the closest possible contact with the people and that the capacity for doing so - without which the work achieved could not have been accomplished - must not be lost. A leader who loses contact with the people is sure to lose very soon the qualifications for leadership. No other movement has been better able than National Socialism to speak the language of the people. Its teaching is therefore immediately understood and all the measures initiated by it become effective forthwith without the necessity for prolonged deliberations as a preliminary to action.

The National Socialist Government has dissolved the trades-unions and the federations of employers. It will oppose anyone and anything tending to divide the people into groups. Every factory and every undertaking constitutes a unit, and nothing must be done to interfere with its unity. Works' leaders and employees must decide for themselves, as far as this is possible, how matters are to be arranged. They must find their way to one another, must look upon themselves as an inseparable community, and must cultivate the spirit of comradeship. Their destinies are in their own hands. We have told them: We cannot and we do not interfere with you. Those who assert the contrary want to deceive you. All we can do is to teach you how to master your destiny. We can supply you with the weapons which you need in your struggle. But do not forget that no one can relieve you of that struggle.

No one can dissociate himself from that community or defy it or cowardly hold himself aloof. Every man and every woman, old and young, employer and employed, are governed by the same destiny if they are jointly working in the same undertaking. Their own destiny and that of the undertaking are identical.

Whenever the undertaking is prosperous, they are prosperous also; and whenever it has to face adversity, they have to do so too. They are members of a living community.

It would be completely wrong to imagine that it would be contrary to National Socialist principles to engage in economic activities in a private capacity. It is a fashion with some people to cry out against materialism and materialists. But without material things, there can be no life. We therefore do not despise them. Sometimes there have been moralists who advocated the separate identity of body, soul and mind; but such a view is untenable. If we take away the body, neither a soul nor a mind will be left. If we take away the soul, all that is left is a cold and unemotional creature; and if we take away the mind, the result will be a poor, miserable idiot. The three things belong together. We shall and must retain command of all material things; and we shall and must wrestle with materialism day after day lest it should acquire command over us. Providence has given us reasoning powers and a creative mind, which enables us to mould the material things as we like, to make new inventions, and to ponder over them. But we always need material things when we wish to give practical shape to the new ideas our brain has conceived.

There is therefore nothing disagreeable in our concern with material things. What would be the good of all our Socialist projects if there were no persons capable of calculating, organising and doing business?

Members of another school of thought desire to persuade us that business and idealism mutually exclude each other and are mutually contradictory. That allegation, too, is not correct. I maintain that the very opposite is true. A real idealist anxious to render a genuine service to mankind must have both feet on solid ground. If he has not, he becomes a visionary and a dreamer, and all his idealism becomes worthless and futile. No one derives any benefit from his ideals and ideas. But it is also true that no economic undertaking can prosper unless it is planned and managed and organised in a genuinely idealistic spirit. In every other case, sham prosperity is the best that can be hoped for.

Thus, business and idealism are not contradictions, but rather supplement one another. No idealism can be of any use if it lacks a material foundation.

Our paramount duty is of an educational nature, and our ultimate aim is to establish true national solidarity. Socialism is neither a gift nor a message. It is not a lifeless object manifesting itself in dead paragraphs. Socialism is justice. The workmen in the new Germany know that they do not belong to the great mass of those who, despite the heavy and burdensome work they do, are merely able to earn a scanty livelihood, whilst a small number of more privileged persons can indulge in all the pleasures of life. They know that their welfare is being constantly looked after, that this world and all the things it has to offer exist for their benefit also, and that they are not mere outsiders to all that. It was certainly no easy task to convert convinced Communists and Social Democrats into wholehearted supporters of the principle of national solidarity. Fine words alone were no use - they had to be supplemented by deeds.

Those who had an uncompromising faith in their ability to convince the German workmen of the justice of the claims made by the Leader won the day after a hard struggle. We now know that the people are behind their Leader like one man. It is therefore possible to entrust them with tasks that demand sacrifices and retrenchment. The Four Year Plan is such a task, and its fulfilment is assured because of the nation's confidence in its Leader. The great work to be achieved under the plan will prepare the road for the German people's new prosperity. True Socialism always endeavours to create new values, so that the nation can spend more money and can buy more commodities. The peaceful struggle for safeguarding the material independence of the German people and the supply of a sufficiency of raw materials will be brought to a successful issue.

This conviction is almost unanimously shared by Germany's workers. They realise that Herr Hitler is fighting their own battle and that he - who has sprung from their own ranks - is indeed their Leader.

They know that he concerns himself by day and night with the cares of every German. They have therefore put their trust in him and support his efforts for the maintenance of social peace within Germany just as keenly as they support those for the maintenance of external peace throughout the world. The Leader's foreign policy aims at international peace, and his home policy has established social justice. For that reason, Germany is now spared the strikes and the unrest so prevalent in some other countries.

Herr Hitler, as the true Leader of his fellow countrymen, gives effect to the will expressed by them, just as they, in their turn, have willingly and loyally acknowledged his leadership. Thus, there is perfect concord between the Leader and the nation.

SECTION FOUR

THE STATE AND LABOUR SERVICE IN GERMANY

Senior Labour Leader Muller-Brandenburg

Leader of the Foreign Affairs and Intelligence
Department attached to the Reich Labour Leader

IT is not easy to give the foreigner a true picture of the State Labour Service, because this is a National Socialist scheme based upon conditions such as exist in Germany only. If English readers are to form a proper judgment of it, they must first of all know something of the premises upon which its development depended.

The State Labour Service has to fulfil two great tasks, entrusted to it by the Labour Service Law, namely, an economic and an educational one.

Let us deal first of all with its economic aspect. Even before 1914 Germany was an over- populated country. By the Versailles Treaty, she lost 9.5 % of her population and 13 % of her area - a loss which made the pressure of over-population still greater. Moreover, the districts thus separated contained the richest agricultural land of the Reich. In this way was lost 18 % of the area under potatoes and 17 % of that under rye, the percentages for other products being similar. When it is remembered that Germany's defeat in the War was ultimately due to famine, it is not difficult to realise how terrible it was for her to have to yield up twice as much of her crop bearing area as corresponds to the loss of population. Germany thus lost her chance of being self-supporting in the way of food, and as long as a people depends upon others for essential commodities, it cannot be said to be truly free. Independence in this domain is of vital importance to the freedom of every State.

135

It was, therefore, quite natural that Herr Hitler, the Fuhrer and Chancellor, should desire to provide himself, as soon as he had taken up office, with an instrument that would help him to make Germany self-supporting once more. The instrument chosen for that purpose was the Reich Labour Service. Colonel (now Reich Labour Leader) Hierl, to whom supreme command of the Labour Service was given, did not start upon his duties without sound preparation. In 1929 he had already laid before the Fuhrer his plans for the development of a Labour Service and had received Herr Hitler's approval. From that time onwards, he carefully worked out all the details and took all the steps required to establish a National Socialist Labour Service. Although membership was to be voluntary at first, it was to become a national duty for all Germans later on.

The outcome of that preparatory work was that the Reich Labour Leader, who had surrounded himself with a staff of efficient co-operators, arrived at the following conclusions, namely:

We have in Germany large areas of waste or insufficiently cultivated land that could be used for growing crops. Some 2,000,000 acres could be converted into arable land and more than 2,500,000 acres of poor soil could be made to yield far better crops than is the case now if subjected to improvement. In addition to this, there are another 1,000,000 acres, including waste forests, that could also be made profitable. All in all, this amounts to some 5,000,000 acres - an area as large as the Prussian province of Westphalia or Schleswig-Holstein. It is, therefore, no exaggeration on the part of Colonel Hierl when he continually emphasises that the State Labour Service is capable of adding a whole province to the present area of the Reich.

It is actually true that the Labour Service, when it has carried through the programme at present laid down for it, will have provided Germany, within half the span of a man's life, with sufficient agricultural land to ensure an adequate food supply for the whole country. German food independence will then have been won.

The results hitherto achieved by the Labour Service in making the countryside fruitful show that these statements are no illusions. An area the size of the Saar district was cleared and made ready for cultivation between 1933 and 1935.

So much for the economic point of view; we will now briefly examine the educational aspect of the Labour Service.

In this connection it is necessary to remember that all civilised countries, since the coming of the Machine Age, have greatly suffered from the erection of certain social barriers. Briefly, populations have been divided into two great classes, bourgeoisie and proletariat. The bourgeoisie adopted, for the most part, a Liberal Capitalism which amounted practically to a recognition of the principle that "those who have may do as they please," to which the proletariat replied by asserting that "possession is theft." It must be clear to all unprejudiced persons that both these ideas will finally lead to anarchy and Bolshevism. However, the development of all civilised countries has shown that this recognition is lacking, although the troubles from which all have suffered - some more and some less - are largely attributable to these class differences.

Germany, because of her historical development and, above all, because of her rapid transition from an agricultural to an industrial country, suffered from class quarrels in their extremist form, the position being aggravated by her loss of the War and the resultant Weimar system of government. When the Fuhrer attained power, he was faced with the fact that the German people were divided into two sections neither of whom - though using the German language - could understand the other. Indeed, they were even prepared to fight one another to the death. The Fuhrer and his movement succeeded in achieving the impossible by putting an end to class hatred.

Herr Hitler then instructed the Labour Service to be an instrument by which the lack of vision of the bourgeoisie and the class hatred of the proletariat should be counteracted, and a true community of all Germans should be created. On the National Labour Day, May 1st, 1934, when speaking on the Tempelhof Field, he declared:

It is not a mere chance that the party representing class war and class division fought so bitterly against compulsory Labour Service. They lived by the destruction of the nation and it would not have served their purpose to see these divisions set aside. They therefore told the masses that the Labour Service was designed only to steal the labour from the labourer. They had no Labour Service: instead, they had six million unemployed. We have introduced Labour Service and we have reduced the number of unemployed by more than half. We do not want the Labour Service to take the worker away from his place. In view of the number of employed people and the number enrolled in the Labour Service, such an assertion would be ridiculous. But we do want the Labour Service to compel every young German to work with his hands at least once and thus to contribute to the progressive development of his people. Above all, we want those Germans who are in sedentary occupations to learn what manual work means, so that they may find understanding and sympathy for those of their comrades whose lives are spent in the fields, the factory or the workshop. We want to destroy the haughtiness with which, unfortunately, so many intellectuals look down upon the manual workers and we wish them to realise that they, too, will be worth all the more if they possess a certain capacity for physical work. The whole idea underlying the Labour Service is to promote understanding between all classes and thus to strengthen the spirit of national solidarity. We desire that all should learn to know each other so that, little by little, the natural basis may be formed of a true inward fellowship, a fellowship which was destroyed in the course of many centuries. National Socialism is inspired with the irrevocable determination to re-establish it. We all know, however, that this cannot be achieved by mere words or professions, but only by a new kind of education.

This may be said to be a rough description of the principles in accordance with which Colonel Hierl has led the Reich Labour Service.

We will now briefly describe how the educational task of the Service is approached. It comprises physical culture as well as intellectual instruction, the latter having a deliberately National Socialist tendency.

Physical education is designed to improve the entire physique of the worker, and especially to give him suppleness of limb. The successes attained in this direction are already considerable. Last summer I conducted two delegations of officers of high rank, sent to Germany by two important Powers, round some of our camps and showed them what our Service was doing in the way of physical culture. What they saw aroused their astonishment and admiration, although both delegations came from countries which pay great attention to the physical well-being of their populations. "This is undoubtedly a peak achievement," was the comment of a General Staff officer who is an expert, not only in his own country, but who is intimately acquainted with these matters in three other European countries. I can assure everyone that the Reich Labour Service is firmly determined to maintain that superiority, because it is of enormous importance to the health of our people that our young manhood should undergo this physical education.

Then there is the intellectual education, which is National Socialism's appeal to hearts and heads alike. This teaching is not given in classrooms, but rather consists in the actual conduct of life and work in the camp. Experience is the thing that chiefly matters, whilst the instruction in political science is only an accessory. Even this knowledge is not imparted by the methods of the class-room or the barracks, but rather in the form of a kind of labour comradeship, by means of which the Labour Service Leader puts all matters in so simple and comprehensible a way that they are bound to make an impression. The young workers' heads are not stuffed with knowledge (which they would, in any case, rapidly forget afterwards), but they are made to understand more intuitively what our Leader desires and what is the meaning of the National Socialist battle for the people and the State.

The young people live together in their camps, far from the big cities, and break German ground with their spades, so that members of all classes - workers, officers, farmers and salesmen - get to know one another and to respect one another's feelings. In our camps, class distinctions are overcome by the facts of experience. Elsewhere, leading articles are written deriding class struggles, but we abolish them with the aid of the spade and thanks to the community spirit naturally growing up in the Labour Camps. Here the son of middle-class parents learns that the labourer's son is worth just as much as he, whilst the labourer learns to value the student as a true comrade. The most valuable lesson, however, thus learnt by them is that all work, whether done by the hand or the brain, is equally honourable if performed by decent people for decent purposes. Labour Service has, therefore, provided a new set of practical ethics which is above both the bourgeois and proletarian way of thought, and supersedes both of them. In our camps, the conception "bourgeoisie" meets with just as much ridicule as the conception "proletariat," for every member looks upon himself as a German, and nothing else. There can be no doubt that the work now done under the inspiring leadership of Colonel Hierl is of so great an importance to future generations that it can hardly be realised by us, and this is certainly recognised - even if not fully - by the many people who visit us from abroad. We appreciate their admiration, but we must remind them that our Labour Service is not something that can simply be reproduced elsewhere. This, therefore, is what we always point out to foreign commissions wishing to study the Labour Service:

The worst mistake you could make would be the attempt to copy what we have done. Our Labour Service is essentially German, and is based exclusively upon our home needs and our own sense of values. In these matters, each nation must follow the paths laid down by its own needs and its peculiar instincts, because the conditions and circumstances that have to be dealt with are different in each case. From us you can learn only one thing, and that is that the social disintegration from which nearly all countries are suffering cannot be overcome by writing leading articles or by speech-making, but only by means of action. This, and this only, can be learnt from the German Labour Service. Organisation and development must be evolved separately in each country.

In this the Reich Labour Service resembles National Socialism: it is not an international affair, but simply a German one. So German is it that, to the astonishment of the rest of the world, the young German girls will shortly be drawn into a compulsory Labour Service. They, of course, will not handle spades, but will perform woman's work, for the women of Germany are also to learn that no higher lot can be theirs than to work for their nation in the home, at the cooking-stove and amongst their children.

Thus the Reich Labour Service teaches all young Germans to be of use to their country.

SECTION FIVE

THE NATIONAL SOCIALIST WELFARE OGANISATION

Erich Hilgenfeldt

Head of the National Socialist Welfare Organisation

EVERYTHING now done in Germany is prompted by the conviction that our nation will only be able to assure its future existence if we succeed in maintaining the National Socialist regime. National Socialism is not a temporary political expedient, but rather a political creed based upon the recognition of our people's vital necessities. If it is to remain a living force, it must be continually renewed and must be continually applied to the facts of real life. It demands of every individual German that he should be conscious of his responsibilities. Individuals, however, as well as nations, can only possess that consciousness on condition that they are strong.

All the manifestations of our public life - such as our agricultural, industrial, financial, cultural, military and foreign policy - have for their object to guide the activities of every German along healthy lines. The task of creating the educational, hygienic and social foundations for these activities is entrusted to a number of organisations working in co-operation with one another, e.g., the Hitler Youth, the National Labour Service, the National Socialist Women's League, and the National Socialist Welfare Organisation.

The special task entrusted to the National Socialist Welfare Organisation differs essentially from that entrusted to the others inasmuch as it is its business to step in wherever the measures adopted by them prove insufficient to attain the desired ends.

In order to carry out so comprehensive a task, a complete break had to be made with the methods and principles formerly applied to public welfare. Prior to 1933, when a purely materialist view was taken of such welfare work, it was considered sufficient to "dole out" some relief to each individual requiring it, and that relief consisted - for the most part - in money. This view was erroneous. The assistance, for instance, thus given to a habitual drunkard was just as much misplaced as that given to a person suffering from some illness if it was merely enough to provide a temporary instead of a permanent cure. On the other hand, the relief granted to persons morally and physically sound was bound to fail in its object altogether when the recipients found themselves faced with distress due to circumstances entirely beyond their control, e.g., in such "special" areas as the Rhon, the Lower Bavaria, and the Eifel district. Distress of that kind could and can only be combated by concerted action on the part of the whole nation. It soon became clear that there is a mutual relationship between the assistance given to single individuals and that given to a whole section of the people. A strong sense of solidarity strengthens the individual and his family, whilst a strong and healthy family always enriches the nation. A really effective scheme of public welfare work must be based upon the active collaboration of all Germans and must exercise a permanent influence upon the Nation. Uncoordinated measures on the part of the State can never be effective.

For these reasons, the carrying-out of the welfare work here described was entrusted by the Fuhrer to the Winter Help Organisation and to the National Socialist Welfare Organisation, and not to the Government relief offices. The principles underlying their work are as follows: 1. The hygienic standards of the nation must be raised, so that the latter will be able to effect even greater achievements than hitherto. 2. The spirit of national solidarity must be fostered. 3. The physical and moral health of individuals must be improved to such an extent that they will be capable of holding their own in the struggle of life.

The ultimate aim of all this educational work must be to strengthen the sense of national solidarity.

I

The instrument that enables us to make the most comprehensive appeal to the spirit of national solidarity is the Winter Help Scheme, which - for that reason - is a matter especially dear to our hearts. There was, to be sure, a winter relief scheme prior to 1933; but the sum of fifteen or twenty million reichsmarks which the Government placed at its disposal each year (and which was diverted to that end from the revenue) was hopelessly inadequate to satisfy the material needs of the seven million unemployed. The National Socialist Winter Help Schemes of 1933-4, 1934-5, 1935-6 and 1936-7 have been carried through, at the express desire of the Fuhrer, by the people and not by the State. Every German capable of earning an income in some way, the business man as well as the worker, the professional man as well as the mercantile employee, contributes a certain percentage of his earnings to the scheme. Street collections are made once a month, especially, however, on the day of national solidarity, when the most prominent members of the Government and the party, the leading representatives of science and the arts, the heads of the business community, and many others, parade the streets with their collecting boxes. During the winter, every German family is content once a month to have a plain "one course" dinner, the money thus saved being applied to the scheme. Innumerable presents comprising foodstuffs, clothing and money - most of them contributed by anonymous donors - testify to the readiness of all to sacrifice some of their own comforts and to improve the lot of those of their fellow-countrymen who are less fortunately placed than they. The finest reward they receive for their sacrifices consists in the feeling that they have rendered direct assistance to a scheme of nation-wide importance.

The administration of the Winter Help Scheme is vested in the hands of the Head of the National Socialist Welfare Organisation. About 1,200,000 voluntary helpers assist him in his task by collecting and distributing the contributions. The gifts consist of food, clothing and fuel. They are distributed among all who are in need of them, including foreign residents provided that they have shown, by their personal attitude towards our country, that they are worthy of assistance. Jewish residents benefit in the same proportion as all other recipients, a separate organisation - subject to the general supervision of the Head of the National Socialist Welfare Organisation - having been created to look after their interests.

Thanks to the scheme, it has become possible to add from 15 to 20% to the income of the families requiring assistance. When we learn that some 1,500,000,000 reichsmarks have been collected by the Winter Help Organisation during the four winters that have passed since it was founded, we can appreciate the extent to which consolidated action has helped to increase the standard of living of the necessitous sections of the population and we can realise the success achieved by the work of fostering the spirit of solidarity.

The Winter Help Scheme is, of course, a seasonal measure. A similar concentration of efforts on an all-the-year-round basis is utilised, however, to combat the distress to which certain "special areas" are subject. This work is done by the National Socialist Welfare Organisation, which was made solely competent - by a decree of the Fuhrer issued May 3rd, 1933 - to deal with such matters.

The National Socialist Welfare Organisation succeeded within a very short time in convincing by far the greater part of the nation that its ideas and methods are right. Having a membership of 8,000,000 including 1,200,000 voluntary helpers, it is the world's largest organisation of its kind. A good many of its officials and many helpers act in an honorary capacity. Their endeavours have made it possible to discover every family that may be in need of aid, so that there is literally no case of distress that remains unattended to or unrelieved. Everything is done to give effect to the comprehensive measures considered necessary to improve the hygienic, the moral and (as a corollary) the economic standards of the population of the "special areas," where the mal-administration during past centuries has given rise to a wholesale and lasting physical and ethical deterioration. The people living there, on a poor soil and in unhealthy houses badly in need of repair, had lost all hope of ever being able to lead a decent life. The rate of infant mortality was much higher in these parts than the national average, the hygienic conditions were very unsatisfactory, and the vitality of children as well as adults was only a fraction of what it should be. Comprehensive measures have now been taken to eliminate these drawbacks. A great deal of painstaking work is now being done by the population and the Labour Service to re-afforest bare patches and to cultivate the waste land. The water supply is being improved, so that the economic value of the soil is increased and great risks to the health of the inhabitants are removed. The National Socialist Welfare Organisation provides a considerable part of the funds thus required, as well as working clothes and ample supplies of food for all those engaged in this useful work.

It is the hygienic domain, however, to which the National Socialist Welfare Organisation devotes most of its energies. It has caused all the infant children in the Reich up to the age of 2 to be medically examined and has not only given advice to parents (in accordance with the results of the examination) as to the correct food and education of their children, but has also supplemented the food provided by the parents themselves, all this being done free of charge. Through its affiliated organisations it has enabled the mothers and children most in need of it to spend a holiday in other parts of the country. It has established numerous kindergartens for those older children whose parents are at work in the daytime, and their number is being constantly added to. As there is a lack of medical facilities throughout the district, the National Socialist Welfare Organisation has covered it with a network of stations for nurses who can point out to parents, in the course of their periodical visits, the ailments to which their children are subject and the remedies to be applied. Dental disorders are still frequent everywhere. They are being combated by means of appropriate food preparations and by dental surgeons in travelling dental clinics.

Health Stations will be established by the National Socialist Welfare Organisation for infants and their mothers, more stations for municipal nurses will be established, and so on. Special areas will be accorded special preference in connection with the numerous labour promoting measures introduced by the Winter Help Organisation.

One other example may be given of the methods employed by the National Socialist Welfare Organisation to improve hygienic conditions and to give practical effect to the spirit of national solidarity. In the district of Schleiden (Eifel, Rhineland) the barrenness of the soil and the lack of opportunities for earning adequate wages had the result that the housing accommodation of the inhabitants was far below National Socialist standards. The sufferings of centuries had deprived these people of all their vitality, but at the suggestion of the Public Works Organisation they created a self-help organisation for the purpose of remedying the existing defects. Everyone contributed his share to the work of providing better houses. The necessary materials were supplied free of charge by the National Socialist Welfare Organisation. Bricklayers, carpenters and others who had been given relief during the time of their unemployment, now showed their gratitude by building the walls, the roofs and the doors of the new houses; and people of all classes and of all ranks and professions were only too glad to render whatever assistance they could. Thus the district - formerly a picture of depression and neglect - has now been improved out of all knowledge; and no trace of their erstwhile dejection can be noticed in the inhabitants.

II

The educational and relief work described above - which concerns itself with the nation as a whole - finds its counterpart in the work done in individual cases. There, too, the economic assistance given only serves the purpose of promoting hygienic and educational aims.

We refuse to alleviate distress by doling out alms, not only because that kind of help fails to achieve its object in any case, but also because it destroys the recipient's sense of responsibility and makes him unfit for self-help. The Fuhrer once said: "If you want to live, you must fight for it; and if you refuse to do so in this world of ceaseless fighting, you do not deserve to live."

We all know that life is one long fight; but we also know that such fighting is of benefit to the fighter, because it increases his inherent strength. Thus, the educational aim of our welfare work is to train the individual for that struggle of life. The ethical principle on which our activities are based is: "We are intended to be active fighters, and not passive sufferers." Only those persons who realise that they must shape their own destinies and who are able and willing to rely on self-help are the objects of our endeavours. To render the individual fit for self-help, we must strengthen the family and the community spirit that animates it. The family, and not the individual, is the fountain-head of the nation's strength. The family is the carrier of the characteristics bequeathed from one generation to another and is the source from which each of its members continually derives additional strength. A strong family is better able to render assistance to its members that may require it than any public relief organisation. Two conditions must be complied with to make the family strong: first, the parents must be enabled to resume those duties towards the family which they tended to neglect during the time of economic distress and during the vogue of woman's emancipation; and second, the family must be made fully efficient again in the hygienic and educational sense.

The National Socialist Welfare Organisation has therefore created several great relief schemes. One of them is called "Mother and Child," whilst the others are intended to provide free board and lodging in deserving cases, to enable town children to be sent to the country, to give assistance to young people, and to fight tuberculosis.

The "Mother and Child" scheme naturally occupies a central position in these endeavours, as the whole life of the family gravitates towards the mother. She looks after the education of all its members, provides their food and regulates the domestic routine. The connection between the National Socialist Welfare Organisation and the "Mother and Child" scheme is effected in such a manner that each local group of the former has affiliated to it a relief station which is in charge of a woman and which is required to deal with all applications and to give ethical and practical advice to mothers. By far the largest part of this work is done on a voluntary basis, about 24,000 relief and advisory stations being run by more than 100,000 helpers in an honorary capacity.

The three objects which the organisation endeavours to achieve are:

1. To co-operate in the fight against economic distress and its moral and hygienic effects. 2. To promote the health of mothers and their children. 3. To promote, more especially, the health of children prior to school-age.

The economic relief work includes such material assistance as the gift of clothing, household utensils, baby outfit, etc. Moreover, care is taken to ensure that the mother need not supplement the family income by doing outside work and that the opportunities for such work are made available to unemployed married men, more particularly those who have to support large families. In suitable instances, funds are provided by the National Socialist Welfare Organisation to finance part of the expenditure incurred in the building of homesteads, to enable families with a large number of children to obtain dwelling accommodation that is hygienically suitable, etc. In addition, the Minister of Justice has authorised the National Socialist Welfare Organisation to act as a mediator in all disputes between landlords and tenants so that these may be settled out of court. The success achieved is so great that about 90% of the disputes concerned can now be settled that way.

The hygienic assistance given under the scheme is equally comprehensive. During the first two years of its operation not less than 106,016 mothers were sent to special recuperation homes where they were able to spend from five to six weeks in each case. The corresponding number last year was just under 70,000. Medical attendance is also given them when there, as well as advice on physical culture and on food problems; and our observations have shown that this arrangement has proved highly beneficial. If, for one reason or another, it is impracticable to arrange for such accommodation in a recuperation home, it is generally possible to enable the women concerned to spend about five days a week in the fine gardens and parks of the National Socialist Welfare Organisation and to supply them with good food, whilst sending the children to some kindergarten. During the mother's absence from her home, her domestic duties are performed by some member of the Women's Voluntary Labour Service unless some friend or relative is available for that purpose.

Expectant mothers and those recently confined are given especially nourishing food, and they are also advised on matters of hygiene and the upbringing of children. Preparatory knowledge of this kind is systematically supplied by the Reich Mothers' Service Organisation attached to the National Socialist German Women's Welfare Association, this being additional to the advice given by the relief stations of the "Mother and Child" organisation.

The measures taken on behalf of young people also serve the purpose of assuring the future welfare of the family. Whereas the" Mother and Child" organisation is a direct product of the National Socialist State, the scheme under which children are sent to holiday homes originated during the terrible years of the War when, owing to the blockade there was not sufficient food for the town children. Notwithstanding the beneficial results then attained the scheme quickly decreased in importance and its scope declined, because it was found impossible properly to finance it. Besides, the party dissensions so prominent in the post-war era had largely destroyed the feeling for mutual assistance and mutual sacrifice.

The National Socialist Welfare organisation has introduced a new method in connection with these matters. Only those children who are urgently in need of assistance are actually sent to holiday homes, whilst the others are provided with suitable accommodation in farms or with people resident in small country towns, where they are given good food for a number of weeks and where they can recover their impaired health in open-air surroundings. The National Socialist Welfare Organisation selects the most suitable accommodation in each case, pays the travelling expenses, and attends to insurance matters. The board and lodging is provided free of charge by the farmers or other householders who act as the children's hosts.

In this manner, it has become possible to send 1,793,354 children to country places during the four years that have passed since the foundation of the National Socialist Welfare Organisation. To us, the work thus done for the children is much more than a hygienic measure. We believe that it will enable the children and their hosts in the various parts of our country to arrive at a better mutual understanding of their provincial or regional differences and that it will help to bridge the gulf between the towns and the country. Children who have grown up in an atmosphere of town life learn to appreciate the amenities of Nature and to love their beautiful country and are thus filled with a desire to extend that knowledge in subsequent years.

Another aspect of our juvenile welfare work is the educational one. In this respect, too, we have benefited from the unsatisfactory experience made in the past; and here, too, we are guided by the principle that prevention is better than cure.

In former years, the public authorities competent to supervise the training of those young persons who were exposed to dangerous social influences or difficult to educate did not commence their activities until it was too late; and the only remedy then available to them was to prescribe institutional treatment for the boy or girl concerned.

The most effective method by which we can assist in the upbringing and training of children is that afforded by means of kindergartens. There is no intention of relieving mothers of their duty to care for their children, because, after all, the proper place for the latter is their parental home. But there are cases in which the parents are unable, either because of their work or their inexperience, to carry out that duty themselves. The National Socialist Welfare Organisation has therefore established seasonal kindergartens in which the young children of peasants and farm labourers can be looked after during the harvesting season by trained helpers, as well as a number of permanent kindergartens. There are at present 2,360 of the latter kind, and the children sent to them are looked after by qualified kindergarten teachers. Most of them will be found in the industrial districts and in the distressed areas.

As we have great faith in the benefits secured by them, we intend to increase their number considerably. Whilst there, the young children are not only protected against all sorts of moral dangers, but also learn to regard themselves as members of a community. Thus the foundations are laid for making these children good citizens.

The practice adopted by the National Socialist Welfare Organisation of removing social and hygienic defects rather than giving temporary relief of a haphazard kind can be studied with particular advantage when we consider its two schemes exceeding the juvenile sphere, viz., that of providing facilities of recreation for men and women in need of it and its tuberculosis relief scheme. Under the former, necessitous applicants are provided with free board and lodging along lines similar to those applicable to the corresponding scheme for children. Whenever the ailment is of such a kind that a stay in one of the country's health resorts or spas may be expected to be really effective, the persons concerned are sent to one of those places for a cure.

The other scheme named has had the effect that there is practically no case any longer in which a lack of funds makes it impossible for patients suffering from tuberculosis to obtain the right kind of treatment.

Apart from the above schemes, the National Socialist Welfare Organisation is carrying out innumerable activities of importance to which no exhaustive reference can be made in this place. Thus, for example, it has distributed so far not less than 897,000 beds free of charge; it is constantly engaged in giving advice on matters of welfare legislation and on any problems that may arise; it co-operates in the fight against infectious diseases, in the financing of homesteads and in remedying the destruction wrought by natural catastrophes, not only through the personal efforts of its helpers, but also by the supply of the necessary funds. When the educational and hygienic tasks have been successfully accomplished, it takes pride in granting such economic relief as will enable the beneficiary to stand on his feet again and to take proper care of the members of his family. In short, it is impossible to express in words the full extent to which the National Socialist Welfare Organisation has rendered and is still rendering prompt and practical assistance wherever it is wanted; but some idea of the magnitude of its work may be obtained when we learn that it spent about 81,700,000 reichsmarks on its various social improvement schemes in 1936 alone.

III

In this manner we add to the strength and health of the nation and prepare the ground for our further activities, that is to say those that deal with the health of the family. Roughly speaking, we may say that the guiding principles that have moulded and will always continue to mould our destinies are: a readiness to make sacrifices for the benefit of the nation; a belief in the pre-eminence of the family; a sense of honour; a knowledge of our responsibilities, and a determination to hold what we have. We have faith in the ancient saying that a sound mind and a healthy body are mutually inter-dependent.

Our work, therefore, not only teaches our nation the importance of health, both morally and physically, but also enables every individual to obtain a proper idea of his responsibilities towards the nation and towards his family. By developing all our intrinsic abilities we make up for our country's lack of valuable raw materials and for our inferior degree of economic and political power as compared with other countries. The more we contribute towards the establishment of fundamentally healthy conditions at home, the stronger and healthier will be the influence exercised by all our national manifestations, be it in the realms of economy or science, in our domestic and our foreign policy. We are proud of the assistance we can give towards the realisation of the high aim once defined by the Fuhrer when he said: "The question of the national progress of a people is largely a question of creating a healthy social atmosphere, that will make it possible to provide each individual with the right kind of education."

The Results of the 1936-7 Winter Help Campaign

Year after year the response of the German people to the appeal made to them on behalf of their suffering compatriots has gained in strength, and the figures showing the results of the 1936-7 Winter Relief Campaign are no exception to the rule. More than 400,000,000 reichsmarks were subscribed and collected - about 50,000,000 reichsmarks more than previously. The nation has thus proved the extent to which it is capable of giving practical effect to the principles of charity.

The report on these activities was submitted to Herr Hitler by Dr. Goebbels at the end of April 1937. The number of persons in need of relief has undergone a regular decrease in successive years, that decrease corresponding to the economic progress made by the country. The figures have been as follows: 1933-4, 16,600,000; 1934-5, 14,000,000; 1935-6, 13,000,000, and 1936-7, 10,700,000. These persons had to be assisted under the Winter Help Scheme in supplementation of the welfare work done by the State and the municipalities.

People abroad have often wondered what is the object of all these "collections." Well, their main purpose is to make it abundantly clear to everyone that he must at all times be conscious of his duties towards his fellow-men and women and that he must act accordingly. It is not sufficient that the well-to-do classes should contribute fairly large amounts towards the relief of suffering and distress. Every wage-earner - no matter whether he or she is a manual worker or a brainworker - voluntarily contributes towards it, however modest the amount may be. As a rule, the street collections take place once a month during the winter months. People are then asked to buy badges at 20 pfennigs each. In the winter of 1936-7 the value of the collections was as much as 38,000,000 reichsmarks-twice as much as in 1935-6. The German people regard these collections as a firmly established institution, and gladly respond to the appeal for their co-operation.

The number of badges sold last winter was 131,500,000, which is 100,000,000 more than it was when the Winter Help Scheme was first introduced. The work of manufacturing them provided in itself considerable relief to the industrial workers in many a distressed area.

The maximum amount collected in one single day was 5,600,000 reichsmarks. That result was achieved on the Day of National Solidarity, when all those who occupy a prominent position in the State or in the party appealed to their compatriots by taking an active part in the street-collecting work.

In addition to the street collections, large sums were obtained in the form of voluntary deductions from salaries and wages; and indeed, the money thus contributed represented the major part of the scheme's income. The figure for 1936-7 was 162,000,000 reichsmarks, compared with 138,000,000 reichsmarks in 1935-6. These contributions are truly in the nature of sacrifices on the part of those from whom they originate. In acting as they do, they receive their inspiration from the words of the Fuhrer, who said that a sacrifice must really be a sacrifice.

Great credit is also due to the street collectors and other voluntary helpers, who spent many a cold and rainy day in collecting. They, too, realise that their action helps to bring relief to those of their countrymen and women who need it most. The guiding idea is that no one living in Germany should suffer from hunger or cold or inadequate dwelling conditions, least of all in winter. Everybody is conscious of the duties he has towards those less fortunate than himself. It is essential that everybody should be anxious to help those who render assistance to others. The work done under the Winter Help Scheme is probably the greatest - and certainly the most comprehensive - charitable action ever accomplished by one single organisation. Its scope is not confined to German nationals, but extends to foreign residents as well. The number of foreigners assisted in 1935-6 was about 89,000.

In thanking all those who had collaborated in the splendid work, Herr Hitler has repeatedly emphasised that the Winter Help Scheme is of particular value inasmuch as it helps to train the German people along the lines of social and national consolidation.

PART III

HOW GERMANS LIVE - LEISURE

SECTION ONE

GERMAN SPORT

Hans Von Tschammer Und Osten

Reich Sports Leader

WHEN Herr Hitler asked me, in 1933, to become the Leader of German Sports, the conditions then existing were deplorably bad. On the one hand, there was a people anxious to practise physical exercises, whilst on the other I found a narrow-minded bureaucracy incapable of satisfying that desire by providing the necessary organic foundation. In the course of a century, a kind of sports organisation had developed which looked upon itself as more valuable than the objects it was there to promote. Critics have sometimes asserted that there was no need for us to subject the organisation of German sports to the same process of drastic change that has been applied to our country's political constitution, its economy, its laws, and all its other activities.

It cannot be the object of these lines to go into all the political considerations that have been at the root of that great change. All I can do is to furnish my readers with a general account of the manner in which it has manifested itself.

I may take it for granted that the previous organisation of German sports is a matter of general knowledge, so that the briefest possible reference to it ought to be sufficient. Since the turn of the century, physical culture had ceased to be an organic unit and had become so much a matter of excessive specialisation that its true purpose was entirely lost sight of. There was a complete lack of uniform direction and proper cohesion. Each branch of sports was organised on lines of its own. There were numerous local clubs, district associations and regional associations devoted to football, hockey, golf, handball, bowling, billiards, swimming, rowing, paddling, hiking, mountaineering, fencing, boxing, wrestling, jumping, running, and so on, and in each case there was a national federation which comprised all of them. For a long time, however, there was no central organisation directing the sporting activities of the country in their entirety.

It is easy to see that so much specialisation combined with the absence of general and uniform direction was bound to produce an adverse effect upon sporting exercise in Germany; and the fact that German sports - despite these drawbacks - had attained a very high degree of efficiency was not the outcome of the work done by the then existing organisation, but of their inherent merits. Even before the close of the War, there were many who predicted that nothing but disaster could result from so misdirected a development, unless the existing drawbacks were abolished; and I wish to point out, in this connection, that great credit is due to the men who succeeded in setting up the first really comprehensive sporting organisation covering the whole country, known as the Reich Committee for Physical Exercises (Deutscher Reichsausschuss fur Leibesubungen), which may be described as a forerunner of the now existing Reich Federation for Physical Exercises (Deutscher Reichsbund fur Leibesubungen). It gradually acquired the status of a centrally conducted authority, and its activities soon received the wholehearted support of the Army, the schools, and the municipalities. It was thus able to play an important part in our country's cultural and political life. The fact that the organisation of the Olympic Games held in Germany in 1936 was universally acknowledged a great success proves that the world at large appreciated the work achieved by the Committee.

And yet, this form of organisation could not completely satisfy us when we started to reshape our political life in accordance with National Socialist principles. What we desired was a peak organisation rigid enough to ensure uniform direction and yet elastic enough to adapt itself to progressive development in the domain of national sports. This was an ideal which the Committee failed to realise. Gymnastics, athletics, and so on, were not merely treated as special types of sporting exercise, but the associations cultivating them were at the same time endeavouring to promote their own ethical standards and their own educational aims. Thus, for instance, the German Gymnastic Federation (Deutsche Turnerschaft), a huge organisation with a membership of more than 1,600,000 representing about 13,000 subsidiary associations and clubs, constituted an educational unit whose principles were fundamentally at variance with those advanced by the greater part of the individual associations. Moreover, the unfortunate division of our people along denominational lines proved a serious handicap to the progress of sports. The largest denominational sports organisations - the Roman Catholic Deutsche Jugendkraft and the Protestant Eichenkreuz - had a combined membership of just under 1,000,000. When Herr Hitler entrusted me with the task of creating a central sports organisation genuinely representative of the nation as a whole, I did not trouble to ascertain the number of independent associations then existing. At a rough guess, there may have been some 300 of them. If we assume that they had a total membership of about 6,000,000, we can work out, by a simple exercise in mathematics, how many different shades of opinion were represented by them. How much greater could have been the influence of sports and games upon the national health and the standard of physical culture if the money and energy thus spent on the promotion of divergent aims could have been used to strengthen the bonds of union.

When, therefore, a revolutionary change was effected in the organisation of German sports after the advent of the National Socialist Government, it was not intended to enthrone centralisation for its own sake, but rather to raise the biological standards of the whole nation, to safeguard its cultural assets, and to restore social, religious and economic peace. The first practical step was the dissolution of the Marxist associations for physical exercises and the incorporation of their members in the organisation to be newly created. Before there was a real possibility of setting up that body, a great deal of preparatory work had to be accomplished. It was necessary, above all, to break down the barriers that separated those who differed from one another in their spiritual outlook, without damaging the sporting interests that linked them together. Within a year of ceaseless effort it became possible to give effect to the first few measures intended to ensure fruitful co-operation among the various sporting and gymnastic associations as a preliminary to their final amalgamation. All this had to be done without jeopardising the valuable international connections maintained between German sportsmen and sportsmen abroad. I am happy to say that my endeavours received the willing support not only of the members of the associations concerned, but of the whole German people. When, therefore, the Deutsche Turnerschaft celebrated the 75th anniversary of its foundation at Coburg (Whitsun 1935), I was in a position to give expression to the thoughts which all sportsmen, owing to their National Socialist views, expected to result in their own sphere of activities from the fundamental transformation in all domains of public life. It will always redound to the credit of the executive of the Deutsche Turnerschaft that they voluntarily resolved upon the dissolution of their great organisation and that they enabled their large number of members to join the Reich Federation for Physical Exercises in a body.

Although the Reich Federation has abolished the associations, it has, of course, left intact the "cells" of sporting and gymnastic exercise. All these clubs, of whom there are approximately some 49,000, have retained their individual character without modification. The 1936 Olympic Games showed the efficiency already attained by the Federation.

It goes without saying that 49,000 clubs cannot be centrally administered from Berlin. Such a plan would not only be technically impossible, but equally objectionable from every other point of view. All parts of the country have their specific characteristics, and proper regard has to be paid to them. Thus, the Federation has been made to consist of sixteen regional groups, and each of these comprises a certain number of sub-regional groups, whose duty it is to maintain contact between the national sports executive and the individual clubs. This fourfold sub-division (Reich, regional groups, sub. regional groups, clubs) holds good for every aspect - sporting, educational, and economic - of the organisation.

It is a source of special pride to me that the task entrusted to the organisation of German sports and games has been - and is being - efficiently carried out. I believe that the less we hear of the work done by an organisation, the more efficient it is. When we watch the joyful display on the sports grounds, we ought to be perfectly unaware of the huge efforts without which it could not go on at all. The organisational work done by the Federation is enormous; but it is carried on quietly and "behind the scenes," as it were, and there is no danger of a "hierarchy of sports organisers" coming into being. One demand, however, will be made upon all these organisers: they must remain in immediate contact with life itself. In order to enable them to do so, the House of German Sports has been built on the Reiehssportfeld. It provides accommodation for the executive and its administrative organs. It is surrounded by buildings and grounds where the sporting and athletic life of Berlin manifests itself. Everyone whose duty it is to act in an organising and administrative capacity can watch the games from his office window. He can no longer shut himself off from these realities, but is bound to identify himself with them. Such intimate contact is of very considerable value, and I expect that highly beneficial results will follow from it. The "organising official" must see all that is going on in the sports grounds, but must himself be seen as little as possible.

The new type of gymnastic instructor will be trained on the Reiehssportfeld and in the Reich Academy for Physical Culture. He is to be the representative of the State within the sphere allotted to him. It is in this domain that the aims pursued by National Socialism in office are especially far-reaching. It is realised that the efficient training of youth is of outstanding importance to the country's manhood. In future, the gymnastic instructors in all categories of schools, from the elementary ones to the universities, will be able to further those great aims. The education to be given to all boys and youths must conform, from the very outset, to the necessities of the State. The gymnastic instructors are the guarantors of the manly strength continually tested and continually augmented. Since the accession to power of National Socialism, the physical education supplied by the State has been supplemented by the voluntary training available within the party and its organisations. When Herr Hitler announced that "the party directs the State," he did not mean that a condition of vassalage should govern the relations between the two; but he did mean that fruitful collaboration should be established between the organisations already in existence and an organisation of the elite. By such mutual co-operation the National Socialist party communicates to the State organism the spirit and the elan of its revolutionary ideas, whilst the State places at the disposal of the party the substance of the public institutions, which those ideas are to permeate.

There is, therefore, a close relationship between the elementary schools (for boys up to 14) and the Jungvolk between the vocational and secondary schools (for boys from 14 to 18) and the Hitler Youth, and between the universities, institutions of university rank, etc., and the S.A., S.S., and P.O. organisations of the party. The Voluntary Labour Service fulfils a similar purpose, as it is not an instrument created for the furtherance of military objects, but is to be a training-ground enabling every German, especially every intellectual worker, to appreciate the value of honest manual labour. Like the schools and the party organisations, the Labour Service is intended to provide practical training in the principles of German Socialism. Education, more especially political education, is to be one of the objects for which the party and the Labour Service exist. Through such a system of political education, every German youth must be enabled to understand the essentials of National Socialist thought and to undergo, co-ordinated with that teaching, a course of physical training capable of developing his body. It will be noticed that physical training is an essential part of the work performed by all educational institutions, and that it cannot be omitted at any stage unless the continuity of the education supplied is to be seriously endangered. It is designed along lines which are identical in all these institutions. It is a means to an end and provides the foundation on which the military training of Germany's manhood can be safely established.

Such military training naturally constitutes the final addition to the whole edifice. Even though physical culture is overshadowed, in so far as the defence forces are concerned, by the training in purely military subjects, the military authorities are well aware that it will be a great advantage if every young recruit is good at his sports. That circumstance alone will facilitate his military training in the narrower sense of the term. A considerable amount of time is therefore set aside for the physical training of recruits; and even though it is only possible to deal with its principal aspects, no means are omitted that will tend to make them physically strong and mentally alert.

Germany is now governed in accordance with the leadership principle, that is to say the Chancellor - Herr Hitler - does not merely exercise administrative functions, but is in supreme control of the country's domestic and foreign policy and assumes personal responsibility for everything done by the Government. In addition he is the head of the National Socialist party - a party which, when it first began to struggle for political power, proclaimed the totalitarian principle. Now that it is in possession of such power, it will firmly uphold it. As regards the organisations for the promotion of physical exercises, this principle will therefore have to be applied in its entirety, failing which there would be a danger of a renewal of the dualism between reality and organisation. In my capacity as Reich Sports Leader, I intend to let myself be guided by that principle. I have accordingly made arrangements between the Reich Federation for Physical Exercises and the National Socialist party and its organisations (more especially the Hitler Youth) on the one hand, and the Labour Service and the Army authorities on the other, which will ensure collaboration for all time. In like manner, co-operation has been established between the Reich Federation on the one hand and the schools and their teachers on the other, which will benefit both sides.

National Socialism has replaced complication by simplicity, artificiality by reality. What it proposes to do and has already done in the domain of physical culture, has been set forth above.

SECTION TWO

GERMAN CULTURE AND LITERATURE

Dr. Hans Friedrich Blunck

Honorary President of the Reich Chamber of
Literature, Member of the Reich Culture Senate and
of the Senate of the Academy of Literature.

AT first glance it may seem strange that a poet and writer of fairy-tales has been chosen to write this article on German culture policy, when so wide a choice from among leading politicians was available. Perhaps, however, the selection was symbolic, because creative artists in Germany today are concerning themselves, as never before, with the rising and falling fortunes of their fellow-countrymen. Certainly that romantic age which consigned the writer to an isolated garret existence has gone for ever. If only in this respect, we, in Germany, have turned from the romantic period of Europe to the classic, when some of the great creative thinkers were also leading personalities in the State.

Another motive made me particularly happy to accept the invitation to co-operate in the writing of this book. I was born in Schleswig-Holstein, a country jealous of its Anglo-Saxon heritage, where we are all intensely aware of our relationships and where also, since the time of Storm and Kroger, we have been fully alive to the dual nature of the creative artist's work. This duality, so frequently found in England, is probably a common inheritance.

Galsworthy, who was my friend during the last year of his life, always seemed to me to be the perfect example of a well-balanced individual, who possessed at the same time the attributes of a strong leader. He was an Anglo-Saxon of the type that we, in this Hanseatic land, appreciate and love, not only from personal empathy, but also for old time's sake.

Occasionally I discussed with Galsworthy the part that writers could play in our restless Europe, and I still remember the tolerant smile with which he said that we writers would never be able to act and write as statesmen, because our ideals, conceptions and convictions must always be bound by some inward necessity. Perhaps, he said, our position may be, for this reason, particularly strong, and perhaps it may not be a bad thing for the people of our respective countries if, by using our imaginations, we can cover with some sort of nobility even the coldness and self-seeking prevailing in European politics.

In considering Germany's present culture policy, a starting-point must not be made at the complacent and satisfied Europe which was commonly shown to the British and French reading publics before the German revolution. Instead, we must examine those terrible times through which our country passed, when it seemed impossible that it could ever rise again from defeat and hopelessness, especially the latter. A military collapse can never produce such bad effects as an injustice; the broken promise that lay between the Armistice and the Peace Treaty was probably that which most deeply hurt the feelings of our humanitarian population, and indeed still does. For long it seemed that all attempts to build up a new Reich were condemned to failure, and as if a death dance had begun which would end in the complete ruin of our thousand-year-old State.

Let it not be forgotten that the Communists were on the point of securing the largest representation in the Reichstag and that all the restraints of the old order were breaking down. The middle classes, supporting a liberalism which they did not understand, and pervaded with the instinct of self-seeking and self-preservation, were apparently no longer in a position to offer any resistance. The currency, after one breakdown, was threatened with yet another collapse. Thousands of peasants were driven from their homesteads, which thus became the property of the mortgagees, and the workers - sick of unfulfilled promises - were definitely hostile to the bourgeoisie. Hundreds of pretentious developments in the sphere of the arts were hailed for a moment as substitutes for religion, only to disappear a few weeks later. Words and figures were bandied about, only to sink again into obscurity, like spooks which had strayed for a moment from the land of shadows. A small gang of alien immigrants from the east drew their profit from the sorrows of a whole nation, spreading like a blight over the country. The cradles stood empty, and everyone lived for the hour or the day because there seemed to be no future. Whatever sensibility or pride remained was destroyed by humiliations suffered through our foreign policy.

These were the conditions out of which National Socialism arose, and beneath its wing our "Wartburg Circle," literature's adventure against the forces of decay, was formed. The "Academy" remained firmly a left-wing institution, while the powers of progressive conservatism collected around Johst, Beumelburg, Munchhausen, Kolbenheyer, Grimm, Schafer, and Vesper (the author of this article is, of course also a member of this group). The glowing poetry of certain younger men, amongst thern Anacker, Schumann, Bohme, Moller, Nierentz, Eggers Meusel, Brockmeier, Oppenberg and Helke formed an accompaniment to the political development of the times. Amongst the dramatists, I would specially mention Rehberg, Bethge, and Langenbeck.

There is no doubt that these groups were the first to awaken a response in the minds of the common people throughout the country. Post-war artistic achievement had no wide appeal, based, as it was, either on eroticism, or concerned with expressionism or cubism, and directed only towards a small public. The right-wing opposition, however, succeeded in winning the appreciation of the youth. Readers, turning away in disgust from the eternal psycho-analytical studies, found a young art flourishing in their midst, that reminded them of their national history, that made their country-side bloom again and whose subject matter was not limited to descriptions of city life. Here were poems, tales and essays for which the man in the street, almost unknown to himself, had had a secret longing. In short, the rift between writers and people, that had yawned wider and wider during the post-war years, started to close again. Here was a literature which - though not ignoring the old forms - was rooted in the countryside, was closely in touch with the feelings of the people but was also vitally connected with the political happenings which were then heralding a new era.

The culture policy of the State has shown clearly enough that the debt of gratitude to creative artists has not been forgotten.

Perhaps it should first be made clear what is meant by this expression "culture policy," for misunderstandings arise only too easily in the babel of modern Europe.

It is the duty of the State to cultivate harmony between the political and private life of the people - neither more nor less. Therefore, without limiting, or acting against, the achievements of the individual, it seeks to promote the broad conception of "People's Culture," to encourage their inherent taste for decoration, for picturesque celebration and for their own ancient customs, and to direct these so that they conform to those "Christian ethics" which are valid throughout Europe. The German State also accepts it as a duty to discover those who are capable of speaking for the people, and who, every now and then, have tried to gain the light of day, only to be overshadowed by the acceptance, formerly so readily accorded, of foreign values. Those who wish to know something of this subject should read the book, The Tyranny of Greece over Germany, published by the Cambridge University Press. German history can reveal over and over again how the so-called educated classes kept their distance from the mass of the people, and attempted to form their own autocracy. The present Government, on the other hand, seeks to emphasise the connection between the old literature and the new, and the relationship of both to the people. This is not achieved by laying a compulsion of any sort upon the creative worker. The Government does reserve to itself, however, certain rights of choice and the right to issue recommendations. What other more fortunate nations accept as a matter of course, namely the possession of an art inherently national had still to grow up in Germany and to be assiduously cultivated.

This problem was solved in 1933 with comparative ease, largely thanks to the opposition of the "intellectuals" to the former regime, an opposition that had sprung up before the revolution.

Thanks are also due to the energetic preparation of the ground and to the intellectual values which the modern conceptions "Nationalism" and "Socialism" had been given in Germany since the pre-classic, the Sturm und Drang period, and since the time of Herder and the youthful Goethe.

Nothing, surely, could make a stronger appeal to the artist's sense of justice than Herder's conception of "Nationalism" - that is to say, the ordering of Europe in accordance with the self- governing rights of the nations, and the refusal to recognise any interference on the part of neighbouring States. I am well aware that the word "Nationalism" has a different meaning in every European country, and it is one of the Continent's greatest misfortunes that this apparently universal expression creates nothing but misunderstanding and that we all mean something different when we use it. Nationalism in England means more or less the same as "Imperialism"; in France it means "Chauvinism", while in Germany it means exactly the opposite, namely, the right of all nations, in the sense of Volkstumer, to develop along their own lines, within their borders. In Germany, in fact, it means nothing but an aspect of the old longing for freedom, the dream of a Europe in which the free nations live peacefully as neighbours.

Again, the religious sensibilities of the artist cannot be more profoundly stirred than by the conception of true Socialism, as the fittest expression of national solidarity. The rationalist, or Marxist, foundation of Socialism was overthrown because it was based on class warfare, but it was a Socialism grounded in religion that attained power in Germany with the arrival of National Socialism. I must go further: I must maintain that it did not only attain power, but it gave Europe the most perfect example of living Socialism extant, so far, of course, as this could be achieved by a people which disposed of no raw materials. It is hardly a matter for surprise that the artist, who ever inclines towards the essentials of faith and pity, eagerly embraced the theories of the new State, that he accepted Nationalism as self-government of the people, Socialism on religious grounds, and that at the same time he rejoiced exceedingly over the new and intimate relationship with all his countrymen, without the barrier of class prejudice that was the gift to him of the new State. I will not conceal that it was the younger writers of the new movement who passionately accepted the change, which was a difficult matter for those who had fought hard and long in the ranks of the opposition, and upon whose individualistic ideas the demands of the time placed hardships, which forced them for a space into loneliness. It may seem paradoxical, but I am quite sure that the new leaders of Germany are fully aware of the essential loneliness of the creative artist. All the same, however, German writers today know what happiness it means to stand before a crowded, youthful audience on a winter evening and to read to them ballads, stories or essays that meet with true appreciation. The writer who stands up and reads his works to a crowd of factory workers, and who sees the meaning of his words truly understood by them, realises enough to want to hold firmly to the relationship between writer and people, which seemed at one time to have been utterly lost.

Perhaps I have dwelt too long on the consideration of that background against which the astonishing change in Germany took place. I thought it necessary because so many of my English friends interest themselves in various details of the organisation of the Third Reich, but know little of the intellectual "behind the scenes" of the change; I might jestingly say that we, the third - or continental - Anglo-Saxon group, feel that we have a certain responsibility towards the Reich on behalf of our next of kin in the United Kingdom, and that we would so gladly restore the bridge that existed for five centuries between England and Germany, so perhaps my discursiveness may be pardoned. In compensation, I will answer more pointedly the questions - What were the practical measures taken in connection with culture policy in new Germany? and How was the close relationship between the State, the people and the artists - desired by National Socialism - achieved? For (and of this there can be no doubt) the relationship exists, even though the voice of complaint is now and again raised, and even though there are aspects of the achievement that could be improved. These things are unavoidable when sweeping changes take place. On the other hand, there is no organised opposition group, a fact that has led our neighbours (who cannot believe that it is really lacking) to suppose that it does indeed exist, but has been artificially suppressed. My friends, anyone who knows anything about the soul of a writer and about the courage of the creative worker, must surely also know that a real opposition cannot be suppressed, and must realise that the wonder of the German unity is that it is actually based upon true community of heart.

This miracle of which I speak is the more remarkable in that the economic situation of the artist was anything but rosy - as is probably always the case in times of revolution and change - during the first few months of the new regime. Adherence to it was, therefore, a sacrifice rather than an exploitation. It must be admitted at once that the State very soon took steps to ameliorate the initial difficulties, but such emergency assistance is not to the taste of the artist, who wishes to live by his work. Nevertheless, financial assistance given to artists during the first two years of National Socialism amounted to more than had been available for two decades before - a sign of how seriously the situation was taken. It was not long before the new theatre replaced the old organisation destroyed by the revolution, and before Kulturgemeinden (Culture Communities) were created which, even in the smallest German towns, invited writers to deliver lectures and readings, and made them the principal speakers at country gatherings. At the earliest possible moment attempts were made, through the organisation Kraft durch Freude (Strength through Joy), to bring to the ordinary workers their past and present heritage in literature, music and art. From the moment that National Socialism achieved power, it strove to make of the "proletarian" the "fellow-countryman," equal heir with all to Germany's intellectual kingdom. In 1936, no fewer than two million workers visited exhibitions and attended plays, and often lectures, organised in the factory buildings. Two literary "agencies" were set up, and helped in their own way:

endless patience was expended in the reading of manuscripts, and it was recently announced that all the writings "hidden away in Germany's old chests and cupboards" had now been examined as to their literary merit. Everything of value was handed to one or another of the great publishers, but in future it will be the task of the latter alone to make their selections.

Among the great organisations in modern Germany, there is scarcely one that has not concerned itself, either more or less, with the arts: they all possess literary departments. Successes have not everywhere been equal, but this was hardly to be expected during a period of four years of drastic change. However, good will has nowhere been lost, and we must realise that when we see excellent cheap reproductions of the classics and the best of the moderns being eagerly read in peasants' houses, in the labour camps and in the barracks; our public buildings decorated by the work of living sculptors, and finally, the love of music being cultivated in villages as well as in city concert halls, then we must also see that work of much value is being done, which outbalances the occasional failures. This revolution, that outwardly forced political aims and social necessity so much into the foreground, and that found so many bitter words to utter against the "anti-social influence" of the arts, has, in spite of everything, greatly profited from the teachings of history. It is fully aware that artistic achievements alone are able to justify to posterity a change in the form of government. This new Government, composed as it is of members half of whom are men who originally intended to devote themselves to some creative work, knows, because of its inward religious convictions, the importance of artists as mediators. This government, rooted in opposition against rationalism, is well aware of the nameless longings of the people it governs, of their dreams that sway between heaven and earth, which can be explained and expressed only by the artist.

Perhaps more important than anything else that has been mentioned so far is the legislative attitude of the State towards the sphere of the arts. The position of the arts in the State was defined by the Chamber of Culture Law of October 1933, which represents something entirely new in Europe.

Probably the clearest description that I can give of this law is that it has given practical shape to the establishment of an artist's guild or corporation. The principle of the Corporate State, which has been applied to some of the changes made in Germany, has, for many decades past, been expressed in political writings. Other countries than Germany have concerned themselves with this idea: Literary Congresses in various countries have constantly urged that the relationship between the arts and the State should be defined, British and French delegates having been particularly insistent on this. No better solution has, however, as yet been found than to demand an unlimited "liberalism"- whilst the corporate suggestion was consistently rejected.

The newer governments have sought another way out by reviving the idea of autonomic "Companies of Artists" such as existed in medieval times. The Chamber of Culture raises the groups of artists from the ranks of the people, and makes them self-governing. The duty of self-observation is also laid upon them. For the present the State has withdrawn various privileges, a withdrawal which certain individuals regard as limiting, and which they describe as "bureaucracy." These privileges have been replaced by a Corporate Constitution, providing for several sub-Chambers, each of which is entrusted with the task of ordering the professional relations between its members and of assuming responsibility for their professional affairs. Each is invested with full legislative power. It should be mentioned that the activities of the Chamber are limited to German nationals, and that artists of foreign extraction are directed to set up their own organisations.

Altogether there are seven such sub-Chambers, those of Music, the Plastic Arts, Literature, Wireless, Press, Theatre and Cinematograph. They are united under the control of a central authority, whose decisions are binding upon all. A Reich minister stands at the head of the Chamber, and the individual sub-Chambers are mostly under the presidency of creative workers. For instance, the architect, Herr Honig, was at the head of the Chamber of Plastic Arts and Richard Strauss was the former president of the Chamber of Music, which is now under the leadership of Peter Raabe. For two years I was privileged to be President of the Chamber of Literature, and I was succeeded by Hanns Johst, the famous dramatist and lyricist. Another writer, Rainer Schlosser, is at the head of the Theatre Chamber, but the Radio and Press are managed by experts in each subject, rather than by artists.

The decrees made by the Press Chamber have received more attention than those received by any other. There has been approval as well as disapproval. The latter is doubtless caused by certain hardships that are bound to be the result of any revolution: nevertheless we have through these prevented our revolution from assuming the proportions of the one in Spain, and I am convinced, however much the duress may irk the individual artist, that, even in this, we have pursued the right path. The great change in the press that has so served to stimulate and refresh us, is what I might call the "publicity" of subscribers and editors, which has completely swept away the influence formerly exerted by anonymous contributors of money, by certain economic circles and by interested denominational groups. The reconstruction is proceeding apace, and is based on the principle of the personal responsibility of the newspaper proprietor and his editors. Anyone acquainted with our press as it was towards the end of the parliamentary democracy must be well aware to what a degrading dependence upon industrial concerns it had sunk, and how many cliques - preserving touch with our foreign enemies - attempted to influence home policy in order to serve their private ends. All who lived through those times realise today how sane an effect the application of the principle of personal responsibility for word and deed has had.

I have nothing to hide or to extenuate, and I am perfectly aware that, at the inception of the revolution and for a short period afterwards, it was impossible to express a free opinion. This has rapidly changed. So long as attacks are not made on the State itself, and so long as nothing is published that could lead to a disturbance of the public peace, there is no ban placed upon the free expression of opinion. Do not let us always return to times that lie behind us, but when did the makers of any revolution permit any opposition propaganda to be published? Let us rather compare soberly the question of dependence and independence as it works out in Europe today, and, if we do so, we must admit that in the majority of countries around Germany (I forbear to mention names) where the press is still in the pay of economic groups and political parties, the freedom and security of an editor are far more severely restricted than in Germany. I think that in this respect (as in many others) the fact is not sufficiently appreciated abroad that a strong opposition is lacking not because it is suppressed in Germany, but because the conviction of opposition is also lacking.

The number of newspapers sold, which decreased between 1933 and 1934, has once more gone up, so that in many cases the original sale of the papers has been greatly increased. The attitude of the general reading public is most clearly indicated by their demand for those publications known to be free from any suspicion of outside influence, i.e., periodicals, magazines, etc. In 1935, their sales figures increased by 9% as compared with 1934, and a further increase of 15% is estimated to have taken place in 1936. These figures apply in connection with about 1,500 important magazines and periodicals. The Press Chamber, like the Chamber of Literature, dispenses a considerable relief fund, which expended over two million marks in 1934, and the same sum in 1936. An Act that came into force in April 1938 provides pension schemes for all editors of newspapers.

The Chamber of Music, apart from giving great support to the cultivation of music throughout the country, has issued regulations governing the fees paid to musicians. The International Congress for the Protection of Authors' Rights, which recently met at Berlin, confirmed the fact that Germany had found the surest and quickest way of dealing with this distracting task. If we should now approach our neighbours with a legislative suggestion to make authors' rights more secure internationally, we should do this not so as to snatch at a leading position for ourselves, but simply because, so far, we have in this respect gone further than any other country. What is probably the greatest proof of this statement is that unemployment amongst our German musicians, which amounted in 1934 to 50%, is today insignificant. Every British visitor to Berlin, Munich or Hamburg knows that the repertoire of operas has been enlarged and that our opera houses are often "sold out" long before the dates of the performances, whilst - in 1932 - our actors and actresses frequently played before empty or half-empty houses.

The most difficult position in those earlier days was doubtless that occupied by the Chamber of Plastic Arts. The bourgeoisie that, perhaps without much taste, took pleasure in supporting the efforts of sculptors and painters, withdrew the greater part of its custom in this respect after the economic crisis of 1929, which led not only to the unemployment of the artisan, but also to that of the artist. The new Government felt itself compelled to set an example, and very soon no public building was planned without an artist having a share in its design. The State has erected many buildings in the past few years, but the position is still very difficult. The new stratum which is to give private orders and commissions to the artist is forming very slowly. During the year 1935, the Chamber of Plastic Arts, apart from large sums expended on travelling, provided 800 old and young artists with holidays varying between fourteen days and four weeks in length. Further sums, reaching a very high total, were also spent in giving relief to artists who had fallen into poverty, and the Chamber instituted, or provided the stimulus for, between three and four hundred competitions offering valuable chances and prizes. The chief work in this connection is the provision of new facilities for exhibition and the training of a new class of would-be purchasers, a task which has met with very considerable success during the past couple of years. Europe's finest exhibition building, the Haus der Deutschen Kunst, at Munich, was inaugurated by the Fuhrer himself in 1937.

The Chamber for Wireless reports that the number of listeners increased from about 4,000,000 to 7,500,000 within the space of four years. I do not know whether this increase corresponds to those recorded in other countries. But I do know, from what I heard when I paid visits abroad, that the German programmes are popular outside the borders of the Reich, especially those broadcast by the Deutschlandsender and the short-wave transmitter, which are designed to keep our countrymen abroad in touch with the mother country.

There is little to say regarding the activities of the Cinematograph Chamber, under the first-rate managership of Professor Lehnich: the international prizes awarded to German films are sufficient witness of their effectiveness. The number of people who go to the cinemas has increased by 10% per annum since 1935.

The Chamber of Culture Law has probably been most effective in the domain of the Theatre and in that of literature. The theatres, which after 1928 grew emptier and emptier, and which could attract a public only by producing the most sensational plays, were not in 1933 instantly able to win back their audiences. The continuous appeals of the new Government to the theatre-going public to encourage the arts, and the influence exerted by the theatre-goers' organisations (which, for the first time, included the workers) little by little produced a change. The visitor to Berlin today is frequently surprised to find that all 40 theatres of the capital are playing to full houses, and that the theatre is actually in the midst of a great boom. The number of State or municipally owned theatres mounted from 155 to 178 between 1933 and 1936, and the number of people employed in theatres increased from 20,000 to 26,000. State subsidies to the theatre amounted to 12,000,000 marks a year, and were principally placed at the disposal of theatres with ancient traditions, which had fallen on evil days, but which nevertheless remained fully conscious of their local or classical importance. I have not space here to relate anything about the new plays that have been performed, or about the open-air theatre or the people's theatre, which can accommodate up to about 5,000 persons. It would be better to hear an expert in these subjects, and still better if English people would make a trip through Germany and see for themselves what is being done.

Under the Chamber of Literature are organised not only writers, but also booksellers and libraries and everything that has to do with the production and distribution of books. When the Chamber of Culture Law was passed, the book trade had an ancient organisation of its own, and there was also an Authors' Society of little importance, which concerned itself solely with financial matters, and which was becoming more and more an institution of the great cities alone. It is putting the situation in a nutshell when it is said that the movement of 1933 was nothing more nor less than a rising of the regional instinct against the exaggerated centralisation in the capital. It is certainly true that literature very plainly revealed that its support was for the healthy movement, rooted and grounded in the people and the country, against the circles of eastern emigrants and undesirable groups in the capital. In spite of the unrest of the times, a strong impetus has been given again to regional forces in literature.

Economic protection remains, of course, an important part of the Chamber's work. The advisory bureau on legal matters has been re-established, and disputes between publishers and authors mostly yield to arbitration, both parties being members of the same Chamber, Subsidies from the State, and privately offered contributions, make it possible to give assistance in cases of real distress, through the instrumentality of the Chamber.

All these, however, are means that were employed before, and they do not suffice for the work of the present Chamber. Soon after it came into existence and was provided with full power under the Chamber of Culture Law, it started to fight for the new rights of the arts. It has opened its own book trade school, at which hundreds of young people not only learn to know the literature of the Middle Ages, the Classical period and the Romantic movement, but learn also to form their own opinions regarding our present-day literature by discussing it with their fellows. Not only this, it has caused the 10,000 lending libraries of Germany, some of which catered for a very inferior taste, to increase their stock by about 33%, in which they had to include the classics and some at least of the best modern writings selected from the literatures of all nations. The Chamber of Literature was also able in 1935 to offer a number of prizes, which were the result of private subscriptions and which represented a value of about 2,000,000 marks.

One of its best ideas has proved to be that Book Week, organised each autumn, in which everyone is asked to examine his books and to buy whatever he can afford to improve his library. Book-buying, which had markedly suffered, has, since 1934, increased each year by about 15 % This is a large increase when it is considered that political books, which were heavily bought during the pre-revolutionary years, monthly lose in popularity, and that book-buyers are found more and more amongst the youth of the country, who are eager purchasers of the omnibus collections published by the Insel-Verlag, the Diederichs-Verlag and the Muller-Verlag.

The passing of the Chamber of Culture Law was followed up by the formation of a Reich Senate authorised to deal with Germany's cultural problems. It is composed of the presidents of the various sub-Chambers and a number of the foremost young writers and artists. From amongst these, experts are chosen to see that the new law is properly applied, and from them the State seeks to forge the instrument by which the intellectual leadership of the people may be made to march side by side with the political.

This is the position after four years of ceaseless, breathless action. We know, of course, that changes which give specific rights to the company of artists, the effect of which can hardly be appreciated as yet, need a decade or two in which to develop. We are pleased that, during these vital years, we have laid the foundations for the new order. We know that we have made a great many mistakes, but it is surely better to achieve something, even if mistakes happen, than to sit with folded hands awaiting the fate that seems to threaten the whole Continent.

Germany's revolution is not yet over: the smoothing of the paths, the rounding off, is just beginning. We know that every revolution produces a number of restless spirits who have to sow, as it were, their wild oats before they can adjust themselves to the new order of things. Our task is not over: it has only just begun. But we are pursuing a road that daily becomes clearer. We are in the midst of a time which is characterised by a will, surely everywhere perceptible, to create juster principles of religious brotherhood and freedom amongst the nations, a Weltanschauung by which the arts are no longer regarded as belonging exclusively to the intellectuals, but as instruments in the hands of an all-pervading Power that guides our human destinies.

I have often spoken about these things with my friends abroad, many of whom still seem to think that the writer should be lying in the sun when he is not puzzling his brains at his desk. How in the world, they say, can you, for instance, who have just read us your poems and fairy-tales, possibly occupy yourself with matters of State? What have they to do with you?

I have already told of Galsworthy, who felt differently about this, and who devoted a great part of his life and his writings to the service of his people. I believe that we, the peoples inhabiting countries whose shores are washed by the North Sea, hold similar views on these matters, and that we also understand the dual task which has been laid upon our shoulders. And if people go further, and ask me whether I approve the restraint that is used and the "Prussianising" of the arts, then I, poor innocent, merely shake my head over the wisdom to be found in this world. Does anyone really believe that we, with our solid peasant stock and honest bourgeoisie, would permit restraints to be placed upon us that we did not voluntarily accept as a means to bridge over the difficulties of the moment? Does anyone believe that we - who, after many a hard struggle, have just regained our national unity - would be content with the policy pursued by the new Reich if, in our hearts, we disapproved of it? Does anyone think that we artists are so unemotional and passionless that we would calmly tolerate circumstances we were unable to support with all our heart - belief in a better world and a new fulfilment of our God-ordained task?

We will not utter reproaches, though it is often a bitter thing to be misunderstood. We want nothing but to build up our own State without external interference, and in the way we think best both for our people and for the young art that is flourishing with us now. May people learn to leave us alone, if they cannot understand us, because we have no designs on them and only desire to complete in peace the great work we have undertaken. But where we find sincere friendship we return it with friendship, and we only ask our friends to be patient for a little while, if they cannot comprehend everything that happens in the Reich. Our people, since 1918, have been compelled to bear almost unendurable burdens - is it then surprising that they are longing for a newer and juster world? We have won through to inward and are now awaiting outward peace and justice. We artists are probably the most strongly desirous of peace, because we are building the new homes of the four arts, and believe we are building them well.

Does this sound arrogant? I do not think so. We should learn to be more tolerant not only of the old, but also of the young. It should be realised that the spirit permeating our continent is one that has many aspects, and that it is variously expressed in every nation. Let us also always remember that the nations are not really so far apart from each other as jealousy and unrest would have them believe, and let us hope that the feeling of European solidarity, which our thousand-year-old history has taught us to appreciate and in the development of which we Germans would like to take our share, may once more be awakened. We artists of the Reich are teaching this creed to the children of our people. But we still miss the outside response.

SECTION THREE

THE MOTOR HIGHWAYS
BUILT BY HERR HITLER

THE PLANNING, CONSTRUCTION AND
IMPORTANCE OF THE REICH MOTOR ROADS

Dr. Todt

Inspector-General of the German
Road and Highway System

IN order to form an adequate idea of what has actually been achieved by the National Socialist Government in their vast road construction programme, it is necessary to make a brief historical survey of the period following the War and bring some light to bear on the general conditions prevailing then, and whence National Socialism sprang into existence. For the construction of the Reich motor roads must also be judged within the framework of certain other important undertakings, and the whole idea is due to the personal initiative of Herr Hitler.

The general decline which set in as a consequence of the lost war was not confined to political spheres, but had a really catastrophic effect upon all sections of German life. Certain faults and weaknesses associated with the German people as a result of their history were accentuated to an immeasurable extent when the collapse came. The main contributory factor in this connection was the lack of unity between the various provinces and parties. After the termination of the Thirty Years' War which brought dire disaster to Germany, the development of the German nation was at least 200 years behind that of other countries. Whereas in England and in France a strong central power could develop, which brought these nations all the advantages of firm resolution and thought, Germany could never entirely succeed in making up for the lack of a clear-sighted and broad-minded national policy, despite all her competency, industry and straightforwardness. Nevertheless, the German people have always felt a deep longing for unity and strength, and this desire existed even in difficult times. Finally, it needed a Bismarck to forge the broken links closer together, and he succeeded in adjusting the special dynastic interests of the individual States.

But the influence of the smaller middle-class communities could not be eliminated in a State which, up to 1918, comprised a number of petty States in which the denominational cleavage had never ceased to exert its disastrous influence since the Thirty Years' War. It is true that before the last War, Germany was closely connected with events of international economic importance, thanks to the industry of her population, her technical progress, and her scientific ambitions. But the inner power and clarity of vision displayed by the political leaders were not in conformity with the outward splendour of the second Reich. Moreover, the sharp distinction which existed between urgent social problems, economic liberalism, and the power of traditional conceptions was too great not to threaten, sooner or later, the outward structure of the Reich.

The Marxist treason of 1918 brought about the collapse of the State edifice. The Army, which was the most vivid expression of German national power and unity, was dismembered. Elements of alien origin were rampant in the political sphere. The imitation of a democratic form of Government, which did not harmonise at all with the sentiments and conceptions of the German people as to what a real democracy is, put the finishing touch to the intellectual confusion, which culminated in the splitting-up of the people into 40 parties. Particularism blossomed forth once more and became so powerful that it undermined the last pillars which held the Reich together.

The German transportation system also presents a true picture of the nation's political history. Its development and condition prove that the entire life of a people is dependent on whether they are able to act in a clever and reasonable manner in important matters where their destiny is at stake.

The formation of the German Customs Union in 1833-4 was not only a preliminary step towards the political unity of the Reich which followed under Bismarck, but also prepared the way for the wonderful development of the Railway System in Germany. The actual extension of the German railways went hand-in-hand with the establishment of the German Empire at Versailles in 1871, which brought in its train a powerful economic revival.

The German Postal System also owes its development to the Bismarck Government. The same applies to the German Mercantile Fleet. The old German Hansa, mighty and magnificent though it may have been at times in its history, had finally to succumb to its competitors, for the limbs could not live without unity in the entire body represented by the German nation.

Is it therefore a matter for wonder that the German transportation system was heavily hit after the War? The pressure from without through the Versailles Treaty, and the disintegration and paralysing of all forces within, were bound to have an influence on transportation. The mercantile fleet had to be surrendered, and the railways were forced to assume heavy war charges. In the period following the World War the century of the motorcar started, but in Germany, where this marvellous invention originated, it was hardly noticeable that a new era in mechanical transportation had commenced. Whereas other countries were able to benefit more and more from the technical and economic progress of motorisation, Germany, which had always been ahead in traffic arrangements, remained far behind.

The State Administration was also unable, because of the number of individual States, to launch out on an extensive programme for improving traffic conditions. While in other countries they had started to adapt the old high-road system to the requirements of the most modern vehicle, the motor-car, things in Germany remained much as they were before. Germany was ten years behind the United States in adopting the modern technique of road construction. But there was no sign whatever of the systematic extension of the prevailing system or of a really modern road. Motorists could proceed for perhaps 20 kilometres on a well-constructed road in some district or other, and when they wanted to reach a place at some distance they found themselves suddenly on routes which seemed to remind them of war territory, or which at best were suited for a mail-coach from the good old times. The bureaucratically-minded governments of the individual States offered no new ideas and proved quite incapable of pushing matters forward in order to be in line with the requirements of the age and the technical progress made. There were 700 Road Construction Offices which worked side by side in this way, though in many cases it must be said that they worked against each other.

How could a modern road system, which could only meet half the unceasing progress of the motor-car, emerge under such conditions?

At that time it was hardly noticed in Germany how from year to year we got further and further behind in comparison with the United States, Great Britain, France, Italy, or other countries. The distress and the daily struggle for existence were so great and the permanent state of uneasiness so pressing that one had become almost accustomed to a continual drifting state of mind. Whereas in the United States, Great Britain and France the motorcar factories were working at top pressure and had thus gained a considerable technical and economic advance, unemployment in Germany increased terribly.

The possession of a motorcar was looked upon as a great luxury for rich people, and Bolshevik class hatred took care that an increase in motorisation and in the possession of motor-cars should not be looked upon as a natural advance on the road of progress, but as an occasion for proletarian envy and the spread of hatred. Such points of view had even managed to affect legislation and the administration of justice, so that it could be said that there was a hostile feeling towards the introduction of motor-cars in general.

There was only one man who thought otherwise in these gloomy times. He was the man who by day and night motored hundreds of thousands of kilometres along the German highways. In his indefatigable struggle for Germany's freedom and honour, he appeared in all parts of the country in order to gather his followers together. That man was Adolf Hitler! Even in the midst of the most difficult political conflicts, he found time to deal with all kinds of problems. Amongst these, that concerning transportation was not the least important. Adolf Hitler was a friend of the motorcar and thoroughly appreciated its various uses and advantages. No other man was in a position to gain such practical experience concerning the motorcar and the road. The distances which he covered by motorcar during the ten years when he was engaged in his political struggle correspond at least to a voyage ten times round the globe! With such knowledge of the matter, the idea occurred to him long ago to launch out on the great schemes, the realisation of which we have before us today in the vast road construction and motorisation plan.

With the introduction of railways, the importance of the road decreased from decade to decade. The value of the high-roads became less and less, not only as a medium for transportation but also from the military point of view. At the end of the last century, however, when the motorcar came into its own, its progress was greatly handicapped, as there were no roads which were even half equipped to meet the new demands. This applied to the whole world, for nobody had foreseen the incredible development of the motor-car. Road construction was limited to very modest attempts, the main object of which seemed to be to keep the roads more or less free from dust.

The Great War did for motor traffic what it did for aircraft, and an unprecedented revival set in. For the first time, the motorisation of transports and supplies was a decisive factor. Indeed, the employment of masses of motorised columns in the World War was the first step in practical motorisation. It is only natural, therefore, that the experiences gained in the War were used for the technical and economic development of a modern motorcar industry. The United States, France, Great Britain, and Italy led the way. Only Germany, for the reasons already given, remained far behind. The development in road construction suffered the same fate, and only a few of the more progressive States and municipalities managed to put their roads into good condition, whereas the others left their roads in a state of sad neglect. The whole business was characterised by one fundamental error: the lack of legal provisions authorising the Reich to intervene in the question of road construction. Party strife and the jealousy animating the various competent authorities made it impossible for the Reich to pass such a law. Some private companies and associations attempted in vain to propagate the necessity of modern road construction. The success of their efforts was confined to narrow limits, and they achieved practically nothing. Technical progress in road construction, as in the motorcar industry, was severely handicapped. For the time being, German road construction had to be restricted to piece-work. In the race between the technical development of motor vehicles and modern road making, the latter was far behind.

This was the state of affairs when the Third Reich was founded in 1933. Immediate intervention on the part of the State was indispensable if the German transportation system was to be saved from permanent damage.

The Leader himself at once took the personal initiative to put the whole system on a fundamentally new basis. At the opening of the 1933 International Automobile Exhibition in Berlin only 11 days after taking over the reins of Government, he announced a reform in the taxes on motor vehicles. The second measure, and one covering a far greater range, was the Motor Road Law issued on June 27th, 1933, which the Chancellor, in spite of much opposition, announced in a memorable speech delivered on May 1st, 1933. This law provided for the formation of an undertaking known as the Reich Motor Roads, conferring on it the power to construct and put into operation an efficient system of motor roads. Simultaneously it was announced that an Inspector-General was to be put in charge of the German Road System. A few days later, the Leader appointed the author of this article to that position.

The subsequent development proceeded at a pace such as has never been witnessed in Germany before. All the people were extricated from their state of annihilation and lethargy into which they seemed to have fallen since they lost the War. The National Socialist revival was showing its effect and all forces were welded together towards the common aim.

In the first place, effective legislation was introduced in order to pave the way for practical work and to eliminate all bureaucratic obstacles. Starting almost at the bottom of the ladder, work was commenced with courage and fierce energy. From June to September 1933, feverish preparations were made for the work in hand. A motor-road system was drafted, with a total length of about 7,000 kilometres, spreading over the entire country and connecting all economic, cultural and political centres.

As early as September 23rd, 1933, the Leader in person inaugurated the constructional work, and made the first cut with the spade at Frankfort-on-Main amid the enthusiasm of the workmen.

The planning and the legislation, but above all the rapid and decisive way in which the construction work was started, caused great surprise in road construction circles at home and abroad. The German people themselves were no less astonished. The majority of the experts had imagined that first of all the existing system of the old highways would have to be extended to comply with the increasing requirements. The Leader, however, chose the opposite method, and ordered the construction of a completely new road system. His reason for doing so was that he foresaw the great traffic, as well as the economic and political possibilities which such an undertaking would open up for Germany, and indeed for the whole of Europe. The Leader knew that the construction of a motor-road system was the most important preliminary for comprehensive motorisation. The object he had in view was that Germany, which was so many years behind other countries in this respect, should pursue a course which would make up for arrears and should be pushed forward by all possible means so as to prepare for any future development.

After four years of work on the part of her great National Chancellor, Germany is indeed the first country in the world where road construction is in advance of the technical development of motor-vehicle construction. This gives an impulse to the motor-vehicle industry and traffic development which will outlive the present generation. It was an event of historical significance that at the International Motor Show in Berlin in 1937, the Reich motor roads completely dominated the whole exhibition, and that the whole motorcar industry had to adapt itself to the achievements which the modern motor roads demand from the cars. Who would have thought it possible a few years ago that Germany should possess roads today which practically place no limits on the capacity of the automobile? The relationship between road and car has changed fundamentally. Today the motorist in Germany has no cause to complain about the bad condition of the roads; on the contrary, he is now asking the motorcar industry when it will be possible to build the car that will be able to make full use of all the advantages and possibilities which these magnificent roads offer. The great idea represented by the Reich motor roads was everywhere apparent at the International Motorcar and Motor-Cycle Exhibitions of 1937 and 1938. It is already the guiding principle which controls the constructional development of the motorcar industry, and applies to vehicles of practically all kinds. This factor will become more manifest from year to year, as the great Reich Motor Road System will be extended from year to year and the entire Reich Road System will be adapted to the ever-increasing motor traffic.

The appointment of an Inspector-General for the German Road System put a rapid end to the previous un-systematic work of the Road Construction Authorities in the various States and provinces. In a decree issued on November 30th, 1933, it was announced that the Inspector-General would be directly under the Reich Chancellor. By this act on the part of the Government, the roads have again come under the sovereignty of the Reich, which had not been the case since the time of the powerful mediaeval Emperors. The construction of the Reich motor roads will only be fully appreciated when the road construction in the new Germany is seen as part of the whole comprehensive programme dealing with motorisation, road construction and the supplies of motor fuel. German motorisation was preceded by a provision by which newly-manufactured passenger cars were exempted from the motor-vehicle tax, whilst older vehicles were afforded tax facilities and replacement parts were free of tax also. The success of this measure was enormous. The number of licences granted to motor vehicles rose from 104,000 in 1932 to 475,000. The production of motor-cars increased from 51,000 in 1932 to 293,000, whereas the number of persons engaged in the motor industry went up from 33,000 in 1932 to more than 100,000 in 1937. In the supply and accessory industries, the number of people employed went up in at least equal proportion. About the middle of 1932, there were nearly 400,000 passenger motor-cars on the roads in Germany: now there are about 1,000,000 of them, so that there has been an increase of 150% In 1932 there was one motorcar to every 100 inhabitants, whereas in 1936 every 54th inhabitant had his own car.

The following table shows the number of new passenger car licences each year:

Year	New Passenger Car Licenses
1932	41,000
1933	93,000
1934	130,000
1935	185,000
1936	200,000

This means that the number of licences granted is now five times as large as it was before Herr Hitler came to power. The number of motor-vehicles of all kinds has long since exceeded the 2,000,000 mark. The production and sale of motor-trucks also show an impressive upward trend, the number having risen from about 7,000 in 1932 to roughly 40,000 in the year 1936. The same applies to motor-cycles, where the number admitted to the roads has risen from 56,000 to 140,000.

Apart from the administrative and tax measures carried out directly under the supervision of the Reich Government, it was mainly the execution of the vast Road Construction Programme which gave a fresh impulse to motorisation. Our road construction is the best guarantor for our motorisation. In German motor-racing, the same powerful initiative which is behind all progressive movements, resulted in a whole series of astonishing international successes, such as had never before been experienced in the history of German racing. On the motor-tracks themselves a number of new world records were set up.

The construction of Reich motor roads is an economic measure, the effect of which is rarely properly appreciated. This vast undertaking can only be compared with the construction of the railway system commenced a century ago, which introduced a new era in traffic and international trade. It took about 70 years to develop the railway system until it was completed in its main sections, whereas it is reckoned that it will require about 10 years for the construction of the new Reich motor roads and putting the entire German road system on a modern footing.

In view of the vast amount of unemployment which prevailed in Germany before National Socialism came into power, it goes without saying that the tackling of this problem was a main consideration in the construction of Reich motor roads. Through their construction, 130,000 men are directly kept at work on the building sites. This is when the work is in full operation, which has been the case since 1935. A further 130,000 men find additional work and their daily bread in the supplying and consuming industries, that is to say in stone quarries, cement works, ironmongery working shops, bridge-building plants, building-machine factories, etc. The increased consumption of foodstuffs and purchase of clothes by this host of workmen who are again able to earn their own living is a factor which carries considerable weight. The prosperity of the building industry largely depends on the season of the year, but in spite of this the number of workers employed on the Reich motor roads was only cut down for a period of a few weeks, when frost and ice rendered constructional work difficult. But even during that short period, 50,000 workmen were kept constantly employed. The building of the Reich motor roads made it possible for the first time in Germany to carry out constructional work on a large scale through the winter months.

In addition to the construction of the 7,000 kilometres of new motor roads, a comprehensive road-construction programme will be put into effect for modernising the former long-distance roads of the various States and provinces, i.e., the present Reich roads. About 40,000 kilometres of such roads have been taken over by the Reich, and are either in course of reconstruction or extension. About 150,000 additional men are directly or indirectly engaged on this work, so that a grand total of more than 400,000 men who were previously out of work are now living again under normal conditions.

Within the framework of other important measures undertaken by the National Socialist Government in its fight against unemployment, the construction of new roads was the first and foremost, and remains so up to the present day. Unskilled workers, amongst whom the greatest distress was to be found, formed the majority of those who re-entered the ranks of the employed thanks to the road-building scheme. About 15,000 of these are trained every year to become road building experts. Modern road construction requires such workmen in increasing numbers, as the technical aspect of road-building has continually improved. The consequence is that there are practically no unemployed trained workers and building assistants, such as are required for the construction of the Reich motor roads. Thus it happens, for instance, that workers have to be fetched from the Saar territory for work to be done in Wurttemberg, and from Saxony to carry out building undertakings in Franconia. This, of course, means that the number of working camps on the Reich motor roads, amounting at present to 140, has to be considerably increased.

Through the measures adopted for the revival of the automobile industry new workers have been engaged on an extensive scale. As against an approximate number of 60,000 employed in this capacity in 1932, there are now about 200,000 men directly or indirectly engaged in the construction of motor-vehicles in Germany.

The motor roads, as a means of providing work, have an essential advantage as compared with the emergency measures adopted by previous Governments for providing employment in as far as they do not represent work which is given to tide people in distress over a certain period, but offer the possibility of regular and continuous work for a long period.

Hence, the economic effect of the undertaking is very considerable. A few figures will serve to illustrate this point. Up to the present (1937) trade has benefited to the tune of about 1,500,000,000 reichsmarks through the construction of the new motor roads. It may be assumed that approximately 400,000,000 reichsmarks will be spent annually on construction work. About 3,600 kilometres, or half the length of the main system planned, are already in course of construction. The first 1,000 kilometres were opened to traffic in the autumn of 1936 At the end of September 1937, 1,553 kilometres were already in operation, and by the end of this year a total of about 2,000 kilometres will be open to traffic as complete motor roads. The following are the roads in question:

The Motor Highways Built By Herr Hitler

Hamburg - Bremen Hamburg - Lubeck Hanover - Berlin Berlin - Stettin Berlin - Frankfort-on-Oder Siegburg - Cologne- Dusseldorf - Duisburg- Reckling-hausen Giessen - Frankfort-on-Main - Heidelberg - Karlsruhe Stuttgart-Ulm Halle - Leipzig - Bayreuth - Nuremberg Dresden - Chemnitz - Jena Konigsberg - Elbing Breslau - Forst Munich - Salzburg (frontier)

As well as a few smaller sections. With the completion of the Leipzig-Bayreuth-Nuremberg section, more than one-third of the entire length of the future Reich motor road from Berlin to Munich has been opened to traffic. Another very important piece of work performed this year is the continuation of the Reich motor road from Berlin to Stettin across the River Oder, thus effecting a connection with the great Baltic main road.

In this context the Berlin circular road which, when completed, will play a most prominent part in the traffic system, is especially worthy of mention. A large section of this highway was opened to traffic this year. That means a direct connection in the East, via Erkner, between the Stettin section and the Reich motor road from Berlin to Frankfort-on-Oder, and the development of the Southern and South-Western portion of the Berlin circular motor road will also be actively pushed ahead. At the present time, the section from Hanover to the Western industrial territory, which is of great importance to the capital, is in course of construction, and when this is completed the construction of the Reich motor road from Cologne in a southern direction as far as Frankfort-on-Main will be proceeded with. Further to be mentioned are the Hamburg-Hanover-Kassel, and above all the Dresden-Breslau roads as sections on which constructional work has been started.

The machinery equipment is more important than any used up to the present for such an undertaking, and the following are in constant operation:

50,000 tipping waggons 3,000 building engines 1,000 modern building machines 3,000 kilometres of building tracks.

The amount of soil which has to be moved in performing the work constitutes a record for all time, and even now it exceeds by far that which was necessary for the construction of the Panama Canal. The country has received important orders for bridge and steel constructions, and through the construction of motor roads, natural stone for the purpose of bridge building has once more come into its own. We are again building many stone bridges, for experience has shown that they last longer and are of more pleasing appearance. The Regensburg stone bridge is 1,000 years old and still carries the heaviest traffic.

The roads are laid in such a way as to offer the most perfect security from the constructional and technical standpoints. There is no crossing, no traversing of rails, no driving through towns or villages, and the departure and arrival stopping-places are arranged in such a way that the cars gradually enter into the moving traffic. The most important point of all, however, is that the Reich motor roads consist of two separate tracks, so that the traffic can only move in one direction. It is therefore impossible for two vehicles to meet. The only possibility of contact is when one car overtakes another in the same direction. This can only lead to an accident in the case of very careless driving, for the total width of the Reich motor roads is 24 metres. They consist of two tracks, each of which is 7.50 metres in width, a middle-strip 5 metres wide with trees and grass, and side footpaths each of which is 2 metres in width. Thanks to the care bestowed on the construction of the driving-tracks and the special attention paid to the sub-soil of the road surface, the Reich motor roads have proved themselves trustworthy in times of frost and when they are slippery. Already in the winter of 1936-7 a regular service was introduced for strewing the roads, which of course will be further developed in the coming years. This will finally mean that every "road master" on the Reich motor roads will have a sufficient number of motorised vehicles at his disposal to enable him to keep the sections under his charge in order and free from snow and ice. Apart from this, the system of signals introduced last winter as a warning against slippery ice proved of excellent worth. The experience thus acquired will be used for the further development and perfection of the winter service. Later on, this winter or signalling service will operate in such a way that every pumping station on the Reich motor roads and every road master of the Reich motor roads will be able to tell every driver the exact condition of the section along which he wishes to proceed. This will be of special use to heavy long-distance motor-lorry traction.

The importance of the Reich motor roads judged from the point of view of traffic policy can best be gauged by considering the fact that out of 50,000 German towns and villages, only 18,000 have direct railway connection. Despite the fact that the German railway system is of great density, we have great possibilities for cars and roads to use the space available and for house-to-house traffic, which can only be effectively done by motor-car.

In the whole development of the system, the sapping of energy and strength through an exaggerated competitive struggle between railway and motor traffic will be avoided in Germany. The development will be slow and gradual, and will be based on sound organic principles. It was, therefore, for very good reasons that the Reich Motor Road Corporation was founded as an affiliation of the German National Railways. Moreover, since the Leader liberated the latter from the last fetters of the Versailles Treaty, they are again in full operation in the service of the Reich and can fulfil their great political and economic tasks without fear of being checked in their initiative, as is often the case with private railway companies.

In order to arrive at a proper adjustment of the German transportation policy, a special law governing long-distance goods traffic was issued, whereby the overland motor-lorry services are combined in a special Reich organisation. The independence of each undertaking is fully protected by the Association. German traffic policy strives in principle towards the systematic distribution of traffic between the railway, shipping, motor transport and aircraft, and this in such a manner that each of these traffic organisations shall discharge the duties which are best adapted to its special sphere and technical development. In other words, instead of senseless competition against each other, an equitable division will be effected, so that each will render of its best. This policy, which by no means excludes healthy competition, will best serve the interests of political economy. Within the sphere of these fundamental principles, a wide field will be open in future for motor transportation in Germany. For instance, all the possibilities of closer traffic relationship between the various Works have by no means been exhausted. In this connection, the erection of new and large industrial production workshops under the Four Year Plan is an important factor. The home production of motor fuel from coal, the erection of important staple fibre factories, the opening-up of important ore and mineral deposits, and the development of the country's own food supplies are all measures of far-reaching consequence which would be unthinkable without a corresponding road construction policy.

Traffic statistics available up to the present point to the fact that the entire long-distance traffic on the roads is going over to the Reich motor roads. Their advantages do not only consist in a saving of time, but also less wear and tear and a lower consumption of motor fuel. This is of great economic importance, and apt to be overlooked.

In the huge undertaking represented by the Reich motor roads, many steps have been taken towards a solution of the social problem. These measures were symbolic and were adopted by the entire building trade for its motto. They are, moreover, entirely in conformity with the conceptions of a National Socialist State.

The motor road workmen are paid according to tariff, and also receive bonuses formerly unknown. For those who, on account of the long distance of the building sites from their dwellings, could not be properly accommodated, lodging-camps were erected. In addition to clean sleeping- barracks, these camps have special canteens, with kitchens. The storage rooms are fitted with the most up-to-date refrigerator apparatus. Hot baths with shower-rooms, steam-heating, etc., are provided everywhere. To ensure smooth co-operation and cleanliness in these camps, there are special leaders with a staff of their own. On an average, each camp accommodates 200 men. The National Socialist Culture and Kraft durch Freude (Strength through Joy) organisations see to it that the workmen get plenty of change and entertainment. There are a stage of strolling players with good artists and an excellent programme, touring cinemas, sports requisites, libraries, newspapers and games for every camp. The price of meals is kept at the lowest level, and the workman gets everything he wants at cost price. Those who are injured by accident are sent to the best and most up-to-date hospital in Germany, at Hohenlychen.

The State and the building contractors work hand in hand, and it is a point of honour with them to make the lives of the Reich motor road workers better and more beautiful. Married workers get a free railway pass in order to go home for week-ends, and the wife of the worker has the assurance that part of her husband's wages will be placed to her account or directly remitted to her. This is a much better arrangement than the previous ones, when it frequently happened, especially in the building-trade, that the man spent his entire weekly wages on drink, leaving his wife without a penny. In any event, constant efforts are being made to render the life of a building labourer, which is a hard one, easier and more comfortable. Unemployment is no longer a factor as far as the motor road organisation is concerned. Indeed, it can be said that unemployment in Germany to all intents and purposes has been eliminated. "Where can we be sure of finding the necessary workmen for building the motor roads?" That is the question now asked.

In the drafting of the scheme, the motor road authorities attached the greatest importance to the fact that the roads should be absolutely adapted to the German landscape. It is to their everlasting credit that they are pioneers in the Third Reich in as far as they have built not only useful motorcar roads, but above all beautiful ones. Their endeavour, in the construction of this gigantic road system, to perform something of real value, has made us recognise that beautiful roads are not more expensive than unattractive ones, and that a perfectly and beautifully built road is at the same time really the best and most serviceable. The lay-out of the roads, which absolutely fits in with the surrounding landscape, is the best, and a beautiful highway attracts traffic like a magnet.

It is a fundamental error to imagine that the roads present the appearance of endless dreary racing-tracks. In all parts of our German homeland where work is being done on the roads, efforts are being made to avoid the errors committed in the last century, when the construction of railways was planned without paying due consideration to other factors. From the very outset the aim has been to build this huge network of roads not only with the mathematical instruments of the real builder, but also with artistic feeling and a love of Nature and her soothing influence.

The deeper and spiritual movement of the National Socialist revolution, which signifies a psychic and cultural renovation of the German citizen, is plainly detectable in this undertaking. The white ribbons of the motor roads are carefully embedded in the landscape, and their lay-out is harmoniously adapted to them. Wherever large viaducts or similar structures are necessary, the same zeal has been shown to combine what is technically serviceable with the special features of the German landscape. These efforts to make out of Nature and technique one perfect unit characterise the work of the Reich motor roads as one of great importance and one which covers the greatest range. Technique and art, nature and life are to take on a new form as a result of this creative spirit. This is a task the immensity of which can only be appreciated by those who understand what the harmony of these things means to our people, and indeed to the whole world.

We can state with pride that the adaptability of the Reich motor roads to the German landscape has already been achieved on a large scale, and is tending more and more in this direction. The roads rank not only among the most modern, but also among the most beautiful ones in the world.

The new roads lend a new character to the German landscape. The open stretched lines which pass through the landscape force the eye to follow their direction and the starting-place and destination are more clearly marked. German men and women will see these roads and the vastness of the scene will help them to think on broader lines than was heretofore possible. This is a matter of extreme importance, and the roads built by Herr Hitler represent the most vivid expression of the unshakable unity of the Reich.

The great importance of the Reich motor roads has long since been recognised in foreign countries. The great achievements and efforts made by the Third Reich in the sphere of road construction were fully appreciated at the 7lth International Road Congress (1934) held in Munich and Berlin, and at the 2nd International Congress for Bridges and Overground Structures (1936) held in Berlin. An official resolution of the Road Congress stated that the construction and planning of the German motor roads is exemplary and the press of all large countries has nothing but praise for the work accomplished. Numerous foreign visitors have come to Germany for the express purpose of inspecting the motor roads, and the number of foreign cars in Germany is continually on the increase.

Road construction in Europe means closer and more rapid communications. The building of modern roads for the purpose of rapid transport is being discussed in nearly all countries, and in some cases Germany is taken as an example. Even in countries where such is not the case, as for instance in France, they are adopting the German word autobahn (motor-track) for similar projects. New road-construction plans are considered in Denmark, Belgium, Holland, Austria and Poland. Germany has made an agreement with Italy to establish motor road connection between Berlin and Rome. We may safely say that the German initiative in road construction has caused quite a lively sensation everywhere.

In September 1937, a special British delegation ("German Roads Delegation") paid a visit to this country to study our new motor highway system. We are sincerely glad to see that our efforts met with the approval of our visitors; and the farewell speech delivered by Lord Wolmer in the Gurzenich building, Cologne, will always be remembered by us with much pleasure. The German suggestion, he said, that Germany's road system should be studied by British experts had been received with great interest. He referred to the delegation headed by him as the most representative unofficial body of Englishmen that has ever visited Germany. It consisted of 225 members of Parliament and representatives of the British road-making and motorcar industries. Although British traffic problems are different from the German ones, the members of the delegation have been able, Lord Wolmer said, to collect many valuable impressions and suggestions. These have meanwhile been summarised in a comprehensive report. We are proud of the complimentary remarks it contains on the safety of the traffic on our motor high-roads and are highly gratified to see that the adoption of the German system by Great Britain is recommended. ("We recommend that the principle of the motor-way system be adopted in Great Britain".) The advantages of our system are considered so great that it is described as desirable to make an immediate start with its introduction. (" ... an immediate beginning should be made with those lengths of the national plan which are urgently required to relieve the pressure of traffic on the existing roads, and to reduce the risk of accidents.") Since then it has been possible further to strengthen the relations so happily inaugurated between German and British road experts. Future visits have already been arranged, including one by the chairman for road-making in the University of London, and who intends to visit us with his students in the summer of 1938. Before concluding this article, I wish to express my cordial thanks for the welcome which was accorded to the delegation of road experts headed by me when we visited Great Britain in November 1937. The German road system is certain to derive great benefit from the opportunities we had of studying London's traffic problems and from the talks I had with British experts, notably with Dr. Burgin, the Minister of Transport.

Germany will be very happy if the construction of her motor roads is viewed in the light of what it really represents, that is to say as an achievement in the domain of European civilization. If all Europe could become engaged in such peaceful work, there would be enough to do for 20 or 50 years. Literally and figuratively speaking, it would bring the nations closer together, and that would be the greatest achievement which technical progress could claim in the twentieth century.

PART IV

GERMANY AND THE WORLD

SECTION ONE

GERMANY'S POSITION IN WORLD ECONOMY

Dr. Hjalmar Schacht

Reich Minister and President of the Reichsbank

I

THE trade and prosperity of a country as well as its intellectual and cultural life depend on a flourishing world trade to such an extent that we must never tire of stressing the need for international economic co-operation. Although the leading economists in practically all countries have directed attention again and again to the national losses resulting from the world-wide economic depression, and have endeavoured to formulate recommendations for a real improvement, ignorance of the steps that must be taken to effect this purpose is still quite general, and there are no signs of a vigorous policy intended to reanimate trade intercourse between the various nations. Seeing that questions affecting world trade are always sure to attract intelligent interest in a country like Great Britain, I am glad of this opportunity for stating once more my views on these matters, more especially in so far as they affect the attitude of the new Germany towards world trade. I shall try to give a brief account of the conditions which, in my opinion, must be fulfilled before we can look forward to a genuine economic recovery throughout the world.

II

Even a cursory glance at the remnants of what is called "international economy" shows that the economic relations between the countries are largely in a state of utter confusion. Instead of making the world's abundant supply of raw materials and foodstuffs available to all nations through the medium of commerce, valuable commodities are wilfully destroyed. Elsewhere, the production of certain goods is artificially restricted, although there are countries that are in urgent need of those very products. Long-term commercial treaties have been replaced, in numerous instances, by absolutely unsatisfactory arrangements concluded for periods that are far too short. International merchandise credits are indispensable to normal trade intercourse; and their scarcity has produced disastrous effects. Owing to the political insecurity, preference is given by financiers to short-term loans; and the erratic movements of the capital thus used have given rise to heavy fluctuations in the rates of exchange and have seriously affected the currency policy of the countries concerned. The position is made still worse by the excessively high tariff walls, by the maze of import quota regulations, import prohibitions, and clearing arrangements. Finally, there are many countries that have been forced by the shortage of foreign exchange to establish a special regime of currency administration that has resulted in the partial resurrection of the primitive system of barter transactions.

In one of the League of Nations reports issued some time ago, it was stated that the total value of world trade in 1934 was less than that of the combined foreign trades of Germany, Great Britain and the United States in 1929. This is not only due to an enormous shrinkage in the volume of trade, but also to the huge decline in prices, which - in the case of some commodities - was at times even more considerable. The demoralisation of the price-level started in the markets for raw materials and caused widespread selling, with disastrous effects upon production and employment in all countries. The currency devaluations (merely resorted to in some countries for reasons of commercial policy) further added to the existing demoralisation, and were so many heavy blows to the development of international economy. The subsequent rise of prices in the world's markets has been of limited range only and has failed so far to restore sufficiently the vanished purchasing capacity of the countries depending upon the exportation of raw materials. Many countries have now put their faith in measures intended to revive their domestic trade and industry, thus tending more or less to establish economic autarchy. Too often, however, the close interdependence of the home market and the foreign market is ignored. A trade boom in the former can only last on condition that it is supported by a healthy export and import trade. It is gratifying to note, therefore, that a few hopeful indications of an upward movement have lately appeared, even though it would be premature to infer from them that a structural improvement had already occurred.

III

Germany's present world economic position is probably more troubled than that of most other countries. Prior to the War, the equilibrium of her situation in this respect was ensured by the proceeds derived from her flourishing foreign trade, by her important investments abroad, and by her large colonial empire; but the ruinous terms of the Versailles treaty put an end to all that. The victor Powers were guided by a foolish desire to keep her down for all time, economically as well as politically. This is the only intelligent reason that explains the excessive indemnities and the harsh economic conditions imposed upon a country already completely exhausted by war. The seizure of practically all our foreign investments, the forced surrender of valuable assets, the cession of provinces particularly important because of the foodstuffs and raw materials obtainable from them, and the refusal to return our colonies, have gravely endangered our future development and threatened our very existence.

But this was not all. The war indemnities demanded of Germany were of an extent incompatible with the most elementary economic considerations. For a long time, her rulers endeavoured to pursue a "policy of fulfilment" at all costs. The efforts made by her to that end have never been duly appreciated abroad. They were, however, bound to be in vain; because the only possible way of redeeming those political debts, i.e., the exportation of merchandise and the rendering of services, was barred by the creditor countries, anxious - as they were - to protect their home industries against the inrush of German products. Today it may be regarded as practically certain that the inevitable effects of the Versailles system upon world economy were left out of account when the "peace treaty" was drawn up. I believe I may claim some credit for having passionately protested, from the very outset, against the senselessness of the reparations policy, and for pointing out that the German colonies should be returned by the mandatory Powers, not only for the benefit of Germany, but also for that of the world as a whole.

War loans and reparations are the root causes of the foreign-debt problem. During the period 1924-30, the immense sum of more than £2,000,000,000 (reckoning the British £ at 12t reichsmarks) was advanced to Germany by foreign creditors. The resulting debt was about equal in amount to Germany's pre-war assets abroad. The proceeds of the loans, however, did not benefit Germany's national economy in their entirety, a large part of them being required for reparation payments. The impression thus created that Germany possessed a satisfactory capacity for transfer was erroneous. It was bound to be shattered by the events of 1930 and 1931, when the foreign financiers, after first declining to grant any more loans to Germany, suddenly asked for the repayment of the short-term credits, the amount of which was very considerable. Grave sacrifices had then to be demanded of the country's body economic, and almost all the reserves of gold and foreign currency had to be relinquished, but thanks to these measures the foreign indebtedness could be reduced to about £900,000,000. Still, even that sum is so large that the country's diminished foreign-trade earnings are insufficient to provide the money required to pay interest and redeem the principal of the debts. Foreign critics are apt to ignore the fact that Germany, more than any other debtor country, has complied with her obligations to the limits of possibility. Although the Reichsbank, too, sacrificed all its gold and foreign currency reserves in order to satisfy the claims of the foreign creditors, it was necessary to resort to the partial suspension of the debt service. An even greater sacrifice was the introduction of a currency regime, a measure which is naturally liable to serious objections from many points of view. Germany has never wavered in her determination to pay back her debts. It may be assumed that this fact will gradually receive universal recognition. All the same, it is a great pity that foreign observers took so long a time before they realised the economic absurdity of demanding the payment of capital debts by an industrial country (which, in the long run, can only make such payment by the exportation of commodities), whilst at the same time placing every obstacle in its way - such as tariff walls, import quotas, import prohibitions, boycotts, and similar modern devices - that will tend to render such exportation difficult.

The attempts of the victor Powers to extort from their defeated enemy "the uttermost farthing" led to so much general impoverishment that even now the country has not yet recovered from it. As Germany is so very closely linked up with the world's economy, it was inevitable that such a situation should react upon international trade. In spite of all the existing difficulties, she still ranks third in so far as foreign commerce is concerned, being preceded by Great Britain and the United States only; and it is obvious that so important a purchaser country cannot be cold-shouldered without serious consequences to all other countries concerned.

IV

In order to counteract the effects of the continued world-wide depression and to avert further menaces to the country's body economic, the new Germany had to subject her foreign trade to systematic Government supervision. Although the term "plan" has been applied to the measures thus adopted, it does not follow that a system of "planned economy" has been or is going to be introduced. We continue to look upon individual initiative as the most valuable asset of our economic activities, more especially in the field of foreign trade. Our present economic policy is in no way influenced by any tendencies towards "planned economy."

The New Plan (Germany's "New Deal") was announced by the Government in the autumn of 1934. Its objects are to adjust the amount of foreign exchange used for import purposes to the reduced amount of it earned by our export trade and to prevent any increase in our indebtedness to foreigners. We perfectly realise that measures such as these must complicate immensely our trade relations with other countries, and it was with a heavy heart that we decided to introduce them all the same. But as a certain minimum of foreign exchange is indispensable to us for the importation of vital necessities and as the amount earned by us is constantly shrinking, no other choice was left to us. We had to protect at all costs the good reputation enjoyed by the German merchant as regards his capacity and willingness to pay.

Another object we had in mind when introducing Our New Plan was to base our trade intercourse with the various countries upon a more satisfactory foundation. It is through no fault of ours that, in a large number of cases, that intercourse is now governed by irksome bilateral arrangements concerning the interchange of goods and the methods of payment. Numerous foreign countries have seen fit to satisfy by way of clearing the claims of their nationals upon German firms, claims arising out of goods as well as capital transactions. I wish to emphasise, however, that we intend to comply with our obligations - as far as we possibly can - in any case, and that no compulsion is needed to make us do so. In our dealings with Great Britain we have already furnished proof of our earnest will by acting accordingly. We shall always be prepared to start discussions with any country whose commercial dealings with us have become subject to rigid bureaucratic methods, for the purpose of giving greater elasticity to expand again.

The fact that we have been able to improve our balance of trade proves that the New Plan is working successfully. With a view to the acquisition of a trade balance sufficient to meet the necessary capital and other liabilities, we have tried to increase our exports whilst maintaining imports at about their previous level. It is estimated that the export surplus thus obtained for 1937 amounts to some forty million pounds sterling. The trade figures also indicate the difficulties our commercial policy has to face. Imports at the rate of approximately thirty-five million pounds a month are barely sufficient to cover our requirements of raw materials and foodstuffs. Owing to the continued activity of our domestic markets, the consumption of goods is steadily increasing. There is presumably no country in which the demand for foreign foodstuffs and raw materials is more pressing than it is in Germany. Our country is not interested in customs barriers or other measures tending to make the import trade more difficult. All we ask is that other countries should absorb a sufficient amount of our industrial products, so that we may obtain the foreign exchange we need. Such foreign exchange would not be hoarded by us, but would be used for the importation of foreign commodities and thus for the stimulation of international trade.

All countries naturally want to export their products, but a good many of them are by no means equally willing to import. That willingness, however, so essential to a general trade improvement, is nowhere greater than in Germany. We hear it said every now and then that these imports are solely required for the manufacture of armaments with which to threaten the peace of the world. Apart from the fact that our present arms policy is merely intended to provide us with adequate means of defence and to make up for past delay, it should be clearly understood that only a relatively small percentage of our imported raw materials is used by the armaments industry, whilst the major part of them is absorbed by the manufacture of articles for domestic consumption or for export.

Seeing that our own soil does not yield a sufficient amount of foodstuffs and raw materials, we are as yet largely dependent upon products of foreign origin in order to keep our industries busy and to safeguard the vital needs of our people. Germany does not want something for nothing. She continues to be capable and willing to supply the world with the superior grade products turned out by her industries. Accordingly, those in charge of her economic policy regard it as their principal task to cultivate close trade relations with all countries and to improve and expand them wherever possible.

V

Germany is a sincere advocate of international trade, because she realises that she is certain to benefit from it. We do not think, however, that normal conditions likely to last can be restored to world economy by arbitrary and unnecessary measures in the domain of currency policy. I do not believe, therefore, that the devaluation of the reichsmark would contribute in any way towards the improvement of the international situation. It is quite impossible to effect such an improvement by currency manipulations. The latest wave of devaluation, far from improving the existing conditions, has only added fresh difficulties. The lack of stability in the world's markets has increased, because some of the devalued currencies are subject to much fluctuation - a circumstance which deprives merchants of the safe basis of their calculation and confronts them with mathematical puzzles which, in many instances, admit of no solution at all. One reason why it cannot be said that the currency problem has been disposed of is that no definite ratio has been fixed so far for the principal currencies.

If international economy is really to return to healthy conditions, currencies must be internationally stabilised, and the restrictions imposed upon the interchange of goods and services between the various countries must be withdrawn as far as possible. In that way, a natural equilibrium will be established between the available production surpluses. The nations interested in world trade must therefore collaborate with one another and must compose their political differences. Mutual confidence must be restored. These conditions are indispensable if the disturbing factors are to be eliminated. Unfortunately, there is no evidence so far that a common basis for negotiations towards that end will be discovered in the immediate future.

VI

So long as Germany remains unable to satisfy in full her large requirements of raw materials and foodstuffs in the world's markets, the Government must take steps to ensure that the utmost use is made of the resources that are open to her at home. In that way, the difficulty of obtaining an adequate supply of foreign exchange can be partly overcome. Besides that, the Government is animated by a legitimate desire that the opportunities for work provided in recent years by our own efforts and without foreign assistance for the benefit of the many millions of industrious workers who were forced to idleness during the years of deflation, shall continue to be available.

Germany is making every endeavour to widen her food basis in a systematic manner and to augment the home production of raw materials by means of the new Four-Year Plan. To those of our critics who assert that the measures adopted by us are intended to establish an autarchic regime, I would reply: If you will withdraw your protectionist legislation and thus enable us to find sufficient markets for our manufactured articles, we shall be much better able to cover our requirements of foodstuffs and raw materials by paying for them with our exports. So long as this remains undone, we shall be forced to adhere to our present policy and to deal in those markets only where people are willing to buy our own manufactures under the terms of barter arrangements. The difficulties imposed upon our export trade must necessarily determine our commercial policy and therefore react upon world trade in general; but it would be wrong to hold us responsible for these results. Formerly, most of our surplus of manufactured articles was absorbed by the European countries, which are our natural markets, and most of our imports were purchased in the overseas countries, which are our natural purveyors. For a variety of reasons we should be glad to see a return to these conditions, although we can quite understand that world trade may possibly prefer different channels in future.

Countries or political entities like the British Empire or France constitute almost self-sufficient economic units. Their resources include nearly all the vitally important raw materials and foodstuffs, and their foreign trade is increasingly concerned with territories subject to their own sovereignty; but opportunities like these are possessed by very few nations only.

VII

In this connection I would like to briefly touch upon a subject to which I have referred several times elsewhere. It is the problem of Germany's lack of space, or, in other words, her colonial problem. I submit that its bearing upon the return of normal conditions in international economy is far from being adequately appreciated. Italy and Japan, who were faced with similar problems, have solved them in their own way, and have thus joined the ranks of the "satisfied" nations. Germany is now the only Great Power without any colonial possessions of her own. Her demand for the return of her former colonies - at present governed under a mandatory system - is the best possible proof of her sincere love of peace, because it is extremely unlikely that those territories would be of any use to her in the event of a war. The reasons advanced by the mandatory Powers for their refusal to comply with Germany's wish have been refuted so often that I need not refute them again. I have repeatedly explained my views on our Colonial problem, for instance before an audience at Frankfort-on-Main and in an article contributed to the American periodical, "Foreign Affairs." All I want to emphasise in this context is that the return of our colonies would solve the problem created by our lack of space and would also dispose of the raw material and currency questions. The conviction that something must be done to repair the injustice inflicted upon us by the Versailles treaty in depriving us of the use of our colonies, is gradually gaining ground throughout the world. Thus, for instance, the Paris representative of *The Times* contributed an article to that paper some time ago entitled, "Colonial Revision," which contained, among other matters, the following:

> The colonial problem will be the next great question to be faced in Europe. Here as in England there are thoughtful people who think that revision of the distribution of colonies is inevitable sooner or later, and that the sooner the fact is frankly faced the easier and less costly revision will be.

As far as Germany is concerned, the colonial problem is essentially an economic problem. Her vital rights cannot be withheld from her for ever. Although the return of our colonies could not immediately relieve us of all our troubles regarding raw materials and space, it could and would render valuable aid to us in our reconstruction programme. In addition, it would tend to diminish the pressure of our exports and to increase our purchasing capacity, and would thus assist in promoting world trade and general prosperity.

VIII

When, on September 30th, 1936, I made a statement on behalf of the Government and the Reichsbank regarding the Three Power Currency Agreement, this was interpreted, in some quarters, as a refusal on the part of Germany to collaborate with the other Powers concerned. Nothing could be further from the truth than such an allegation. Germany is quite willing to enter into any discussions of the currency problem. It is certain, however, that a mere devaluation of the reichsmark would not alter the existing conditions in any way.

The point that matters is the restoration of normal methods of making international payments and thus the re-establishment of the freedom of international commerce. A mere devaluation will ensure neither the one nor the other. That can only be done by tackling the international debt problem and that of raw-material supplies. No discussion will produce any positive results unless and until these questions are made part of it.

SECTION TWO

THE COLONIAL PROBLEM

General Ritter Von Epp

Reich Governor in Bavaria, Reich Leader of the Colonial League
and the Colonial Board of the National Socialist Party

GERMANY'S demand for the return of her Colonial possessions has given rise to an animated world-wide discussion that still continues, thus showing that the Colonial problem is one of those most urgently in need of a satisfactory solution. It will be observed, however, that the most essential aspect of the problem. i.e., Germany's claim that she has a right to demand the return of her former Colonies - is frequently ignored in the discussions. This circumstance suggests the probability that some writers on the subject lack a clear perception of the arguments by which Germany supports her claim, and that they are not familiar with her Colonial necessities as such. The following account of Germany's standpoint may therefore be found of some use, as it is doubtful whether a successful outcome of the discussion can be hoped for if it is not based on a sound knowledge of the facts.

Germany was a late-comer in the Colonial sphere. She only entered it in the last quarter of the past century, when it became apparent that the unclaimed regions of the world were about to be finally distributed among the Powers. She then acquired certain territories in Africa and in the Southern Pacific of which it could be expected that their possession would satisfy at least some of her economic necessities. Her action was in no way prompted by Imperialist motives, but was the direct outcome of a development that had converted her from an agricultural into a highly industrialised country within a few decades. The more she became industrialised, the greater became her need of imports from abroad, as her own resources of raw materials have always been insufficient. Two reasons combined to bring about her industrialisation: first, the large increase in her population, and second, the unique technical progress achieved ever since. In 1800, her population amounted to about 20,000,000; a century later it had risen to 56,000,000, and in 1914 it had reached a total of 67,800,000. It had thus more than trebled; but as the size of the country had remained almost unchanged, it follows that the "space forces" had decreased by two-thirds.

Additional industries were constantly growing up. A large part of their output was exported, whilst those raw materials and foodstuffs which could not be produced at home were imported. Without such an interchange of commodities, it would have been impossible to provide enough food and work for the steadily growing population. All this development, however, was based on the then existing system of universal free trade. It was taken for granted that peace would continue indefinitely, and that the sanctity of private property and the business man's initiative would continue to be respected as usual.

The acquisition of Colonial territories by Germany was intended to provide her with a reservoir of supplementary "space forces," a matter which has at all times been considered the premier aim of all Colonising activities. How firmly this conviction was shared by all the Colonial powers may be gathered from the conclusion of the Congo Convention (1885), which was signed by Britain, Germany, France, Belgium, the United States, Italy, Portugal, and a number of other countries. Article I I of the Congo Act provided that, should any power exercising in Central Africa the rights of sovereignty or those conferred by a protectorate be involved in war, the others would endeavour to ensure that its Central African possessions should be declared neutral, and that they should be treated as though they belonged to a neutral State. The term "Central Africa," as here used, included not only the whole of the Belgian Congo, but also the whole of German and British East Africa, about one-third of the Cameroons, Uganda, Nyassaland, a small part of Northern Rhodesia, and about one-half of French Equatorial Africa. All these wide domains were to be kept outside the range of a possible European war, and their integrity was to be respected.

Germany vigorously applied herself to the opening-up of her Colonial Empire as soon as the initial difficulties had been overcome. The task was enormous; and Germany had practically no experience as a Colonising power. Large parts of her Colonies had never been explored previous to their peaceable and lawful acquisition by Germany. The natives had to be brought in touch with the administrative system. For reasons of internal policy, the capital required for all these purposes did not flow freely into the Colonies during the first couple of decades; but their opening-up proceeded apace in spite of that drawback; roads and other means of transportation and communication were built, and economic progress was unmistakable. The value of the Colonial export trade increased from 25,000,000 reichsmarks in 1903 to 160,000,000 reichsmarks in 1913; and the importance of the Colonies as markets for manufactured articles was steadily growing. By 1914, after less than thirty years of opening-up work, a state of development had been attained that promised well for the future.

It is quite true that Germany's trade with her Colonies formed a small fraction only of her total trade in those years; but this circumstance has no bearing upon the present economic situation. In the pre-War days, when Free Trade was a fact and not a mere name, and when no obstacles were placed in the way of any country's foreign trade, Germany was not actually dependent upon the produce of her own Colonies. Besides, she was a large creditor country; she had invested huge sums in all parts of the globe, and she could buy all the necessary raw materials and foodstuffs without endangering her currency.

And then the War broke out. The solemn undertaking given by the signatories of the Congo Act was ignored by Germany's opponents. On August 2nd, 1914, Dr. Solf, the Colonial Secretary, relying upon the provisions of the Act, advised the administrative authorities of German East Africa by telegram that the Colonies would not be involved in the impending war, and that the European settlers need not fear any complications. A few days later, Great Britain started hostilities in East Africa, and the Colonies became a theatre of war.

This obvious violation of a given undertaking was afterwards sanctioned at Versailles, although those who dispossessed Germany of her Colonies had no legal title to do so. On December 14th, 1917, President Wilson stated before Congress that the War was not to be terminated by an act of revenge, and that no nation and no people should be robbed or penalised; and on February 11th, 1918, he added, that "there shall be no annexations, no contributions, no punitive damages." This was also implied in the fifth of the President's Fourteen Points, which provided for "a free, open-minded and absolutely impartial adjustment of all Colonial claims." Germany accepted the whole of the Fourteen Points by her note of October 3rd; and the Allied and Associated Powers also accepted them after the precise meaning of Point Five had been explained in the so-called Lyons wireless message of October 29th, 1918, which was a report drawn up by American delegates at the request of Colonel House, the President's confidential adviser. As regards the "justified Colonial Claims of Germany," it was said in the message that Germany must have access to the tropics and their raw materials, that she needed space for her excess population, and that, in conformity with the proposed terms of peace, the conquest of Colonial territories did not give her opponents a legal title to their possession. In the note of the American Secretary of State (Mr. Lansing) dated November 5th, 1918, it was stated again on behalf of the Allied and Associated Powers that President Wilson's Fourteen Points were to be the sole basis for the contemplated peace.

In spite of these unambiguous declarations, Germany was forced to surrender her overseas possessions (Art. 119 of the Versailles Treaty), although the unwisdom of making her do so was pointed out in many quarters. According to the secret minutes of the Council of Ten (January 24th, 1919), the Allied and Associated Powers were very far from viewing the whole question with unanimity. President Wilson expressed himself as follows:

> The world will say that the Powers first of all divided among themselves the defenceless parts of the globe and then proceeded to create a League of Nations. The naked truth is that every one of these parts has been allotted to a big Power. I wish to say quite openly that the world will never tolerate such a proceeding, which will make the League of Nations impossible, and we shall have to revert to the system of competitive armaments, huge accumulations of debt, and the heavy burden of large armies.

Today it is only too evident that the President's forecast has come true. As the Powers did not want to lose their hold on the German Colonies, the mandatory system as set forth in Article 22 of the League Covenant was invented. It is interesting to recall the following remarks made by Mr. Lansing in 1921:

> It may appear surprising that the big Powers lent their support so readily to the new method of gaining an apparently limited control of the conquered territories, and that they did not try to acquire full sovereign rights over them. There is no need to look far for an adequate and very practical reason. If Germany's Colonial possessions had been divided among the victors in accordance with the usual method, and if they had been transferred to them with all the rights of sovereignty, Germany would have been entitled to

demand that the value of such ceded territories should be credited to her reparations account. The League, however, was supposed to distribute the mandates in the interests of the inhabitants; and the mandates were to be regarded as obligations, but not as a means for the acquisition of additional territory. In this way, the mandatory system deprived Germany of her Colonies, the value of which would have considerably reduced her indebtedness towards the Allies, whilst the latter acquired the Colonies without losing any claim to compensation. Actually, therefore, the apparent altruism of the mandatory system favoured the selfish and material interests of the Powers by whom the mandates were taken over.

In order to justify the seizure of the Colonies and their transfer, under mandates, to the supreme control of the League, it was asserted that Germany was incapable of administering Colonial populations. In the notes dated July 16th, 1919, it is stated among others that:

The Allied and Associated Powers are satisfied that the native inhabitants of the German Colonies are strongly opposed to being again brought under Germany's sway, and the record of German rule, the traditions of the German Government, and the use to which these Colonies were put as bases from which to prey upon the commerce of the world, make it impossible for the Allied and Associated Powers to return them to Germany, or to entrust to her the responsibility for the training and education of their inhabitants.

These charges were based on the "Report on the Natives of South-West Africa and their Treatment by Germany," issued by the Administrator's Office, Windhoek, South-West Africa, concerning which the District Council for South-West Africa unanimously resolved on July 29th, 1926, that it was an instrument of war, and that the time had come for discontinuing its use. General Hertzog, the South African Prime Minister, stated on January 28th, 1927: "The unreliability and worthlessness of the document in question were sufficient to condemn it to the same disgraceful oblivion as all similar documents dating from the time of the war." And it is interesting to note in this connection that Mr. Amery, the former Secretary for the Colonies, expressed himself in a similar manner in January 1937, by way of replying to my explanation of the German view on the Colonial problem, when he said: "As regards Germany's inability to rule native populations, that is an assertion like many others made in the speeches and even in the official documents originating in the unhealthy atmosphere of those days." This latter statement should be read in conjunction with a remark on President Wilson and the mandatory system made by Mr. Lansing: "His noble mind and his lofty views made him blind to the base motives which seem to have been at the root of the general consent given to his beloved mandatory system."

It follows from the foregoing explanations that the alleged reasons for placing the German Colonies under mandates, and therefore those for the continuance of the mandatory system itself, are untenable. Contrary to a belief prevalent in some quarters, there has never been any actual annexation of the Colonies by the mandatory Powers. If it were otherwise, the question might well be asked: Why should there be any mandatory system at all? And what is the use of Article 22 of the League Covenant, which was intended to form an integral whole together with Article 119 of the Versailles Treaty? The fact that, in accordance with the last-named articles, Germany had to surrender her Colonies to the principal Allied Powers, does not imply a transfer of her sovereignty. (Cf. the corresponding provisions respecting Memel and Danzig in Articles 99 and 100.)

Germany, therefore, has a proper legal claim to the return of her Colonies. The German people are profoundly conscious of having such a claim and regard the existing position as a serious discrimination against themselves. It is evident that the question of the Colonies is at the same time a question of equality of status.

Germany's demand, however, is not only based on legal and moral grounds, but is supported by weighty economic reasons as well. There are many people outside Germany who do not realise the exceedingly unfavourable conditions which she has to endure in many respects. The Versailles Treaty has deeply undermined the foundations of her economic life. Apart from the loss of her Colonial empire, that treaty also forced her to surrender 13% of her territory at home, together with the valuable mineral and agricultural resources contained in those parts, as well as her entire mercantile tonnage. The confiscation of German property abroad was sanctioned by the terms of the treaty. Germany's foreign investments, which represented a value far exceeding £ 1,000,000,000 gold, were taken away from their rightful owners by a stroke of the pen. In addition, she was asked to pay fantastic sums by way of reparation. After she had done so for a number of years, it was seen that a continuance of these payments was an absolute impossibility. In order to make the payments on reparations account, she had been compelled to contract so large a foreign debt that, after the lapse of ten years or so, her liabilities towards her creditors abroad were almost as large as the value of her pre-War foreign investments. This foreign indebtedness accounts for the gigantic losses her gold and foreign-exchange reserves have sustained since 1931.

As time advances, it is becoming increasingly apparent that the Versailles Treaty has brought about a serious disturbance in the world's equilibrium. It has given rise to an economic development throughout the world the ultimate effect of which has been to reverse completely pre-War conditions. Before the War, the markets for raw materials were unfettered by any restrictions, and long-term commercial treaties guaranteed the freedom of international trade. The economic era, however, which dates from Versailles, is characterised by protectionist, selfish, and monopolist tendencies. Most countries, notably the United States, the United Kingdom and France, have surrounded themselves with high tariff walls, and have introduced every possible device for promoting trade within their own territories and for preventing the products of other countries from entering them.

Thus, present-day Germany finds herself confronted with the following facts: Considerable territorial losses in Europe and abroad; the complete loss of her foreign assets; a large debt resulting from her reparations payments, and the impossibility of importing sufficient quantities of those commodities vitally necessary for maintaining the standard of living of her population and for ensuring the continued existence of her national economy itself. The consequence of her declining export trade was that the foundation on which her economic system had been based for more than a century suffered a considerable contraction. Even though her Colonies may have been relatively unimportant to the balance of her foreign trade in pre-War time, present economic conditions are so different that the possession or non possession of Colonies is a question of the very first importance.

All these circumstances have to be taken into account by those who want to understand the justice of Germany's Colonial claims on economic grounds. The fact that governs the whole situation is this: The centre of Europe is inhabited by a nation which, despite every effort made, finds it impossible to safeguard the foundations of its existence by making use of the resources provided by its native soil.

Before the War, Germany had started to develop, on systematic lines, all those resources of the areas subject to her sovereignty which were -

and which are - necessary for the maintenance of her surplus population. At Versailles, however, her Colonial empire (which, although but small, was of great importance to her) was divided among nations that were in no need of additional Colonial possessions. Besides, these nations had so many other matters to attend to that they were not in a position to engage in the work of opening-up the mandated areas. It can be shown that the development of the mandated territories - not only as regards the production of raw materials, but also in connection with many other items - has received far less attention than that of countries adjacent to them where the climatic conditions are very similar. It is very instructive to compare, for example, the export totals of oleaginous seeds and fruits from Togoland and the Cameroons with those from the Belgian Congo and Nigeria, those of timber from the Cameroons with those from French Equatorial Africa, and those of cotton from German East Africa (Tanganyika) with those from Uganda and Kenya. Comparisons such as these indicate that the Colonial possessions of the European countries concerned are developed far more systematically than the territories under mandate. The development of the transportation system in the latter has almost come to a standstill since the advent of the mandatory administrations, as may be seen from the following figures:

Railways open to traffic or in course of construction.			
	1914.	1934.	Increase.
East Africa.	2,171 km.	2,215 km.	44 km.
South-West Africa	2,178 km.	2,357 km.	179 km.
Cameroons	327 km.	442 km.	115 km.
Togoland	443 km.	504 km.	61 km.

Thus, almost the whole railway system of the mandated territories dates back to the twenty odd years of German rule, whilst the mandatory Powers have hardly done anything since to extend it. Equally slight has been the increase in the export trade of the Colonies since their taking-over by the mandatory Powers.

During the period from 1908-13, i.e., within five years, the total value of their exports went up from £1,400,000 to £8,000,000, which is undoubtedly a clear proof of Germany's successful Colonial work in

Africa and in the Southern Pacific. By 1936, after seventeen years of mandatory rule, that figure had only risen to £10,000,000 gold. The increase, therefore, has been remarkably slight.

Even in their present state of development, the Colonies could do much to ease Germany's economic difficulties. They could supply considerable percentages of the raw materials she requires. Based on the export statistics for 1936, these percentages work out as follows: Oleaginous seeds and fruits, 14 per cent.; flax, hemp, etc., 43% (for sisal alone, 261%); cocoa, 61%; coffee, 13%; bananas, 61%; mineral phosphates, 49%. Other important raw materials that could be imported from the Colonies are hides and skins, cotton, timber, wool, rubber, and various cereals.

No attention has been paid so far to the considerable possibilities of future development. In view of the relative neglect of the mandated territories by their present rulers, we are justified in assuming that their production totals can be greatly augmented within a short period of time. Experts with a good knowledge of all the facts have ascertained that, on a conservative estimate, the value of the exports can be raised to £30,000,000 gold within eight or ten years, provided that intensive methods of cultivation are employed. This means that the mandated territories could supply Germany with 12 or 15% of her import requirements. It is obvious that this would materially ease Germany's foreign-exchange position and her international trade relations and would, above all, give her a feeling of economic security.

To make such an increase possible, it would be necessary, of course, to accelerate very considerably the pace at which the opening-up of the Colonies takes place, both through private initiative and by means of Government assistance. A typical example of the great success that can be achieved by systematic work in the right direction is afforded by the Gold Coast Colony, where the cultivation of cocoa was introduced about the turn of the century. In 1906, about 8,000 tons of it could be exported; and by 1936 that figure had risen to as much as 306,000 tons, so that the Gold Coast is now the principal producer of cocoa.

As the climatic and geographical conditions of the Cameroons are very similar to those of the Gold Coast, it would seem quite possible to increase the cocoa production of that country very greatly within a short time. The same possibility presents itself for a number of other products that are of value to Germany as foodstuffs or as industrial raw materials, e.g. timber, oleaginous fruits, sisal, and rubber.

Before the War, there was no need for Germany to adjust her foreign trade with an eye to her Colonies. Today, however, large quantities of Colonial produce could be used to cover the needs of the mother country; and the part not thus used could be sold in other markets. In this way, foreign exchange would become available for purchases in other countries. All the suggestions put forward with a view to making Germany renounce her Colonial claim fail to do justice to the requirements of the country's body economic. It has been said that Germany ought to make use of the numerous facilities afforded by "the open door." But if we look at that "open door," we find that it is very carefully locked indeed. It has already been emphasised that the principal countries of the world have adopted undiluted protectionism since 1924. Great Britain, more especially, has secured for herself a very favourable position in the great raw material markets by the Ottawa agreements. She, therefore, can hardly claim the right to speak of other countries' freedom of access to raw materials.

A glance at the customs lists and import regulations of practically all parts of the British Empire, Dominions as well as Crown Colonies, shows that the products of non-British countries (more particularly finished articles, in the export of which Germany specialises) are treated far less favourably than those originating within the British Empire. Another example of the tendency on the part of the large Colonial Powers to establish a privileged position for their own products is Britain's policy in Nigeria and the Gold Coast Colony where a quota system for textiles based on the import figures for 1935 has just been introduced. This step is a serious handicap to the trade of the non-British countries, as 1935 was in many respects a year of bad trade. Since then the purchasing capacity of the inhabitants has considerably improved, so that Great Britain alone will reap the resulting advantage. Besides, nearly all the Colonial territories have established a system of discriminating export duties that make it difficult for Germany to obtain a sufficiency of Colonial produce. All this shows how threadbare is the assertion sometimes heard that the have-nots need only set aside an adequate amount of foreign exchange if they want to share in the Colonial wealth. The very fact that payment must be made in foreign exchange puts us at a disadvantage. Besides, nations deprived of their investments abroad can only obtain foreign exchange by selling their goods. Experience has shown that Germany is not in a position to sell large quantities of her manufactured products in the mandated territories. This applies still more to the actual Colonies of the European Powers, in whose trade the latter-as a rule-have the lion's share. France's share in the import trade of Morocco is 43.7%,

Great Britain's share in that of Nigeria is 55.2%, and Belgium's share in that of the Congo is 43.4%, whilst Germany's share in the trade of these and numerous other African territories is very slight. Her trade with them is for the most part passive, because even now imports from them considerably exceed her exports to them. The mandated territories are no exception to this rule, notwithstanding the status of economic equality supposed to exist there. Everywhere the Colonial Powers predominate in the import trade of their Colonies and in that of the mandated territories administered by them. Their nationals are sure to get all the orders from public authorities and also those of any importance from most private firms.

Since all the big Colonial Powers have taken successful steps in recent years to cover an increasing part of their import requirements within the areas subject to their political influence, it is difficult to understand why Colonial possessions should be a burden to the countries that own them - an assertion sometimes made to refute Germany's Colonial claim.

The share of the United Kingdom in the import trade of the British Empire went up from 31% to 42% within twelve years, and that in the export trade from 41% to 49% The same tendency may be observed in regard to France, where the share of the Colonies in the import trade of the mother country increased from 10% to 26% in ten years and that in the export trade from 14% to 32% Such developments could only take place at the expense of other countries, largely at that of Germany. But even apart from these facts, it is strange to hear it sometimes said that Colonies are of no value. If that were true, the return of the German Colonies would be felt by the mandatory Powers as a relief, and not as a sacrifice. In Germany it has been noticed with interest that such a view of the Colonial problem has frequently been advanced by British writers on the subject.

From all that has been said it may be inferred that the Colonial question is not simply a "raw-material question." There is no chance of Germany ever being able to extend her trade unless she is reinstated in the possession of her Colonies. The point of cardinal importance, in view of her foreign exchange position, is that she must be enabled to obtain from territories subject to her own sovereignty, where her own currency circulates, a considerable part of those raw materials and foodstuffs that have now to be paid for in foreign exchange. In this way alone will it be possible for her trade to gain that measure of security and stability which she so urgently needs in the economic domain. Customs facilities and the removal of trade restrictions are insufficient to do justice to her requirements, however desirable they are in other respects.

Germany asks only for the return of territories that were her own property before she had to relinquish possession of them. She demands nothing unfair, and has no design upon the Colonial possessions of other countries. She only desires to recover those overseas territories to which she has a legal title. It is evident that her claim is directed in the first instance against Great Britain, whose Government was chiefly instrumental in depriving her of their possession. In addition, most of the Colonies are now administered by countries that are constituent parts of the British Empire.

It has been shown that Germany has an unchallengeable claim to the return of the Colonies, based on legal and moral grounds, and on the right of every nation to safeguard the interests vital to its existence. This latter necessity is especially urgent in Germany's case because of the many restrictions to which her commerce is subject. Her demand is not prompted by a desire to stop up any temporary gaps in the system of her supplies, but rather by a determination to pursue a Colonial policy intended to bring about the economic assimilation of the mother country and the Colonies. Her sole aim is of an economic kind; and all allegations to the effect that she wants to turn her Colonies into military bases are groundless. The Anglo-German naval pact ought to be sufficient proof of the futility of such allegations.

The great task with which the statesmen of the present generation are faced is to establish a lasting peace among the nations. No Government anxious to collaborate in it can want to maintain indefinitely a policy by which a nation of 68,000,000 people is to be deprived of its vital rights. The Versailles doctrine of the advantages to be derived from a system of arbitrary restrictions must be abandoned, more particularly in so far as it applies to restrictions that are meant to be of a punitive kind. Germany therefore expects that the Colonial clauses of the Versailles Treaty will be made the subject of a revision that does justice to her legitimate claims. The solution of the problem must be effected by the method of negotiations, because - as the Fuhrer has said - "the Colonial problem is not a question of peace or war."

Once Germany has regained her proper share in the opening-up of overseas territories, her economic system will function normally again and - above all - a valuable contribution will have been rendered to the recovery of international trade. Such a solution will provide the basis for the peaceful co-operation of the white nations and will initiate a lasting epoch of quiet development. It is the hope of all right-minded people that common sense - so indispensable to all human progress - will prevail in the method of handling Germany's Colonial problem.

SECTION THREE

DEVELOPMENTS IN GERMAN COMMERCIAL PUBLICITY

Its Reorganisation And Relations To Great Britain

Ernst Reichard

President of the National Board for Trade Publicity

ON the various lecture tours both at home and abroad which I have recently undertaken at the invitation of some of the leading advertising societies, I have repeatedly drawn attention to the importance of commercial advertising in an up-to-date national economy. The general public should, in my opinion, be enlightened as to the value of this side of economic activity, for the more familiar it becomes with the essentials of advertising, the greater the chance of it becoming popular. And if publicity is resorted to for the purpose of bringing something to the notice of the customer, it stands to reason that an adequate knowledge of its main features, its range of possibilities, and its working methods, should be made as general as possible. Advertising advertisement - if I may be permitted such an expression - cannot be overdone. It is certainly true that things have improved in the course of the last few years, but it is not so very long ago that the psychology of advertising in all its various aspects did not rate as a full subject at European universities; at best it was included in the curriculum as a supplement to the study of business economy. There was no such thing as university lectures on the law of advertising. Thanks, however, to the development that has taken place since then and to the systematic and sustained effort made to educate the public, commercial publicity has now acquired a certain standing in Germany, and has, indeed, become a recognised subject of university education. The number of researches into the art of trade publicity continues to grow; literature on the subject, which until recently was negligible, is on the increase, while special training colleges for the proper schooling of agents are being established. In 1936, for instance, the Reich College of Advertising was opened in Berlin. Furthermore, lecture courses are about to be introduced at the universities on the subject of publicity in relation to national and international economy, its legal principles' and inter-state ramifications. All along the line, both in theory and practice, the attempt is being made to do justice to the importance of this indispensable accessory to modern commerce. Above all, it was high time that something was done to eradicate the prevailing prejudice against publicity as such. A not uncommon objection was that advertising added to the ultimate cost of an article; or it was looked down upon as savouring of something cheap; or not taken seriously because of certain degenerate tendencies. This hostility, originally due to an unawareness of the essential aims and qualities of publicity, has now been successfully overcome, for the systematic work of enlightenment has not been without its effects. Once set in motion the ball keeps on rolling, carrying all before it. This is apparent in the gradual spread of appreciation of advertising as one of the vital factors in modern commerce. The time is past when its more unwholesome features were used to condemn it altogether, and the general attitude towards it has now become much more favourable.

In our time, publicity has become the pivot on which all sales possibilities hinge. Hence the close connection with commercial statistics and market research. This data constitutes a helpful ally in the interests of a forward market policy. For, by influencing the consumer psychologically, advertising is intended to awaken a demand or direct an already existing demand into the desired channels. Hence it is a most important element in times of depression. A wise business management, however, keeps on advertising even when times are good in order to sustain as well as enlarge the turnover.

We see, therefore, that publicity is of vast significance to both individual and public economy. This applies equally to all modern industrial countries. In Germany, for instance, about 2% of the public income is invested annually for such purposes. In the United States, in 1934, according to figures compiled by the National Union of Publishers from statistics covering the total expenditure on advertisement of 367 members of the leading national association of advertising agents for publicity in newspapers, periodicals and wireless, amounted to 2,232 million dollars; in Great Britain to 100 million sterling. These figures speak for themselves.

It is quite clear that in view of such immense sums every effort must be made to avoid superfluous and prevent false outlays. For this reason, and more especially for the purpose of raising the standard of advertising ethics and strengthening the confidence of the consuming public - incidentally the greatest capital reserve a nation has - commercial advertising in Germany was subjected to a thorough revision in 1933.

This seemed the more called for as certain practices incompatible with the accepted conception of honour and straight dealing had made their appearance through developments being left to themselves. Newspapers, hoardings, pillars, etc., displayed all sorts of wayward ideas born of unscrupulous competition and of a philosophy dominated by one thought only - "advertisement at any price!" The result was certainly devastating to the countryside! Newspapers bluffed on their circulation, an old dodge. Either the size of the issue was not disclosed or misleading statements were given so that it was difficult, if not impossible, to obtain a clear idea of the coverage, the practical value of the advertisement and, therefore, its actual cost. At the same time, firms in the habit of advertising big were frequently accorded such favourable conditions that on the one hand the merest margin of profit remained for the paper, and, on the other, the person or firm having need only for occasional advertisement, ignorant of the intricacies of the tariff, was very often imposed upon.

These few illustrations chosen at random from a host of unhealthy features are only a modest sampling of the objections which could be raised on the basis of decency and fairness. With the spread of the depression and the attendant struggle for markets, canvassing sins took on sharper forms. Manifold as advertising media were the opportunities of trespassing.

These pathological symptoms were removed by the National Board for Trade Publicity set up by the Law of September 12th, 1933. Cancerous growths were cauterised; the operation was painful indeed, but we can safely say that as a result commercial publicity in Germany has been placed on a sound footing. Wholesome economy presupposes wholesome advertising. Was then, it will be asked, the danger so great as to warrant the setting-up of such an organisation? Yes, seeing that the matter concerned the squandering of national wealth, something which no nation can afford. And the mere responsibility for private enterprise demands categorically that the conscientious business man should be afforded a certain amount of protection against the unprincipled and, above all, that the consuming public be protected against undue exploitation through deceptive advertisements. The outstanding principle underlying reorganisation was: "Advertisement pledges!", that is, everybody investing money in advertising his business has a right to know and to judge whether that money is well spent, and every advertising agent has a responsibility towards private as well as public economy.

The task of instilling this line of thought falls upon the National Board, whose scope of activities is clearly defined in Section I of the Law governing commercial publicity: "For the purpose of uniform and effective execution, all private and public advertising, exhibitions, fairs, etc., are subject to the approval of the Reich."

This provision indicates the position of the National Board in German commercial publicity. The Board may be said to have two fundamental functions: a supervisory one, which is of an administrative kind and is concerned mainly with regulations and suggestions of an educative character, and a practical one, i.e., the promotion of German trade publicity. This, of course, is the more important function since with the lessening of malpractices as a result of administrative activity, the need for supervision diminishes. Incidentally, it signifies better business.

What has been done to rectify existing evils and to create a saner outlook? To begin with, the entire advertising system whether through press publicity, displays, advertising firms, fairs or exhibitions, has been completely reorganised along uniform lines.

This part of the work may now be regarded as concluded. I should like to state, however, that the measures taken are not in the nature of rigid by-laws but represent real assistance in reviving the economy; that is, they are the result of close co-operation with men conversant with economic conditions and requirements. This contact is supplied by the various trade committees composed of leading business men and advertising specialists whom I consult before making my decisions. The Board is at pains - and this has been its guiding principle from the very outset - to work with commerce, for the good of commerce, and in co-operation direct commercial publicity into the desired channels. Nothing could be more erroneous than the allegation frequently heard outside Germany that the Board is a Government affair. On the contrary, everything foreign to commerce, everything that approaches bureaucracy, has been carefully avoided. For, since elasticity is a *sine qua non*, the Board as a kind of Werbekammer (Advertising Chamber), like the ordinary chambers of industry and commerce, has been made a statutory body. It is vested with certain powers, but is by no means a prosecuting body. While preserving private initiative, its objective is to give commercial publicity a new impetus by directing the advertising policy. The extent to which the Board is desirous of making its measures anything but arbitrary can be seen from the fact that it works in close conjunction with the Federated Advertisers, a trade group rooted in the very heart of commerce. In all matters of far-reaching consequence the Federation is consulted. I have even entrusted to it the task of preparatory examination of certain questions, leaving the final decision only to the Board. The latter, being by nature a supervisory body, does not pursue any commercial policy. It does, however, seek to improve business turnovers by advancing publicity - to achieve which defects must be eliminated. As publicity can never be an end in itself but is enlisted in the interests of economy as a whole, it can never be successful unless it is in close contact with the commercial world. Fundamentally, therefore, the Board has nothing whatever to do with politics.

The readjustment as carried through in each individual sphere aims primarily at establishing ethical principles in all matters concerning publicity of any description. The simple formula for the substance of the reforms effected is: "We want everyone engaged in advertising or any form of business publicity to act in accordance with his business principles; we want to purify the business mentality, an essential to sound economic life. Hence one of my first notices reads (No. 2, section 6) - "Anyone engaged in commercial publicity shall act as is expected of an honourable business man. All statements must be plain and truthful and must avoid being misleading."

To prevent disappointment accruing to any person or firm investing money in newspaper advertisement, it became compulsory for the issue size to be given. To put an end to the practice of granting 80% rebates, the third Notice established certain norms for "price loyalty," so that a feeling of confidence in newspaper advertising was created. Apart from general business conditions, the Board set up a uniform tabulation of prices (advertisement and poster rates). The sizes of advertisements and placards, etc., were standardised and the calculation of fees was unified. The idea of this "drive" is to inculcate an equitable and social spirit in the interests of the advertising industry, which has to be safeguarded against unfair exploitation. The implementing of the latter measure was at the beginning not exactly easy for those concerned; it affected publishers' "prescriptive rights" of long standing. In the end, however, the publishing and advertising industries were glad to comply, knowing that it was for the ultimate benefit of both.

In the sphere of fairs and exhibitions, conditions were equally unjust. Individual fairs were in keenest competition; local patriotism waxed important by playing off one against the other with the local producing firms. This sort of thing was at the expense of the country's economy as a whole. Something had to be done; definite rules were laid down for the scope and range of either; their respective claims were "pegged" as it were, and the ensuing calm relieved commerce of an unnecessary burden, at the same time permitting exhibitors clear-sighted publicity for their goods. Radical steps were also necessary in the drug trade, for there more than elsewhere the chances of abuse were legion. My 17th Notice of May 5th, 1936, in close co-operation with the industries concerned, laid down the terms and conditions on which sales publicity for medical remedies, courses of treatment, faith healing, etc., can be carried out. In this sphere probably more than in any other, unprincipled elements made hay by gulling the public to an almost scandalous degree. Now, however, they have to comply with various requirements when advertising their goods to the public.

To the remarks on the administrative tasks of the National Board may I be permitted to add a few on the active commercial publicity which it pursues at home and abroad? Its territory is vast, to name only collective advertising for a distressed area; this is additional publicity, incidentally backing individual or specific advertising in the interests of a larger, common issue -national economy. Collective advertising, needless to say, is not confined to distressed areas, but extends to all spheres demanding public enlightenment on aspects of national economy. Thus, to cite an example of fairly recent date, under the sponsorship of the Agricultural Estate a "Stop that Waste" campaign was carried through, it having been ascertained that an annual loss of some 1,500 million reichsmarks occurs as a result of deterioration and avoidable loss in perishable foodstuffs. To give force to this most important campaign through the medium of newspaper publicity - still the most effective of all - the Federal Committee for economic enlightenment, appointed by the National Board, in conjunction with the foodstuff industries, worked out a plan for collective advertising. The idea is to arouse the masses to the national importance of combating all avoidable loss.

It can be seen from the above what we mean in Germany by collective advertising (Gemeinschaftswerbung) and how it is effected. Naturally, the example cited is only one of many. The nature of such general publicity on a broad scale varies according to the diversity of requirements. In recent years we had publicity campaigns for German newspapers, books and handicraft, etc. At any rate, this form of advertising is one of the chief outlets of an active canvassing policy. Equally important is the promotion of the exhibition mentality by means of enlightening newspaper articles of a definitely national economic tendency.

Relatively difficult is such commercial publicity abroad. Its objective is to strengthen Germany's economic relations with foreign markets. This is a task which demands a wealth of practical experience, and a sound knowledge of the labyrinth of world economic associations.

The highlights indicated above are sufficient to give an idea of the nature of commercial publicity and its reforms. To summarise, I should like to state that our foremost aim is to educate all those associated with the trade to ply it with the right spirit and, above all, to be straight in all their dealings. We do not ask for more, nor less, than that he who advertises should do so as a business man with a sense of responsibility.

The raising of the standard of advertising ethics is no less desirable in international commerce, seeing that trade publicity is not confined to one country but, like trade itself, is international. Where there is light there are always shadows. And injurious practices, even abuses, have crept in internationally as well, readily explained by the keen struggle for world markets. But a high standard of advertising ethics is an indispensable condition to an improved economy as a whole.

In order to place commercial publicity on a footing beyond reproach internationally, I ventured to suggest co-operation in this direction with a view to purging it of scurrilous practices. The International Chamber of Commerce in Paris was kind enough to take up the matter. After a detailed report on the subject which I submitted to it, a Committee of Inquiry was appointed to which I had the honour of belonging. As pointed out in my very first public discussion of the matter, the ideas responsible for the law against unfair competition are closely related to the regulations governing our advertising reforms. It has been found, however, that the more artful offender is not always to be got at by the Law. Apart from this, possible legal procedure frequently entails material disadvantages; litigation, even if successful, proves more than a nuisance, often a burden of extra work and expense, so that one is tempted to apply the bland hospital bulletin - "Operation successful, patient succumbed."

Hence the idea was conceived of establishing an international court of arbitration to deal with possible difficulties. This method of settling advertising disputes was mainly suggested by the conviction that advertisers must be protected against financial loss. The new plan of dealing with advertising offences committed in international commodity exchange is based primarily on practical considerations. Such a solution of the problem was approved by the International Chamber of Commerce, so that the Advertising Committee of the LC.C., which had been set up in response to my suggestion, was able to announce at the Berlin meeting, held on July 2nd, 1937, a set of Regulations governing Advertising that met with universal consent. It was seen that there is general agreement among business men throughout the world regarding the ethics of advertising and that there is a need for such agreement to be expressed in a form that is internationally binding. The Advertising Committee, accordingly, has to examine all questions that concern the regulation of international advertising and has to make suitable proposals for successful co-operation in that domain. The International Advertising Board, however, which has likewise been set up, chiefly functions as a court of appeal in connection with advertising delicts. It is largely due to the initiative of Mr. F. P. Bishop, LL.D., managing publisher of *The Times*, that such an understanding on international advertising has been reached. He has, accordingly, been elected President of the two bodies named; and as I am one of the Vice-Presidents, I shall have plenty of opportunity for close co-operation with him in all matters concerning the reform of international advertising.

To me it appears specially significant that the interest taken abroad in the problems of commercial publicity and their solution is steadily increasing. In addition to Sweden and Hungary, in which countries I have recently lectured by request, Great Britain, above all, where advertising has developed to a greater degree than is general elsewhere, is becoming increasingly alive to the subject and its possible chances of reform. The Incorporated Society of British Advertisers, more especially, whose gathering in London I had the pleasure of addressing a year ago, brings a united attitude to bear on all the burning problems of the trade. In line with these developments several members of the Society visited Berlin not so very long ago to see for themselves how the National Board operates. Mr. C. Taylor, the President of the Society (since retired), subsequently read a paper on the reform of commercial advertising in Germany. He pointed out that the improvements effected in the advertising trade had proved beneficial to business as a whole and suggested the advisability of setting up a British organisation similar to the German National Board for Trade Publicity. Such a body, of course, would have to conform to British ideas and would have to function in accordance with British requirements. The very fact that such a suggestion has been ventilated is pioneer work and may well be regarded as a notable step forward. The mere raising of questions on the subject is sufficient proof that trade publicity is thought to be worthy of careful consideration because of its influence on national and international economy, and that reforms are, perhaps, thought to be advisable. But, as we all know, "Rome was not built in a day."

I can well imagine that in Britain, where so great store is set by personal liberty, any control of advertising activities in the sense of systematic education to certain views would be felt as irksome tutelage. Nevertheless, I have no fear that sustained effort at enlightenment will some day gain its ends seeing that au fond reforms on the basis of fair play really represent a natural development in that direction. Only the good and sound things in life are of lasting duration, and this applies to advertising also. Thus, sooner or later, other countries will have to set about ridding this trade of undesirable dross, not only to the advantage of their own national economy but as something demanded by international trade. Great Britain, particularly, with her large share of world trade, would assuredly welcome the universal observance of a high standard of advertising ethics; without it there can be no real revival in world trade, no real prosperity.

SECTION FOUR

GERMANS ABROAD

E. W. Bohle

Head of the Foreign Organisation of the National Socialist
Party and Secretary of State in the Foreign Office

I WAS born at Bradford in Yorkshire, and spent the whole of my
youth within the British Empire, partly in England and partly in
South Africa. It is generally agreed that the impressions we receive
during the first sixteen or seventeen years of our lives are particularly
lasting in their effects upon our subsequent development. It is but
natural, therefore, that my knowledge of Great Britain and the British
should be more intimate and deeper than it would be had I acquired
it in later life. In like manner, a British boy born and educated in
Germany is certain to have a far better understanding of that country,
and the national traits of the German people, than one born and bred
in England, even though he may have made a profound study of our
country and people when grown up.

My reason for thus prefacing the following is that as Head of the
Foreign Organisation I have been subjected to a great deal of criticism
and my critics have entirely failed to appreciate the significance of the
facts indicated.

I would like, therefore, to give a clear and straight forward account of
the work done by that Organisation and to put right a few mistaken
ideas about it, not by way of parrying the attacks made upon us -
for our conscience is quite clear - but rather to explain the profound
change that has come over the minds of Germans resident abroad
with the transformation that has been effected in the Reich itself.
That transformation has attracted the attention of the whole world for
the past five years with the result that - broadly speaking-people are

now beginning to understand the new order of things in Germany. It stands to reason that so far-reaching a change in the mother country could not but greatly affect all Germans living beyond its borders and the responsible body guiding the changing trend in the right direction is the Foreign Organisation of the National Socialist Party, of which I am the Head.

On January 30th, 1933, Herr Hitler took over the government of Germany. Everybody knows that this step was much more than a mere change of government. It was the definite assumption of supreme political power.

Anyone who failed to realise that difference at the time has had ample opportunity since then to convince himself that the Leader of the National Socialist Party has not only changed the whole form of government but has entirely transformed every other aspect of public life in Germany. What could be more natural than that the Germans abroad should watch these tremendous developments with an interest unprecedented in its intensity? And, having grasped what has been done at home, they have become as fervent National Socialists as the people in the Reich.

That is nothing surprising; it is, in fact, a natural and logical development. For Germans living abroad are no different from those at home; they belong to each other, and they must know of the happenings in the Reich. After five years of effort in maintaining this contact I am proud to be able to state that perfect harmony between the Reich and its nationals abroad has been established - a harmony that will never be shattered.

Anyone who witnessed the enthusiasm of the 10,000 Germans who came from all parts of the world to attend the Fifth Congress held at Stuttgart in 1937 will endorse this statement.

If it be argued that there are Germans resident in other countries who are still opposed to the Third Reich, the answer is that they are a negligible factor. Their existence is no more important than the fact that in the Reich, too, there are still some people who object to National Socialism.

What is of importance, however, is that the National Socialist views on the values of life and citizenship have now been accepted by the vast majority of Germans within and without the Reich. This fact cannot be questioned by any fair-minded person. The inference is that the German element abroad is, as a matter of course, completely National Socialist minded, and that to be a German is the same thing as being a National Socialist.

Once people realise that the terms "Nazi" and "German" are synonymous the former will no longer be used to designate some exceptional type of German. To ensure this must be one of our principal aims if an honest attempt at a friendly understanding is to be made on both sides.

By way of explanation: if a London paper announces "A German speaks in London," this may be of interest or it may not, but there is nothing sensational in it. If, on the other hand, the heading reads "A Nazi speaks in London," it would probably cause quite a flutter, many English people committing the mistake of thinking of a "Nazi" as something out of the ordinary, mysterious, although a Nazi is ipso facto a German and a German a Nazi.

When an Englishman addresses a Berlin audience, he does so as an Englishman and not as a Conservative, Liberal, Socialist or Independent. The fact that we have only one party in Germany is a characteristic peculiar to ourselves.

And another eloquent illustration: supposing a Reich German goes abroad and says he is not a Nazi; similarly an Italian on his travels says he is not a Fascist, nobody would seriously take them to be representatives of their country.

If these things were properly understood in England as the home of common sense, we might cheerfully look forward to the disappearance of many obstacles tending to keep apart two great nations that have so much in common. And if people would only grasp the fact that Germans in the Reich are National Socialists by conviction, they would realise that Germans abroad must likewise be regarded as National Socialists.

This brings me to the object of the Party's Foreign Organisation in Berlin, which is to unite these National Socialist Germans resident abroad by setting up local and divisional groups to foster and strengthen their love of the homeland, that is their National Socialist homeland, and their feeling of national solidarity.

These National Socialist groups in foreign countries are nothing more than voluntary associations of German citizens who believe in National Socialism as the instrument of their country's salvation and who, by joining these groups, want to show their readiness to contribute their share towards building up the new Germany. They are not members of various political parties, but of the only political movement that exists in present-day Germany, and one that has taken a sure hold of the whole nation.

It is no part of their task to propagate National Socialist ideas among the citizens of other countries. Their only function is to encourage their members to conform to these ideas and ideals as closely as their fellow-citizens in the Reich have done and are doing.

It is downright nonsense, therefore, to talk of the members of our Party abroad as "Nazi agitators" or "agents of the German Secret Police" (to mention only two of the many misleading terms that have been used), whose aim it is to infect foreign nations with what is "Nazi poison."

The truth is that National Socialists abroad are expressly forbidden to interfere in any way with the domestic politics of other countries, and the much maligned Party discipline is perhaps the surest guarantee that this injunction is strictly obeyed. When other countries organise their nationals abroad in clubs, societies, associations and the like, nobody takes exception to it, and no country would consider its security thereby menaced.

The same is claimed for the organisations of German residents abroad being similarly a menace to nobody. Not one instance to the contrary has ever been brought to my notice.

It is more than ridiculous when certain persons and certain newspapers persist in raising the bogy of such a menace. The only result of insinuations of this kind is to disturb the relations between Germany and the country involved. And those disturbances are bound to occur if, for instance, young German women employed in foreign households are denounced as "spies," and if every National Socialist is referred to as a "political agent." The point that matters here is not whether the editors of those papers are pleased or displeased at the thought that German citizens abroad are National Socialists, but that they are National Socialists.

In Germany we do not trouble ourselves about the political views of British subjects residing in our midst. There are thousands and thousands of them, and I assume that they are good Democrats. But it has never occurred to us that they might be a source of danger to the existence of the Third Reich. Nor have we the slightest objection to their gathering together as often as they like in appreciation of the benefits of Democracy. We should be justly entitled, however, to put a stop to their activities if they attempted to impose their Democratic ideas upon us on the ground that they were suitable for our country. And with the same right the British people would be justified in prohibiting the propagation of National Socialist ideas in their own country.

But as nothing of the kind has ever happened, the attempts recently made in certain quarters to arouse feelings of hostility against National Socialists living abroad can only be regarded as acts of interference with the internal affairs of Germany. The ideology of Germans living abroad is nobody's concern but their own, just as the ideology of British residents abroad is exclusively their own affair. To take up any other stand on this question would imply a denial of Germany's equality of status; and we all know that the time for such a denial is definitely past.

It is one of the foremost duties of every government to look after its nationals abroad, to help them and to protect them whenever protection is needed. The British Government has always been a model to all as regards the fulfilment of this duty. That truth is so universally recognised that a passing reference to it is all that is needed here. In like manner, the solidarity shown by the British all over the world has always been exemplary.

The official representatives of the British Government have at all times protected the interests of their fellow nationals abroad in the most admirable fashion. They take every care (and rightly so) that His Majesty's subjects abroad shall remain loyal to their King and Country wherever they are. Every other country conscious of its national responsibilities takes the same view as a matter of course.

Some time ago, a Congress of French residents abroad was held in Paris under the chairmanship of the President of the Republic. It was attended by a large number of Frenchmen from the colonies, mandated territories and foreign countries; and several Cabinet Ministers were among the speakers.

Similarly a Congress of Swiss residents abroad was held at Berne. It was organised by the New Helvetian Society, and its importance was underlined by the fact that M. Motta, the Federal President, delivered one of the addresses on that occasion. Many of those attending the Congress used that opportunity of suggesting that the Secretariat of the Swiss foreign groups should be transformed into a Department of State. The Federal President himself is a member of the Committee of Patrons under whom the Secretariat conducts its activities. In Germany alone the Society has at present 37 principal groups and 31 sub-groups.

It is well known that Fascist Italy has had its Foreign Organisation for the past sixteen years. Poland, too, has a World League of Polish residents abroad, with branches all over the globe. It concerns itself in great detail with all questions that may affect its members in any way. It is presided over by a Cabinet Minister. Congresses attended by Poles from all parts of the world are held at regular intervals, and this League has undoubtedly achieved a great deal in keeping the national spirit alive among Poles in foreign countries.

We Germans do not look upon this as a matter for surprise, and we see nothing sensational in it. And strange to say, all other countries feel the same way. It is regarded as the natural thing to do. But as soon as Germany creates a similar organisation for her nationals abroad, limitless sensational charges are made against her and all sorts of ulterior motives attributed to her.

Thus, in outlining the work of our Foreign Organisation it must be understood that there is nothing out of the ordinary about it. As its Head my position was very clearly defined by the Fuhrer when appointing me. Within the scope of the Foreign Office I am responsible for all questions that concern citizens of the Reich living abroad. The fact that I have nothing whatever to do with non-German nationals - either in my capacity as a member of the National Socialist Party or owing to my connection with the Foreign Office - has been emphasised so often as to require no further reference. All statements to the effect, for instance, that I make it my business to organise the German minorities in foreign countries are pure inventions; and nobody knows this better than the governments of the countries concerned. I am here referring, of course, to those of German origin abroad who are citizens of the countries in which they live.

I should like to state categorically that we neither desire nor expect any special privileges from foreign governments for those of our leading men abroad who are not connected with the diplomatic or consular service. This gives the lie to the rumours which would have it that the Foreign Organisation is thinking of appointing so-called cultural attaches abroad.

Great Britain, too, takes a lively interest in all matters affecting British residents abroad, and which nothing could be more justified. In 1920 a very interesting official report entitled, "Report of the Foreign Office Committee on British Communities Abroad," was presented to Parliament by command of His Majesty. The purpose for which the Committee was appointed, was to discuss ways and means whereby His Majesty's Government can:

1. Foster a greater spirit of solidarity among British communities abroad, and

2. Make British ideals more generally known and appreciated by foreign nations.

Anyone who has read this Report, and who is in any way acquainted with the work done by our own Foreign Organisation, can see at a glance that we pursue exactly the same aims. And it should be noted that the Report was drawn up by a Committee appointed by the Foreign Office:

We consider it extremely important that His Majesty's Government should make it known without delay that they take a sympathetic interest in the activities of British communities in foreign countries, and that they are prepared in certain cases to afford practical support.

It is also suggested that British nationals abroad should be induced to register their names with the consular offices competent for their district. It is emphasised that every British child living abroad should be given the opportunity of receiving an English education. The Government is urged to support all associations and societies of British residents abroad that serve to promote British ideals. Stress is also laid on the desirability of establishing British Chambers of Commerce abroad, of organising trade propaganda, of providing English libraries, and of maintaining English schools.

Can the above go by the name of agitation, political or economic espionage? The British Government, and the special associations concerned with British communities abroad, have a perfect right to interest themselves in the affairs of their nationals, provided - of course - that they do not come into conflict with the laws of the countries in question.

Moreover, British residents abroad are perfectly entitled to promote the commercial interests of their country whenever they have a chance of doing so. Similarly, no one can possibly object to our claims to exercise exactly the same rights on behalf of our German communities in foreign countries. This is a birthright, as it were, which we do not wish to relinquish any more than the British people would think of relinquishing theirs.

Cosmopolitan sentiments will never take the place of national sentiment so long as there are different nations. There will always be a British, French and an Italian national sentiment - and there will always be a German national sentiment. Incidentally, the time has passed when people could count on a weaker national sentiment among Germans than among the members of other nations. We Germans of Today, who are National Socialists, demand the same rights for ourselves as do other nations. We do not ask for special privileges, but we feel equally disinclined to put up with discrimination against us.

No fair-minded person can deny that many countries have derived untold benefits, more especially in the cultural sphere, from the German communities that have existed in their midst for a number of decades. Besides, it cannot be questioned that these Germans are peaceful and respectable citizens who have always abided by the law and for whose presence no country has been the worse.

For this reason, surely, the unfortunate practice of suspecting and reviling Germans in other countries, that has lately been indulged in, should definitely cease.

When the Fuhrer appointed me Head of the Foreign Organisation, numerous foreign papers seized the opportunity of designating me as the head of a widespread system of espionage; and no one was more surprised at the absurd charges levelled against me by a clique of irresponsible journalists than I was myself. These outbursts came to a climax when they called me the "Chief of the Nazintern," an imaginary organisation whose existence, I suppose, is confined to their own fertile brains. That such wild accusations could be raised is all the more remarkable as the work done by the numerous groups controlled by our Foreign Organisation must have made it plain to everybody that we Germans look upon National Socialism as something which we jealously treasure as our own property.

These false accusations make it extremely difficult for me to achieve an object which I am most anxious to see realised with the aid of our Foreign Organisation, namely to make the German communities the most popular among the foreign residents of each country in which they are domiciled.

We believe, and every reasonable critic will agree with our views, that the well-disciplined German nationals residing abroad constitute a special element of security for the country in which they live because their own country expects them to conduct themselves in a particularly decent and loyal manner whilst abroad, and because the National Socialist Government will hold each of them answerable for any attempt they may make to interfere in the domestic affairs of other nations, and thus impair Germany's chances of living in harmony with them. Moreover, those of our nationals abroad who may become destitute can never become as heavy a charge upon the country's revenue as the citizens of many another country, as we have a well-organised Relief Scheme for such cases, and resort to self-help as much as possible. We never tire of reminding our compatriots abroad that they must have the highest regard for the nationals of other countries. The very reason why we understand and respect other peoples' ways and traditions is that we love our own.

German residents abroad can surely be trusted when they say that they are staunch upholders of the cause of peace, as it is they who stand to lose most - if not everything - in the event of a war breaking out between their home country and their country of residence. It is therefore particularly infamous to represent them as warmongers.

Ever since the dawn of civilisation people have at times left their homeland to settle among strangers. Indeed, this is likely to continue so long as there is peaceful intercourse among nations. Instead of treating these foreign communities with suspicion and distrust, they ought to be regarded - in my opinion - as the best possible emissaries in the cause of international peace. They know the country from which they come and they get to know the country of their adoption. Who could be better qualified than they to create mutual understanding?

British residents in Germany are the welcome guests of the Third Reich, and not one of them I am sure can honestly say that there is such a thing as anti-British propaganda in our country. It is not usual for German newspapers to slander them or to accuse them of being spies. Nobody molests them, either privately or officially, because of their Democratic principles or because of their faith in the parliamentary system; and I think I may say that we treat our foreign guests with exemplary courtesy.

And even if we should have to arrest one or two on occasion because they happen to be spies, we should never think of generalising from such isolated cases and accusing all British residents in Germany of being spies. We should regard such an attitude as exceedingly unfair and, besides, we have no reason to entertain any apprehension for the security of our National Socialist regime.

There is an English word that has found its way into numerous languages in its original form and that is more appropriate than any other to serve as a basis for approaching all questions connected with our Foreign Organisation and the German communities. That word is "fairness."

It is not fair to reproach German residents abroad for being loyal to the Reich and for being National Socialists. Nor is it fair to hold them responsible for the establishment of the National Socialist regime in Germany, because that is the regime desired by the German people and they want no other. This is known to every Englishman, however slight his knowledge of German affairs may be.

The form of government that exists in Great Britain is a matter of complete indifference to us; and we should never think of giving advice on this subject to any British nationals, whether living at home or among us. That is their own affair, just as it is exclusively ours to select a regime we consider best suited to ourselves. Some time ago an article appeared in a London paper entitled, "Germany Today." That article appealed to me and I would like to cite a few passages in support of my contentions.

> Germany's system of government is Germany's affair; Britain's is Britain's. And there is no sound reason why these two Countries, each governed in the manner that its people prefer, should not live side by side in a spirit of friendly co-operation and human understanding. Such a change in their relationships

would be immensely beneficial to themselves, and an incalculable contribution to the peace of the world.

That, of course, has always been Germany's view of the problem. It is the only suitable basis for all attempts at removing the endless series of misunderstandings that have unfortunately grown up in the relations between the two countries.

We Germans in foreign countries have declared over and over again that we desire nothing better than permission to assist in bringing about a fair and decent understanding among nations. The groups affiliated to our Foreign Organisation are representatives of the new Germany in the truest sense of the term, and are, therefore, admirably qualified to render most useful work in that domain.

But this can only be done if a stop is put to the practice of discriminating against them merely because they have completely identified themselves with the National Socialist Party.

And to this end I would direct an appeal to the British, and I do so not as an absolute outsider. After all, my whole childhood was spent among British boys and girls, and I was educated with them. During the terrible war years I attended an English grammar school and was the only German boy at the school. These facts, I think, enable me to see both sides of the question.

Anyone who knows Great Britain, the British people, and more especially British history, cannot but admire this great nation with its grit and foresight. Similarly, I think that every Britisher who has had the chance of studying German character and the epic history of Germany will be equally impressed with the imposing spectacle presented by the heroic struggle towards national unity which our people have waged for a thousand years, a struggle made all the more difficult by our geographical position. No power in the world has ever been able permanently to dismember our country, though there has certainly been no lack of effort to do so.

Surely, the time has come for these two great and proud nations to grasp each other's hands in friendship and to try to arrive at a sincere understanding even on matters concerning which their views must necessarily differ. They have so many things in common that these differences - which are part of their national characteristics - ought not to stand in the way of a rapprochement.

The Fuhrer has often expressed a desire for such an understanding; and we Germans have noted with much gratification that his suggestions have been received with an increasing measure of approval on the part of the British people. Our Foreign Organisation will do everything in its power to support any such attempt, because we cherish the hope that German residents in Great Britain will be regarded by our British friends as what they really are - the Messengers of German Goodwill.

These National Socialists do not disseminate hatred and discord, but are anxious to deliver the messages of goodwill emanating from a country whose Leader loves peace because he loves his people and wants to make them happy.

The man who raised one of the world's great nations from the depths of misery and despair and made it great and united again, did not do so as a prelude to another war that would throw sixty-five million people back into the abyss from which he had rescued them.

He stands for the cause of peace - peace for Germany and peace for the world.

We National Socialists from foreign countries do the work that the Fuhrer wants us to do. We are his loyal and devoted followers because we know that by carrying out his instructions we shall ensure the peace and happiness of our own country, and assist in healing the wounds inflicted upon a distracted world that knows no peace.

SECTION FIVE

THE PRESS AND WORLD POLITICS

Dr. Dietrich

Secretary of State, Reich Chief of Press

A NEW problem has been added to the big political problems which influence the nations during the last few decades. There is no doubt that press matters have long been among the most interesting questions in social life, and the most important in intercourse between nations; but never before has the work of the Press had such a deep and direct effect upon political happenings as at the present day.

The Fuhrer of the German nation made the growing international problem of the Press the main theme of a great speech which found echoes in every part of the globe. He publicly and clearly showed the results and dangers of destructive Press work, which now has so much influence upon international politics.

Hitler referred to the Press as a political problem of world importance. His speech showed the negative side of a part of the international Press. But perhaps many who heard this address learned for the first time the extent to which the Press has developed into an element in world politics in the last few decades. It may be said that the policy of the Press has become an important part of politics, both national and international. The Press is one of those institutions of which it may be remarked that its shadow is more noticeable than its light. Perhaps it is on this account that some are honestly troubled and regard the Press as one of the misfortunes that afflict mankind. But we have progressed too far for a life without newspapers. The Press has become one of the most important parts of modern life, and the existence of nations without it can hardly be imagined.

The Press bridges time and space in reporting daily happenings. It links up mankind daily and hourly with the surrounding world beyond the range of vision. The newspaper is the mirror of our age, and the Press is always the focus of all big events. It has been called the organ of public opinion, the voice of the nations, and the eye and ear of the world.

To what extent can it fulfil this great task? That is the Press problem of our times. But it is certain that the Press is an important element in political life. It creates the atmosphere, both good and bad, in which politicians must work.

The German Press policy is not always understood in some parts of the world, but I believe that if it were rightly grasped it would help to remove the frequent disastrous effects in which a wrong idea of the Press has often resulted.

It is hardly possible to understand the structure of our Press, or our Press policy, without some knowledge of the fundamentals of National Socialism, of the new school of thought which gave rise to it, of the new conception of State which it produces, and of the relationship of the individual to the whole which lends his existence entirely new expression. National Socialism revolutionised the political thinking of the German people.

As already intimated, National Socialism replaced individualistic thought, which it regards as the error of a whole age, by the community idea. New paths were thus opened which those whose whole life is, so to speak, on another plane cannot grasp. The ideas other peoples use as the base of their school of thought are often not sufficiently far-reaching for their upholders to follow with understanding what has happened in Germany, although they are ample in their own countries. We are here at the cross-road of two schools of thought. This is the true source of all the difficulties and lack of understanding so often met with in international discussions. It is not possible to understand National Socialism with Liberal types of thought. Only those who feel this new community thought, or, at least, endeavour to comprehend it, can understand National Socialism, its age and its works, its language and its voice.

My remarks regarding the progress of human ideas, which has achieved a revolution of thought in Germany during the last few years, apply especially to the Press. When one looks into the standpoints from which the National Socialist Press is criticised, and considers the outlived standards employed, one cannot be surprised at the deficient understanding with which so many foreigners regard the National Socialist conception of the Press. It is true that the Press was born of Liberalism, but the Press of the Liberal age is not synonymous with the "Press" as a whole.

The conception of a newspaper is very different in the National Socialist State. A new age gives the Press new tasks to fulfil. The Liberal Press is characterised by the idea that the criticism or opinion of the individual regarding the State and its public institutions is justified. The individual, no matter whether he be a journalist or contributor, appears as the mouthpiece of public opinion with no justification to this claim beyond his own private opinion. This corresponds to the fundamental idea of individual thought.

The National Socialist community idea, on the other hand, gives the Press a basically different, in fact directly opposite, task - that of publishing the principles of the whole as against the individual. The German people have learned that the idea of pulling together is their greatest treasure.

The National Socialist Party, as the great revival movement of the German nation, has learned from its own history that the uniform political thought of the whole nation is the basis for all national and social success, and that it is the knowledge of common problems of destiny which produces the will to solve them. It sees an element of power in this knowledge, and regards the Press as one of the mightiest means of serving this knowledge.

In a National Socialist State, the Press has not the task of expressing individual opinion against the whole, and of voicing a "public opinion" which is really non-existent. On the other hand, it has to represent the community view against the individual, and to make this comprehensible to those who do not know it. The newspaper thus becomes the warning voice of the nation, and the school of political thought, lending every citizen the knowledge that he is a link in the community chain for good or evil.

Public opinion in Germany is thus not a fluctuating barometer, subject day by day to thousands of influences of uncontrollable individual interests.

Public opinion, as we see it, is the real will of the people, with which National Socialism has direct contact at its source through its close connection with the people. We do not make public opinion, we seek to establish it.

The newspaper in Germany is not the scene of irresponsible criticism on the part of a few who act as advance guard on behalf of anonymous interests and misuse criticism to undermine the authority of the State. Our newspapers are the publicity conscience of the nation, destined to foster instead of to hinder the work of the State, for we have better methods of maintaining the State in contact with the people. This is a very different view to that of the Liberal Press, and we feel sure that it is a better one.

The arguments used by some foreign critics against German Press methods on this or a similar basis thus prove unfounded. They do not touch the essence of the matter, being taken from the Liberal dictionary whose expressions are no longer applicable to our times and our modern conception of the duties of the Press. The German Press also takes the liberty of criticising, but it criticises what harms the people, and not what benefits them. Within the obvious limitations set by the vital interests of the nation, it has in reality more freedom than the Liberal Press. It even takes the liberty of criticising the "freedom of the Press," which is praised with all the passion of which Democrats are capable as one of mankind's most holy possessions.

Even the most independent Liberal pen never dares to criticise the so-called freedom of the Press. Our colleagues in the editorial offices of the "free Democracies" know why. But they are not allowed to say so since such painful publicity would result in their having to seek a change of profession which was by no means voluntary.

The history of the development of newspapers shows what the freedom of the Press is really like. It has been proved that the expression "freedom of the Press" is one of the loudest of empty phrases which has ever fogged the human brain.

The evidence of those who claim Press freedom in their own lands is furthermore a proof that there has never been any real freedom of the Press anywhere, and that in places where this freedom is particularly boasted it is least truly present. I may quote some cases which exemplify the mental slavery of the Press.

In 1913 the American Journalist, John Swinton, stated at the annual meeting of the American Press Association that there was no independent Press in America, apart from the papers in small provincial towns. He went on to say that this fact was known to everyone, but that no one dared to express his opinion about it, while it would never appear in print even if he did. The man who was mad enough to write his own personal opinion would soon be in the street. A New York journalist had to lie and to sit at the feet of Mammon. He had to sell himself and his nation for the sake of his daily bread. The speaker concluded by referring to journalists as the tools and vassals of the rich who sat behind the scenes and pulled the strings. The time and talents of journalists belonged to them, and Press men were mental prostitutes.

This is a hard and drastic opinion expressed twenty-five years ago. Conditions have, however, not improved since.

A New York firm of publishers recently brought out a book entitled *The Washington Correspondent*, in which some extremely interesting statements appeared. The author records the answers to a questionnaire placed before several hundred journalists. The question as to how far the freedom of a journalist extended was often laconically answered to the effect that everyone knew they had to write what the editors wanted, or that they would be thrown out of the editorial departments if they did not write what was wanted. The writer of the book, Leo C. Roston, remarks that in a Society where freedom is a nice slogan, limited by economic reality, a clear conscience is a luxury restricted to those who have enough money to refuse to compromise at the expense of their personal ideals.

This book, which was not written by German National Socialists, but published in the United States, would be excellent reading for those who believe that they can reproach us with lack of Press freedom. Or they should peruse the sensational attack on the American Press which was also published in New York, and by Ferdinand Lundberg, under the title America's 60 Families. The chapter on journalism under the influence of money is especially interesting. In this book the real truth about the freedom of the Press is recognised.

The freedom of the Press is a phantom, a mere label. There is not, and never has been, freedom of the Press in any part of the world. One should have sufficient feeling for realities to admit this fact. The Press is always dependent, and always under obligations to someone.

The only question is, to whom? To business and party politics, to the anonymous power of gold and the destruction of order and morals, or to the responsible Statesmen and Government?

When the National Socialist State was established in 1933, and Press matters were in a state of chaos, Germany was faced with this problem, and decided for the last-named alternative. The purification of the Press in the Reich was, so to speak, the visiting-card, and the reorganisation of the Press the first fruit of the National Socialist revolution.

The reputation of the Press might have been lost among the German people if the National Socialist Party had not made great sacrifices to found their own Press, which fought for years against the old conditions in the newspaper world. Chaos was turned into order, and the new law for editors was issued as early as October 4th, 1933, coming into force on January 1st, 1934.

The structure of the reorganised German Press is clear and simple. The new law changed the centre of gravity of responsibility to the person concerned. The personal responsibility for the editorial part, i.e., for the political and chief part of the paper, was made clear. Just as the individual is absolutely responsible to the whole nation, so those who write in the Press and mould public opinion are likewise answerable to the State and to the public.

This new law also corresponds to the German feeling of right, in contrast to the Liberal conception, that the contributions of free-lancers should be editorially supervised, and that the individual is responsible. The anonymous principle was thus replaced by responsibility.

The National Socialist Press law brought German journalists into direct relations with the State and nation, to whom, as well as to their own conscience, they are answerable. On the other hand, the State guarantees them the necessary legal independence of unfair influences in their work. Formerly the Pressmen could not always repel these.

Personal Press responsibility and rights are the starting point for the new position of journalism in National Socialist Germany. They have effected a fundamental change in the social position of the German Editor. It would be a great mistake to believe that Germany wanted a mechanical State Press, with the editors as mere slaves of State authorities. We wanted a living people's Press in which the personality of the Editor could develop freely, and his journalistic sense of duty could unfold for the benefit of the nation.

At the same time, the German Press is aware that there is much left for it to do. Such a fundamental personal change as we undertook requires time to develop in accordance with the tasks at hand. The legal regulations were absolutely essential.

With the radical separation of business and politics achieved by the editorial law in Germany, the basis for the recovery of the Press is provided, for it has awakened in the breast of every German journalist the inner law of that higher Press freedom which distinguishes the journalistic profession as one ennobled by national responsibility.

The inner power and the national importance of the Press thus becomes clear. Opposed to it is the international power of the Press as a factor in world politics.

The Press is a power in the life of the nations, being much greater than is dreamed of by many citizens in their bourgeois philosophy. It was formerly called the seventh Great Power, but I believe it has been promoted in order of seniority during the past twenty years. In proportion to the approach of the nations to each other as a result of modern transport and telegraphy have the opinions and political atmosphere and reactions of the nations become more important for the political decisions of the Powers. The wires of the Press convey the true or supposed attitude of the nations to all great happenings from one country to another within a few hours. There is no point in saying that the wireless does it still more quickly. The wireless announces the opinions of the Press, which are taken as the barometer of public opinion, and regarded as the voice of the nation, whether it be so or not.

The Press is looked upon as Public Opinion because it most strongly influences the opinion of the public.

On this account it may be designated as the barometer of world politics, its influence over the decisions of many cabinets in the last few decades having become stronger and more direct than many imagine.

This power in the hands of the Press as one of the most influential means of guiding the public has potentialities both good and bad: it can develop for the well-being or to the detriment of international relations. A French Diplomat hence described it as the tongue of Aesop, ans said it was both the best and the worst member. Unfortunately, the bad tongue has made itself much more noticeable in international relations than the good powers of the Press.

Many a time public opinion has been poisoned by untruthful statements in the Press, and by that irresponsible sensationalism which endangers the peace of the nations.

In his Reichstag speech after five years of National Socialism, Chancellor Hitler spoke of this open wound in the life of the nations. He gave a clear answer to those who incite the public, and appealed to the Governments not only to make international arrangements to prevent the dropping of explosive, poison gas and inflammable bombs, but also to stop the publication of all newspapers which have an even deadlier effect on international relations.

There have been occasions when sections of the Press have preached hatred and war between nations whose only wish was to live in peace. No one will seriously try to deny this fact. One or two foreign journals have referred to me as a remarkable Press surgeon, and written about my "Nazi mentality." But I have received private letters from many journalists who agreed with me. These are a proof that my words express the thoughts of many Pressmen who are working under the compulsion of circumstances. It is the same with many Democratic Statesmen as with many journalists. They have long recognised the depressing Press problem, but dare not deal with it. Their own Press freedom forbids them to touch upon these problems. The tragic difficulty in the way of solving what is really a simple problem is to be found in the fact that all who could change these conditions are compelled to be silent because they are politically dependent upon the Press. While other matters in public life are freely discussed, the silence of the grave envelops this subject in the Democratic Press. Only the Leaders of authoritarian Governments have raised their voices against this state of affairs.

For example, Mussolini explained on one occasion to the President of the International Editors' organisation how great was the evil of one-sided reporting. All these incorrect Press announcements created a state of affairs which was serious, and which all countries should help to remove in the interests of peace.

The extent to which the importance of this problem has been recognised in the parliamentary Democracies is shown by statements made by many of their responsible statesmen. Thus, M. Lebrun, the French President, seriously warned the Editors of his country not to abuse the so-called Press freedom. That was at the annual meeting of the French journalists' organisation on February 8th, 1937. The freedom to say everything within certain limits was good, but it was dangerous when one allowed oneself to be led by hate and passion. The French Editors, he went on, would have to consider the different management of the Press policy in the various countries. On the one hand there was something like an orchestra conductor, who harmonised all notes, so that the national will appeared more uniform and powerful. This was a strength which was to the benefit of the country. But where criticism exceeded the bounds, everyone did as he wished. There was thus the danger that exaggerated individualism would compromise everything, and make the desired effect impossible. One should never forget the regrettable effects of false reports, which might endanger that international harmony among the nations, for which one should work more than ever, and jeopardise the peace desired by all.

At a lunch of the Foreign Press Association in Paris, the French Foreign Minister, M. Delbos, recently spoke against the custom of issuing false or unfair reports, stating that the common duty of the Press in all lands was to allay the fever which had arisen. The Press would have, he continued, to do more for the reconciliation and unity of the nations than for their separation.

It was none other than M. Herriot who, according to the Paris Temps of April 16th, 1936, demanded a law against Press slander on the ground that it was unbearable that lies went unpunished in a respectable country like theirs. This new law would, therefore, have to comprise at least two points: firstly that all articles would have to be signed, and secondly that the responsible Editor must not misuse his position; the manager of a paper and author of the article should take over the responsibility.

According to the Prager Presse of April 21st, 1935, the Czechish President Benesch asked whether it was possible to overlook the fact that the moral state of our generation was being ruined by the revolutionary, demagogic, immoral, corruptible, sensational, etc., points of view and aims which guided the Press.

In an address before the Irish branch of the Institute of Journalists, President de Valera asked whether the freedom of the Press should or should not be unrestricted. He said that the expression "freedom of the Press" must have a reasonable explanation, and might not be regarded as meaning power without responsibility. There was a foggy notion of Press freedom in many circles, with the aid of which people spread disturbances of thought which they would not allow their children in private life. The nation would have to be protected against the abuse of the influence of the Press.

Numerous Statesmen have made similar remarks in almost all lands, e.g., the Danish Prime Minister, Stauning, and the Swiss statesman Dr. Meyer, while Mr. Eden, in one of his speeches before the League of Nations, mentioned that diplomatic successes had little news value, while diplomatic failures had lasting results which could long be heard and felt.

The British Premier, Mr. Chamberlain, stated in a speech in the House of Commons that the power of the Press for good or evil was very great in the field of international relations, and careful use of this power, guided by full realisation of responsibility, might have far-reaching effects by attaining a favourable atmosphere for the aims they were striving for.

Mr. Chamberlain was almost certainly thinking of the role played by a section of the English Press regarding Lord Halifax's visit to Berchtesgaden, and of the kind of service it rendered to British Diplomacy. It is a fact that sensationalism on the part of an irresponsible section of the Press has done much to disturb the chances of understanding among the nations. This list is a long one, but it becomes almost endless when one considers the vast positive power of the Press, and what a blessing this could be for mankind if it were wielded with a true sense of responsibility.

One imagines how peaceful the world would be if one did not only write about peace, but if the newspapers themselves would keep the peace. The Press could work wonders in political life. The League of Nations has attempted to arrange international relations. There have been innumerable diplomatic endeavours, conferences and assemblies. The result is very trifling. But perhaps the disappointment at the fruitlessness of these endeavours is the chief cause of the political defeatism which has gripped so many countries in Europe. The nations could have very different relations with each other if they recognised how much the Press could do towards the promotion of collaboration and mutual understanding, and if the positive power of the Press were employed fully for this high goal.

It is not Utopianism to state that mutual respect and understanding could be reached in the atmosphere created by the Press in a few months, whereas this could not be achieved in other ways even in centuries.

Instead of sowing the seeds of dissension and hate, as some papers do, the Press could be one of the most beneficent organs in creating international relationships. The nations want peace, wish for understanding with their neighbours. But the Press in many lands, while claiming to be public opinion, does not allow these wishes to fructify.

The Man in the Street in many lands might well ask why the path of international Press peace is not taken. The nations have all come to an agreement regarding drug-smuggling, the White Slave traffic, and the pursuit of robbers. Why, then, should they not join hands in fighting political incitement and the peace boycott indulged in by some irresponsible papers?

I fully recognise the difficulties in the way of a solution. They are rooted less in the will of the peoples than in organisation conditions and in the structure of the Press. In his Reichstag speech, Herr Hitler gave some clear hints regarding the objections that there are no legal means in other countries of ending lies and slander. In going into this question I have no wish to outline any ideas of my own. But I may remark that Germany and Italy have the practical essential conditions for Press collaboration by means of modern Press legislation. The structure of our Press shows, for the first time, the prospect of achieving aims in international politics which, when properly understood and followed without prejudice, will become a blessing to the nations and to mankind as a whole.

Those who have recognised these practical aims and possibilities are in duty bound to work for their international realisation in the interest of the nations and of peace. The policy of the German Press is guided by this thought alone in trying to adopt the path of reason and understanding in international Press matters by making Press agreements, whether written or unwritten, from country to country.

The Press Agreement made by Germany with Poland and Austria serves this goal, and a further success was attained in the shape of a Gentlemen's Agreement regarding mutual Press relations not long ago, when the Yugoslavian Premier visited Germany. The close friendship between the German and Italian peoples is due by no means least to the attitude of the Press in the two countries, the journalists having visited each other for years, and set up friendships which are now of benefit to both peoples.

The German Press will continue to pursue this policy of non-aggression pacts and agreements between country and country so far as politics and Press affairs may permit.

But there are limits in this respect - not limits to our good will, but to possible negotiations and to the Press morals in some countries. Just as there can be no armistice between two States when one has a well-disciplined army while the troops of the other are in the hands of condottieri who carry on a war of their own, there can be no Press peace when only one party adheres to the national discipline, while the other refuses to accept responsibility and allows itself to be led by the anonymous influence of powers which aim at destroying peace.

Thanks to the national discipline to which our Press is trained by National Socialism, we are in a position to make such agreements and to keep them. What, however, is the position in other countries?

Diplomatic representations are often made regarding unqualified attacks on our people and their form of Government, and the almost stereotype answer is: "We agree that it was untrue, or a grave slander, but we have no basis for effectively interfering in view of the constitutionally guaranteed freedom of the Press."

Such objections are incomprehensible to us, even from the standpoint of the widest Democratic Press policy. What is thus defended as freedom of the Press is not freedom but insolence. Here, the State does not defend freedom but abuse. M. Herriot said that it was unbearable that lies should go unpunished in a respectable land like his. In doing so, he merely expressed what every respectable man thinks in every country, for there is no Constitution which can shield such things in the name of the people. Every government can step in against those who poison the foreign relations of a nation by false reports, and thus endanger their own nation's peace. The wellbeing of the nation and the security of the State are, after all, the first law of Democracy. When the interests of the people are irresponsibly endangered by the publication of untrue rumours, every Statesman should claim the right to seize the edition of the paper in which such reports appear, according to the written and the unwritten law. Countries in which such obvious principles are not applied are not suitable partners for Press agreements.

In many countries the strange custom of holding the German Government responsible for every word printed in German papers has spread. Reserve is demanded of the German Press, while the countries concerned do not feel obliged to act similarly owing to their view of the freedom of the Press. That is unfair banking on our respectability and does not bring the goal of a Press peace any nearer.

We are not prepared to accept irresponsible Press attacks as the reward for our honest endeavours. Any such attack which is not suppressed by the Government of the country in question compels us to resort to the same weapons. No one will doubt we can be plain in defending our rights. We are of the opinion that the bad custom of judging by such unequal standards does not foster international Press reconciliation. We cannot afford to act as peaceful angels when the devil stands before us. Here, we say: An eye for an eye; a tooth for a tooth.

We, too, can only contribute to the Press peace step by step. No one can expect us to keep our arrows unpointed while others launch attacks at us. This must be clear to Statesmen in other lands who consider a Press peace as the best preparation for an all-round political agreement. It is of little use to protest that one wants peace while the Press shoots its poisoned arrows simultaneously.

In Germany, as in Italy, Press reform and legislation have made the first step towards a reasonable Press policy between the two countries, and thus shown the way to a clearing of the international atmosphere.

In a number of other countries, reason is also making itself heard. We have recognised that the moral crisis in world newspaper circles has less to do with the journalists than with those who prescribe their line of action from the darkness of anonymity. As a result, we freed the Pressmen from the invisible shackles of capital by means of our Editor law, and gave the journalist a directly responsible relationship to the nation and State, without in any way interfering with the private ownership of the newspapers. This clear and healthy solution has brought our journalism in order. Now it is the turn of others to follow if they really mean that they wish for peace.

The means they adopt is their own business, in which we shall not interfere. As in the case of foreign politics, National Socialism has its own conception of Press politics. Just as we believe that world peace can only be assured by the existence of free, sovereign and happy States, so do we also hold that world economy can only prosper on a basis of healthy national economies. In the same way, we are of the opinion that only a morally and economically healthy national Press can be the basis of international Press co-operation.

The barriers built between the nations by hate will be pulled down all the quicker the more the responsible Statesmen understand the will of their people in this question in all lands, and the more they find the courage to act accordingly, and thus serve the interest of the nations. The so-called freedom of the Press which they believe they must respect is a phantom, with no more power than the fright it instils, as one of the first European newspaper men wrote in 1827. The real issue should not be avoided for the sake of a mere catchword.

The journalist who exercises his profession has long recognised the true face of this strange freedom of the Press, which is no freedom for him. He knows that the Press is free in theory, but that this freedom is abolished by the power of gold in actual practice, as an American once remarked.

Statesmen who shrink from this power should consider this point, and not avoid it by talk of "a good conscience" and by an appeal to the people's love of freedom.

True freedom does not lie in irresponsibility, but in responsibility. Responsibility towards the community of one's own nation and towards the community of all peoples. This would make the Press an instrument in promoting peace, and not one which separates and incites the nations. This responsibility should be felt by all, both by the men who guide the policy of the Press, and by the journalists who write for the newspapers, whether they work in the editorial departments, or as correspondents abroad. We see the first main basis for profitable Press relations with other lands in fruitful collaboration with the foreign Press representatives in Germany.

Our attitude towards the foreign journalists accredited to Berlin may, perhaps, be the subject of some misunderstanding. I believe that journalistic fairness and national obligation in the Press work of the foreign journalists can well be combined. This presupposes some psychologic understanding of the situation, and of the conditions existing on both sides.

We see the duties of the foreign correspondent as follows. He is to give his countrymen an unprejudiced, truthful picture of a foreign land and its people. Those who view their task in this way can be sure of our assistance at any time, for we then respect in them the representatives of organs of public opinion in their own country. We shall not dispute their right to make objective criticism so long as they wish to serve the interests of truth. But those who harbour feelings of personal or other dislike, or even hatred, for the country they are in, feelings which bring them into constant conflict with their professional duties and make objective reporting difficult or impossible, should not come to us as correspondents. They harm not only our land, but also their own by unfair, one-sided news reporting, and are subject to justifiable distrust which is sure, sooner or later, to lead to a breach.

We are very sensitive when we find a foreign journalist acting in opposition to the endeavours of politicians towards "neighbourliness" with other nations by deliberately reporting in a manner likely to incite other nations against us, deliberately misreporting conditions in the Reich. In such cases we have resorted to the institution of expulsion, which, by the way, is not a National Socialist invention but a measure applied everywhere to journalists who abuse their position and the hospitality of the country they are in. This measure has already been made use of by us, and will be retained in the future. But we understand the peculiar conditions under which the foreign journalists have to do their work. We are not narrow minded, and do not belong to those who believe every journalist must be an objectionable creature if he does not write exactly like a National Socialist. We expect him, as a subject of another land, to think and feel differently to us in many matters, just as we expect a German abroad not to forget that he is a German. We only ask the foreign correspondent to serve the interests of truth, to do his journalistic duty in a respectable manner, and like a Diplomat, to view his mission from a higher standpoint - that of fostering the relations between nation and nation.

It is true that a paper cannot be quite without sensations, but do not the achievements of National Socialist Germany in many fields offer more than enough material for sensational reports? One should not devote so much energy to the quest of the negative when so much positive is available. In exaggerating for the sake of sensation there is the danger of slipping, and thus of falling victim to rumour, and hence to untruthfulness.

Bismarck said that every country had, in the long run, to pay for the windows broken by its Press. He also said that it would be easier to make a good editor into a Secretary of State than to produce a single good journalist from a dozen privy councillors. These words still apply today.

I do not see a destructive, but a reconstructive element in Pressmen, an element which will help us to realise the exigencies of Press politics which constitute one of the most urgent problems in international politics.

Herr Hitler made a difference, in his Reichstag speech, between two kinds of journalists. I should be happy if all belonged to the kind who serve their people by preparing the way for the truth.

One saying may also be quoted, which also applies to the correspondent abroad: "Respect everyone's country, but love your own."

SECTION SIX

GERMANY AND ENGLAND

What Has Been: What Is: What Ought To Be

Freiherr Von Rheinbaben

Former Secretary of State

THE purpose of this book is to enable representatives of Germany to describe the great spheres of national and international activity with which they are especially acquainted, and the task allotted to me is to endeavour to present, as briefly as is consistent with their importance, the essential phases of Anglo-German relations in the past few decades and at the present time. I will explain furthermore how a German who believes understanding and friendship between Germany and England to be the most important part of peace in Europe, hopes Anglo-German relations will develop.

Just as I was setting to work I read in *The Times* a report of a speech delivered by Sir Edward Grigg in Bristol before the Royal Empire Society on November 12th, 1937. This speech struck me as being so very remarkable that I decided to base my work on it:

Sir Edward Grigg said that by a fateful process which all must deplore but none could now correct, the Empire was facing, on the eve of 1938, a problem and a danger strangely similar to that which had confronted it 40 years ago. Since the end of the Great War the Dominions had assumed with us that the world had been made safe for democracy by the victory over Germany and the creation of the League. That dream was now shattered. Once more the central question of foreign policy lay in the relations between the British Empire and the German Reich. History was therefore repeating itself, as it so often did. The problem that had profoundly exercised Joseph Chamberlain's far-seeing mind more than a generation ago was now confronting his son. Joseph Chamberlain's repeated efforts to secure an understanding with Germany had been stultified by a steady refusal on the part of the German Emperor and his advisers to come to frank and friendly terms. The issue had been terrible-and even more terrible for Germany than for us. It was surely not to be endured that two great nations should willingly tread the same disastrous path again. Was it really the case that in the year 1898 and during a short period afterwards the possibility of an alliance or even only of an understanding in "frank and friendly terms" with England was frustrated by "a steady refusal on the part of the German Emperor and his advisers"? No! It was not so. There may have been individual Germans who, vastly overrating their own importance or impelled by ignorance or prejudice, gave an affirmative reply to this question, but the objective German historical view is very different. I believe that it approaches very nearly to what I myself wrote recently in an appreciation of the late Sir Austen Chamberlain's attitude towards Germany:

On March 22nd, 1937, the *Daily Telegraph* published an article by Sir Austen Chamberlain, written shortly before his death, on the negotiations conducted by his father, Joseph Chamberlain, with Germany at about the turn of the century. The tendency of the article is that Joseph Chamberlain honestly wished then, as Minister for the Colonies, to arrive at an agreement with Germany on a treaty basis, and that Bulow had at first deceived him and then wrecked the negotiations, whereupon England turned to another direction.

To this our reply is briefly as follows:

1. It is by no means certain that Joseph Chamberlain's policy would have been approved in its final phase by the Prime Minister (Lord Salisbury) and the Cabinet, to say nothing of Parliament and of public opinion.

What Has Been

2. In view of the existing international situation Joseph Chamberlain aimed at relieving England and the Empire of danger from France and especially from Russia.

3. The then directors of German foreign policy therefore mistrusted the English offers. They wished not to expose Germany to the risk of a

war with Russia (and consequently also with France) to serve English interests.

4. From the historical standpoint, that is to say, bearing in mind the growing British animosity towards Germany from about 1902, England's subsequent engagements with France and Russia, the concealment of the systematic political encirclement of Germany, the secret military arrangements restricting fatefully, when the War broke out, England's freedom to decide to maintain peace – the attitude then assumed by Germany was perhaps after all a mistaken one. That attitude was, however, based on conceptions which ultimately were diametrically opposed to those put forward by Sir Austen Chamberlain, its aim being to prevent the breaking out of a European conflagration. For this there are living witnesses.

This example shows us at the very beginning of our survey how difficult it will be to find in both countries, in Germany and in England, a similar and a universally approved presentation of the same process in the past. It is true, scientific investigation has proved to be of great utility in correcting errors and clearing up misunderstandings; the judgment dictated at the time by hatred and prejudice has been considerably revised in respect of the Versailles war-guilt thesis. However, we need quicker working and more practical methods if we are to reach mutual understanding and to create confidence and friendship. We should not think of settling the matter simply with popular formulas about the "Cousins on the other side of the North Sea," or less even with the catchwords: "Colonies, Czechoslovakia, and General settlement." Sir Edward Grigg was eminently in the right in saying that whatever may be the appearance of the details between 1898 and 1914, it was an unparalleled tragedy that the march of Anglo-German relations in those years ended in an embittered fight, for the first time in their thousand years' history, between Germans and English, each at the head of a coalition of antagonistic forces.

It is assuredly the most important task in the international work of the German and English political leaders to prevent a recurrence of this combat, and at the fitting time, after calm consideration and following sensible principles, to set a foreign political course that will avoid the dangerous waters bordering on war. And therefore no one speaking for Germany Today, and wishing to add something useful to the all-important subject of Anglo-German relations can ignore the question: Why did war break out in 1914?

It was unfortunate that so much misunderstanding concerning the strength of each other's Navy arose during the Dreadnought period. Still more unfortunate, however, was the failure to conclude a naval agreement establishing a ratio of 16 to 10 for the large vessels, as was suggested at the time. The conclusion of such an agreement might not perhaps have had much influence on the actual construction policy, but even without the promise on the part of England to remain neutral in case Germany were attacked, it would have served the German interest by proving once more to the world that nothing was further from Germany's intention than an attack on England. Germany's whole policy rested, then, on two pillars: on progress, including the extension of her trade interests dispersed over the world, and on vigilance lest a sign of weakness should be given in view of the overwhelming coalition obviously antagonistic to Germany, whose own allies were inwardly unstable or for other reasons doubtful friends. How often have I heard such statements made by High Admiral von Tirpitz, whose collaborator I had the honour to be in those years.

On the very verge of the outbreak of the Great War Germany was negotiating with England on the subject of the increase of her colonial possessions in Africa. The Naval question had reached smoother waters, the danger point was safely passed. England was apparently reconciled to a strong German Navy of somewhat less than two-thirds the strength of her own, and thus the more readily as she could reckon with certainty in the case of war on the French and Russian navies. Is it conceivable that in such a situation and in a period of unparalleled economic prosperity Germany would deliberately prepare to attack and strive to obtain dominion over the world?

England, on her part, carried out in the year 1902, by entering into a treaty with Japan, her intention first broached in 1898 to emerge from her splendid isolation and conclude alliances. The Entente with France followed in 1904, and that with Russia in 1907. Germany's natural and rapid growth was regarded as a danger to the interests of England; her expanding naval power, supported by the finest army in the world, would, it was believed, be a real menace to England in the case of war. England thereupon became the moving spirit of a development that directly or indirectly, with the help of her friends, thwarted Germany in every part of the world. It was like a fateful force that with certain interruption pursued its inexorable course. The real political momentum was the objective set up by Sir Edward Grey, which I would describe as the Magna Charta of the English pre-war policy. In his well-known biography Trevelyan has, with all his admiration for his hero, proved once again for us Germans that the determining reason for England's participation in the War was not commercial rivalry, not the tension created by the growth of the German Navy, but the fear that a victory over France and Russia would ensure to Germany hegemony over the continent, upset the European equilibrium, and bring England face to face with the danger of being compelled later on to fight without allies the combined forces of the continent.

Why did England go to war in 1914? Germany stood, at a moment of heavy affliction that threatened the very roots of the existence of Austria-Hungary, by her ally. Austria-Hungary believed that it was incumbent upon her to fight Serbia with the sword; Russia supported Serbia and stood against Austria-Hungary; Germany also was thus against Russia; consequently France sided with Russia, and Germany was opposed to France ...

England acted in accordance with the "Magna Charta" of her pre-war policy. All the rest, the Kaiser's marginal notes and speeches, corresponding utterances by Lloyd George and others, diplomatic mistakes or omissions, dates or wording of telegrams in the course of the month of July 1914, even the march through Belgium, is material only when it is considered expedient to make it so. It does not affect the final verdict of history. In this it will be acknowledged that in the year 1914 Germany went to war in order to defend what was sacred to her. England must answer before the bar of history the question whether, seeing that her desire for peace was as great as was that of Germany, she used her great influence over France and Russia, whose openly declared aims could be reached only by the force of arms, and if she used this influence at the right time in an effort to ensure renunciation of actions that bore upon them the stigma of war.

Without any wish to enter into a polemical discussion, I am writing this only because I believe that Britons should know this German view, and because I wish to make it clear that all English ideas and decisions which, as parallels to 1914, still start from the basis of Versailles regarding the outbreak of the War, can meet with no understanding in Germany. On the contrary, they are energetically rejected. Germans and Britons speak without understanding each other when this basis is adopted, even when they do not discuss 1914, but peace and friendship in general.

What was fateful in 1914 was not strength or weakness of any particular nation but "Collectivism" in the form and character of that period. It was given a new form by the dictated Treaty of Versailles, the form with the halo indicating that its purpose was the maintenance of the status quo, that is to say, the permanent subjugation of a Germany now finally defeated by superior force and the hunger blockade. Was it surprising that the German people gradually awoke from the torpor produced by the collapse, the revolution and the dictated Treaty of Versailles, and strove to find the entrance to the long road back to freedom? I hardly need deal with these matters in detail. There are English publications enough in which the history of the injustices committed and of the opportunities missed, between 1918 and 1933, is given at length.

As between 1898 and 1914 there had been interspersed pauses and hopes for the maintenance of peace through Anglo-German understanding, so now similar episodes occurred between 1919 and 1933 during which it seemed as if reason might prevail and bring about a real peace. In general, however, ruthless advantage was taken of Germany's weakness. Often enough did Germany build "hopes" on England, but on the whole she was disappointed. England could not bring herself to reduce the pressure exerted on Germany mainly at the instigation of France. The great opportunity offered by Locarno was allowed to pass by unused. Economic discernment was lacking to an almost greater extent than political insight. Even in the year 1930 England's representative in Geneva signed a document in which it was declared that disarmament meant Germany remaining on the Versailles level while the other nations discussed what was to be understood from the military standpoint under "effective." At the same time, the Young Plan was forced on Germany, with figures that were still astronomical.

But enough of this, which is, moreover, not written with the object of making reproaches, and is included in the complete picture without bitterness, simply as a statement of facts, with their lesson for the future. A German looking back on this period will say that Providence intended that the opposition encountered by Germany on the natural and obvious way back to freedom should be so great that corresponding counter-forces might be produced in order to overcome it. What an Englishman thinks of those times I can only imagine, but whatever may be the nature of his recollections, there is the eternal truth of Dryden's words:

Not heaven itself upon the past has power; But what has been has been, and I have had my hour.

What Is

There is now once more a Germany with which England must reckon as an important member of the European family of nations. This historical fact was achieved between the years 1933 and 1938 by rapid action accompanied by a far-reaching transformation in Europe and in the world. Would any purpose be served by describing fully in this survey the course of events that led up to that result? I doubt it. None of these events influenced decisively the nature of Anglo-German relations. Germany has regained the external and internal attributes of a great power, and has accordingly acquired increased weight among the nations, though without detriment to England.

It must have been clear to the English-speaking world in the spring of the year 1933 that something absolutely new was occurring in Germany, which European diplomacy would have to take into account. To the great surprise of the German people, however, there was no sign of a new course being adopted. On the contrary, the exultant feeling created by unity, by the overcoming of the antagonism of classes, political parties, creeds, and of the separate States that had heretofore been so fateful, and especially the uprising from humiliation and impotence, was referred to officially at Geneva as "inciting unrest in Europe."

The armament limitation plan submitted by England in the person of the Prime Minister in March 1933 to the Disarmament Conference was repudiated in the autumn of the same year with special reference to Germany. Furthermore, it was suggested that the German nation, just inspired by new impulses and starting on the work of the future, should undergo a "period of probation" before abandoning the one-sided Versailles disarmament in favour of an approach to equality with her neighbours in the matter of armaments. This suggestion was made in spite of the fact that Germany was surrounded by neighbours who were continually strengthening their armaments, some of them being by no means of a friendly disposition towards her.

Germany simply did not understand this attitude on the part of an England so renowned throughout the centuries for her sense of justice and fair play. Was this attitude dictated by consideration for the nerves of her excited French friend? Is it possible that the belief was held in England's Geneva Delegation or in London that Germany was only bluffing, and that she was not in earnest with her demand fanatically reiterated, for the return to equal status in the defence of the home country, even if that legal basis were only partially taken advantage of in the quantity of armaments? I was at that time myself German Delegate at Geneva. I took the greatest pains to convince the other side of the seriousness of the German demand. It was all of no avail. The bow was too tightly drawn. Germany left the Geneva League of Nations, never to return. A new chapter in European politics was opened. Let us look at the milestones of Anglo-German relations in the years that followed.

1934 - Recurrence of English appreciation of the reality of the new development in Germany leads to diplomatic negotiations the aim of which is to find a platform for a European limitation of armaments outside Geneva. In April the French Cabinet definitely declines to come to any understanding with Germany, because some of its Ministers are of the opinion that Germany will soon have exhausted her economic and financial resources. England considers all this. Her Government invites the French Ministers to London. In order to shackle Germany, the idea of an "Eastern Pact" is conceived, and it is suggested to her in all seriousness that she should recognise Bolshevist Russia, which joins the League of Nations soon afterwards, as a supplementary guarantor of the Locarno Treaty. Once again unbounded astonishment is felt in Germany that the English Government should take such a very different view of the situation.

1935 - France continues to reintegrate her policy of alliances, to form a ring round Germany, and to increase her armaments. Germany replies by proclaiming universal military service, in order to meet the growing menace. A long catalogue of points for negotiation drawn up by English and French Ministers has, of course, in these circumstances no prospect of success. Germany is to be rebuked in Geneva for her "bad conduct." England goes to Stresa and joins a "front" whose declared aim is to take sides with Italy, and curiously enough that country's preparations for the Abyssinian expedition are apparently overlooked, or not understood. In May Germany publicly announces her own policy, one of the essential features being "Friendship with England." On June 18th, a treaty is signed in which Germany voluntarily contents herself with a little more than one-third - against almost two-thirds in the years 1913-14 - of the British naval strength. Tentative suggestions for an air pact that at first seem promising are put forward. What is England's answer? She gladly accepts the great advantage over her pre-war level.

For the rest, no reply is deigned to the far-reaching German proposals for the appeasement of Europe. What does happen, however, is that France, England's friend, obtains the approval of the British Government to negotiations with Soviet Russia concerning what could only be called a military alliance against Germany. Once again the German people are disappointed in their hopes of England understanding their view of the necessity for European appeasement including a free and independent Germany.

1936 - The Franco-Russian Pact is ratified. In order to avert imminent dangers, Germany feels compelled to re-establish her full sovereignty in the Rhineland, and to withdraw publicly from the Locarno Treaty which, through no fault of hers, has been invalidated by the new Franco-Russian alliance. At the same time, Germany spontaneously proposes a complete plan for the pacification of Europe. There is nothing in this that conflicts with what has repeatedly been described by England as her own supreme aim, namely, "Peace in Europe." England's reply is participation in condemning Germany in the League of Nations' Council, and, instead of appreciation of Germany's proposals, the despatch of a "questionnaire" that hurt German feelings. Is it so surprising that negotiations in favour of a Western Pact to replace Locarno broke down at the very outset?

1937 - For Germany this year is above all a period in which she completes and consolidates her endeavours to improve conditions for her trade, commerce and food supply. The time of peace plans and constantly renewed offers to negotiate on them is past. The foreground is occupied by internal efforts to enhance the nation's strength. At the very beginning of the year the residue of the Versailles Treaty, in as far as it discriminated against Germany, simply collapses. In the preceding year the German rivers were restored to German sovereignty, and similar measures are now taken in respect of the Reichsbank and the Reichsbahn. All this has to happen through one-sided declarations on the part of Germany, for the other side gives no sign, nearly twenty years after the conclusion of the World War, of appreciating in any sense the urgent German demand for the full restoration of the power of a great nation.

The aim pursued by Germany, which she constantly proclaims, is to render herself to a great extent independent of foreign countries in respect of the production of certain raw material and foodstuffs, but not to withdraw for all time from international trade. The catchword "Autarchy" is an absurdity for a country constructed as Germany is.

In proof of this, Germany has, by straining every nerve, increased her foreign trade with many countries, and has discovered new and better methods by which to overcome the difficulties of currency conditions.

From the foreign political point of view the Spanish war creates many crises and great international tension. The desire for peace cherished by the participating European great powers, not least by Germany, continues to overcome the crisis, and to thwart Moscow's endeavours to foment an inter-European conflict. By the end of 1937 the Spanish war has ceased to be a reason for strife between England and Germany; it is not even a cause of serious differences of opinion. On the other hand, the German-Italian friendship, which has received its first powerful impulse during the Sanctions by the League of Nations against Italy, becomes the Berlin-Rome axis, and thus a powerful counterpoise to the close military and political Entente between England and France announced to the world in the spring of 1936. In the autumn Italy formally adheres to the German-Japanese Agreement of 1936 against the danger of international Bolshevism. From now onward there is an international political "Triangle," which is opposed to the Bolshevist danger, and which cherishes many views in common.

1938 - We are now in the middle of today's happenings. The year began quietly, and not without some prospect of general relief of the tension. Suddenly a Press campaign against Germany was started, the final tendency of which was always the same - the internal conditions and the internal contrasts had become unbearable. The German Leadership proved by the new concentration of forces that just the contrary of these descriptions was the truth.

Soon afterwards developments in Austria demanded further decisions. The Agreement of 1936 had not been utilised there to clear the internal atmosphere, but rather to sharpen the differences, while, at the same time, the Legitimists publicly announced their none too popular demand for the return of the Habsburgs. Everything was confused and done by halves. Those who wish to inform themselves without prejudice on this subject will find confirmation in the book by the former Austrian Chancellor Schuschnigg, recently published under the title Dreimal Oesterreich. The position of the National Socialist section of the populace had become unbearable. Renewed protests against Schuschnigg's Government were to be expected every day. The German Chancellor invited the head of the Austrian Government to visit him, and made proposals for relieving the situation. The result was the outward announcement of a "peace" which was not inwardly adhered to. In obvious self-deception regarding the imagined success of his wireless speech to the world in general, Schuschnigg believed he could arrange a plebiscite which would have been a falsified election, and which, as opposed to the so-called sworn constitution and to the agreement reached at Berchtesgaden, would have promised the Marxists fresh influence. The cup was overflowing. A large section of the population protested; Schuschnigg's power suddenly crumpled up. A new Austrian Chancellor requested the dispatch of German troops so as to prevent bloodshed and civil war. The German troops arrived, and with them the Fuhrer. The vast majority of the Austrians greeted him with bursts of cheers. Under the glow of the spring sun, and with the enthusiastic consent of many millions, Austria became united with the Reich. No force was used, not a single shot was fired. A burst of joy went through the hearts of the 75,000,000 people reunited in a single realm, which found its political expression in the elections of April 10th. The outside world was surprised. Judgment has not yet been brought into line. The British Government was one of those which criticised the happenings; France took up a similar attitude. Other governments welcomed the event, having understanding for the great secret of the bond of race, blood and language, even though these be qualities of another people. The most important factor was that Italy held firmly to her friendship for Germany. The Berlin-Rome axis has been further strengthened by the happenings of the last few weeks. All ideas of playing a game in which Italy opposed Germany, or vice versa, had to be abandoned. A further chapter in post-war politics has reached its conclusion. We are turning over a new leaf. It begins with the question: After all that happened between January 30th, 1933, and the present, what is the attitude of Germany and England in regard to the most important features of their foreign policy and the feelings of their peoples towards each other?

Germany has given clear proof under National Socialist leadership since January 30th, 1933, that her primary need and desire is peace in honour, dignity and strength. How much has been written in these last years in certain sections of the international Press alleging German intentions to disturb peace by force! It should now be much more clearly understood that malicious and obscure forces that have been bought, or are acting from other even more questionable motives, are working in the international Press, by disseminating false rumours about Germany, to create new coalitions against her, and if possible to bring about an open conflict. Is there any hope that this will be grasped? Unfortunately, there is none. I fear that the so-called "Freedom of the Press" will continue to be abused in certain countries for the circulation of false news either because of aversion to the German system of government or, as before the Great War, as the result of envy or jealousy of a strong Germany that has again appeared on the scene.

We Germans must, therefore, reckon with this fact, as with the chance that although we start on an excursion in fine weather there may yet be storm and rain. And what have we to represent in politics the function of an umbrella or of a rain-coat? I believe that if I were to employ in Germany today the method, say, that Sir Philip Gibbs applied to his own countrymen in his extremely interesting book Ordeal in England, I should have to describe the frame of mind produced in Germany during five years of National Socialist government somewhat as follows: "Let a portion of the international Press vilify and misjudge us - after so many years of humiliation we have today a new, magnificent and strong Germany. We shall attack nobody, but woe to those who attack us!" I could make this feeling still more clear to English readers by citing some of what in my opinion are the finest lines in Rudyard Kipling's "Seven Seas":

Stand to your work and be wise, certain of sword and pen, Who are neither children nor Gods, but men in a world of men.

That should have been the spirit pervading "Britannia ruling the waves." It corresponds well, however, with the spirit that once again animates the German people. Who will deny Germany's present Fuhrer the historic merit of having made this national pride, this calm feeling of security, and this manliness the common property of his people? Is all this still to be described as "Unrest in Europe" as on October 14th, 1933, and to be criticised as contemptible, or regarded as an alleged terrible danger to be met with more and more armament measures and alliances?

Why, then, to summarise once more, has Germany increased her armaments to such an extent, and why was she compelled to do so? Because on the other side, including England, the determination to create a preponderating military coalition in the name of the so-called "peace-loving nations" was stronger than the desire to arrive at a fair understanding with a Germany that now had equal rights and privileges.

Why was Germany forced to take in hand the Four Year Plan? Because the seizure, in contravention of international law, of her private property, the cost of the war, the war tributes, and the immense loss of territory and of the products of the soil, together with many other consequences of the dictated Treaty of Versailles, have weakened Germany to such an extent that in spite of foreign credits amounting to thousands of millions of Reichsmarks since the year 1926, her currency can finally be upheld only by special measures on the part of the State, and must be administered according to Germany's special needs. All phrases about the existence of ample raw material in the world thus avail nothing, because Germany cannot buy it in the course of normal exchange of goods.

Why, furthermore, cannot Germany be content to sign new peace pacts, instead of presenting demands for her future? Because among the consequences of the dictated Treaty of Versailles, and notwithstanding the greatest possible internal efforts, her economy and food-supply conditions are anything but satisfactory, and a serious development can be averted only by constantly renewed special efforts.

Why was it that Germany had to act with such speed on her own initiative on March 12th? It was to prevent civil war, to stop a breach of contract against her own interests in the highest task given her of Fate - the union and right of self-determination of the German people in two States which formerly belonged together.

Why did she not leave it to "peaceful revision by international action," as afterwards advised in England? Because Germany had lost all confidence in the efficiency of such methods as a result of the attitude of the other Powers from 1919 until the present day.

Why, finally, does Germany need colonies? In the first place, because their possession is a question of national honour and of equality like everything else that she has herself restored during this period on her own territory. Secondly, although the possession of colonies is certainly not a universal remedy that removes all economic difficulties, it would, assuming suitable administration and development, help in a useful manner towards overcoming those actually existing.

I do not know if these questions and answers suffice to make it clear why German foreign policy, in the endeavour to secure international co-operation, has ever and anon in the course of the past years put forward proposals for a general peace settlement, and why, seeing that these have been repelled, it finds no reason to repeat them. Self-help in the truest and broadest sense of the word has become the watchword of the German people.

Is Germany to blame for this outcome? The answer of the German people is a decided No! The situation existing today both in the armament race and in economy, and finally in the domain of international pacts and treaties, has not arisen through sabotage on the part of Germany, or even through malice or ill-will. On the contrary, it has arisen from the refusal to pay due consideration to German initiative. This again is not intended to be a reproach, but simply a German statement of fact to assist in the formation of a right understanding of the present situation.

Time, however, does not stand still, and thoughts press forward towards the future. Meanwhile it is perfectly clear to us Germans that the so-called "Versailles period" has been brought to a conclusion. For, in the first place, as a result of Germany's own vigorous actions, German sovereignty is no longer restricted in any sense; and in the second, Germany having again become fully sovereign, has re-entered a period of her foreign relations that in more than one way can be compared with the periods preceding the War and in Bismarck's times. The task of giving freedom to Germany and of uniting 75 millions is now to be followed by an equally important one. This is the definite inclusion of Germany in the European community of states and in the world with its economic relations in such a manner that a system of useful collaboration in favour of universal peace may be established by means of the voluntary and sovereign actions of Germany, now fully restored to her position of a great power. This task involves unceasing and continuous exertion. It is certainly not an easy one. That we know. German history perpetually teaches us this lesson.

What, then, is the attitude of present-day England to this Germany? The great majority of English people certainly wish for peace and some sort of friendly relations with Germany, with whom they are racially connected. What is less clear is the position in the numerically restricted circles that have the real political leadership in their hands. Here also understanding is desired. There is certainly no inclination to intensify the differences of opinion that undoubtedly exist. In responsible quarters efforts are made to discourage internal criticism and certain prejudices, so that the great aim "Peace in Europe" may not be thwarted; but it is not rightly known in those quarters what method is to be pursued towards this somewhat enigmatic Germany, that is certainly very often difficult to understand. If this assertion be correct, the reply is facilitated to one question at any rate: What are the reasons for England's not always very clear attitude towards Germany in the years since National Socialism came into power?

I have certainly not the faintest knowledge of the secrets of the Foreign Office or of the Imperial Defence Committee. I leave out every connection with party politics, opposition speeches and questions in the House of Commons. All that I can do is to describe how the individual actions of English policy towards Germany appear to me, and how they may perhaps be explained. I will begin with the impression that in some critical periods, when certain French circles played with the insane idea of a preventive action against Germany by force of arms, London certainly applied the brake. This was undoubtedly the case, especially in the spring of 1933 and 1936. This attitude was supplemented by the establishment of a political and military friendship between England and France of such a nature that it is hardly possible to conceive of a closer union between two sovereign Great Powers.

A section of English public opinion, nevertheless, manifested towards Germany a fair-minded understanding - and much more so than the official policy of every action on German territory tending to the restoration of full sovereignty there. To make a long story short: After many ups and downs a development has gradually manifested itself in England, since the fiasco of the League of Nations, and many other painful experiences, which endeavours to do justice to all currents of public opinion and to combine all possible aims. Such aims include the maintenance of old and the gaining of new friendships, and adherence to the League of Nations, notwithstanding its notorious failure, as an instrument for the maintenance or re-establishment of peace. At the same time readiness to conclude treaties with Powers that are not members of the League is declared, the call "unite the Democracies" is heard, but the warning is expressed against dividing the world into groups with different systems of government. Everything is drowned, however, by the cry for speeding up of armaments ...

To speak clearly and candidly, we Germans do not know today what England's intentions towards Germany really are. We often ask ourselves, when our affairs are discussed on the other side of the North Sea, if English politicians really endeavour to understand Germany's position. The same people who reproached us bitterly before 1914 on account of the "ever-growing German Navy" showed complete understanding for the land armaments against the allied States of France and Russia; now, however, they curse German armaments in every shape and form. Some declare that colonial possessions would be absolutely useless to Germany, while others become excited because Germany has improved her economic position in Central and South-

East Europe by the union with Austria. The same politicians who wish to encircle Germany just as before 1914, and, at least, to oppose her by a superior Coalition of Powers, are surprised or indignant when such pressure naturally results in counter-pressure, and when Germany is compelled to increase her armaments still further. Then they go to the House of Commons, play the role of a Cassandra, and, while referring to Germany, demand once again more armaments for England. A part of public opinion in England is in favour of limiting England's obligations in case of war, while the other part wishes to add to these obligations. Some still call the League of Nations England's salvation, while others refer to it as a hardly veiled alliance between England and France, with Russia in the background. And, in view of so many varying opinions, we Germans ask indeed: How far does the English friendship with France go in regard to all the political and economic happenings in Central and South-Eastern Europe, in which France claims the right of special interest? Does the Anglo-French friendship mean that all France's pacts and alliances with diverse European countries are considered by England to be her own obligations? In a word, where are really the limits for what is still understood today as "Collectivism"?

Before the situation in the Far East became critical Mr. Eden, then Secretary for Foreign Affairs, declared what England would fight for, namely, for the security and integrity of France and Belgium; to keep the route through the Mediterranean open; and to prevent a hostile power from establishing itself on the East coast of the Red Sea.

And just recently, when the differences in public opinion in England were great, and when the opposition and some Government supporters as well wanted Britain to enter into a guarantee for present Czechoslovakia and the question of England's engagements in case of war was generally raised again, the Prime Minister replied in the midst of the storm of public opinion that the greatest interest of the British Empire was peace. England would also fight if certain of her vital interests were threatened. But outside such matters with vital interests, as Mr. Eden stated at a previous date, England could not undertake any automatic military engagements. Existing engagements referred to the defence of France and Belgium against an unprovoked attack, while there were also other obligations towards Portugal, Irak and Egypt, but no special obligations towards Czechoslovakia. England would, even though her belief in the League of Nations were shaken, as a member of this institution, reserve the right to step in to restore peace or order if circumstances were according. Finally a modern war would almost certainly show the tendency to spread to other countries apart from written or other obligations that may exist between a few.

Although we Germans acknowledge the steady leadership of an eminent statesman in these statements, one who would not allow himself to be taken from his considered policy by excited and obviously dangerous advice, we recognise to a great extent the old traditional policy of a free hand and we still miss a real and positive step forward towards guarantees of the peace of Europe by practical action. We are also again and again surprised by the way in which the fateful role of Bolshevism is so clearly overlooked in responsible statements made by British Governments.

Germany is its sworn enemy. What is England's attitude towards it? Does the declaration suffice that no Bolshevist danger exists for England, and that the English policy deduces from this the right to attach small importance to the German view that Bolshevism is the gravest of international dangers? Or have the directors of British policy the Far East in their minds, and think that the antagonism towards Japan shared by them in common with Soviet Russia dictates certain considerations in respect of European conditions? We Germans know nothing of all that. We can only guess. What we see and have to note for the present is the regret that the most important German political and economic aims are judged wrongly by many people in England, and are at times criticised very superficially or even arrogantly. If "Germany speaks," we must give expression to this regret, if we are to be honest.

And while this happens, while a German searches in vain for a clear line in Britain's policy towards his country the world has very considerably changed. The Abyssinian war was succeeded by the proclamation of the Roman Empire, and by a perceptible access of power to Italy in the Mediterranean. The Spanish war, however it may end, will also assist in changing England's position in the Mediterranean. The difficulties in Palestine are growing. Unrest prevails in the Arabian world, where revolution is also showing its head. The white man is losing prestige in Eastern Asia, and whatever may be the outcome of the Sino-Japanese conflict, England's dominant position in the Far East will be impaired. Even India seems menaced, though distantly. Bolshevism is fomenting in its own way hatred and discontent among the coloured races. This is not, moreover, a narrative compiled by a malevolent German, it is what British patriots write in English newspapers.

In this situation England's Prime Minister, the son of Joseph Chamberlain, a short time ago proposed that there shall be understanding and friendship between England and Germany, and in the last month of the past year Lord Halifax visited Germany's Fuhrer. The object of that visit was "to arrive, if possible, at a clearer understanding on both sides of the policy and outlook of the two Governments." The result was according to Chamberlain's own words "a fairly definite idea of the problems which in the view of the German Government have to be solved" in favour of European peace and co-operation.

Then followed, a few weeks later, that momentous decision made in a dramatic session of the House of Commons after Mr. Eden's resignation of the office of Secretary of State for Foreign Affairs. A large majority supported the Prime Minister's policy of discarding the illusions of the past and seeking, instead, new and more successful methods by which to achieve the appeasement of Europe. This, as he said, could best be done by direct negotiations between the chief Powers in Europe, namely, Britain, France, Germany and Italy, on the upholding of their respective interests, the promotion of a better understanding and co-operation. In the meantime negotiations with Italy have led to good results and Germany welcomes the new Anglo-Italian agreement heartily. It means a step forward on the right path.

Between Germany and England, for the present, things remain as they were.

What then ought there to be between Germany and England?

What Ought To Be

There ought to be friendship! Is there such a thing today? No! Something quite different exists between Germany and England at the present time. There are many, perchance very many, points of personal contact. Take, for instance, the large number of sports' events now in Germany, now over in England, ministers' visits, student-exchanges, study-commissions, concerts, meetings of ex-service men and social functions of various kinds. Today, as in past years, many German girls go to England as paying or as non-paying guests, thanks to the ready hospitality of the English people. Many prominent Englishmen visit Berlin and acquaint themselves with existing conditions; they travel to Bayreuth, they listen to the strains of Wagner's music, and watch with interest the proceedings at the party Congress in Nuremberg. All this is doubtless most admirable and extremely useful, and for heaven's sake let us go on with it. But stop! Did not something similar already exist before the Great War, if perhaps less extensively and systematically? I myself, for instance, always spent my annual leave in England in those days. I am still grateful to all those English friends who received me then with such cordial hospitality. But it is precisely such a one as myself who knows full well that such kindly sympathy and personal contact between Germans and Englishmen by no means signify "political friendship." I can even recollect how before the War the culmination of personal visits coincided with the culmination of political tension. No - let us be honest. "Political friendship" is not easy of attainment. It is something to be striven for between Germany and England, and because we do not possess it Today, "it ought to be."

There is much that separates us at the present time, just because "What has been" and "What is" are not forgotten and have not really become things of the past. Nothing definite has as yet been decided as to the future of Anglo-German relations. We are living now in a period of waiting, of considering and of examining. The momentous problem of mutual needs, interests and demands is still an open one. And precisely because we have not yet finished defining the line of demarcation between State and State, nation and nation, we see no sign of real co-operation. To start with, each must show full appreciation of the other's natural sphere of activity. Such appreciation must become a reality. On the one hand stands the world power England; on the other, the great continental power Germany with perfectly definite conditions of life, necessities and aims. On the one hand, the "having and possessing"; on the other, the "not having enough and demanding." On the one hand the "being," on the other the "becoming."

And in accordance with this fundamental, political difference are the feelings of the one nation towards the other which are not yet constant and on a firm basis. In England, provided nothing remarkable occurs, one may probably count on a majority desirous of agreement and friendship with Germany. If that is so then let all concerned bear in mind, that many a criticism, many an arrogant and frequently disparaging judgment passed on our mode of life, our acts and above all on our system of government, are a considerable hindrance to the fulfilment of their wish. We cannot and will not listen any longer to such phrases as: "I love Germany but I dislike the Nazis." Germany and "Nazis" are identical - this fact ought at last to be grasped by everyone. We also object to many English speakers' measurement of

Germany by two different standards. Everything is in perfect order in England, but there is much open to severe criticism in Germany. To be perfectly honest, we are often roused to indignation on noticing that we are made to look as if we were naughty children, deserving of chastisement, if not by the rod, at least by the "governess." Neither are we at all pleased when the Fuhrer's solemn declarations made in the name of the Reich Government are distrusted, and German policy is accredited with irresponsible decisions signifying a menace to European peace by the use of aggressive measures. In view of our own present unified Government we found it hard to credit the rumours whispered in our ears that several obstinate opponents of ours in the Foreign Office do everything in their power to destroy the sincere and friendly intentions of certain Ministers with regard to Germany. And with the same disbelief we listened to certain information stating that one Cabinet Minister is well disposed towards Germany, and another is decidedly hostile.

But whatever has happened in the past, recent events now point to a certain self-examination on both sides. At any rate we are now waiting to see what policy England will adopt with regard to Germany. And since we do not belong to those who look for the mote in the other's eye and neglect the beam in their own, we ask ourselves whether or not certain things and certain ideas of ours ought to be changed, if mutual friendship is to prevail.

I shall attempt to be perfectly honest also when dealing with this delicate question. Yes, indeed, there is much that ought to be different in Germany too. On personal observation, I find that here and there views are expressed over-estimating certain difficulties of the British Empire. According to the holders of such opinions, there are certain weak and vulnerable parts in it and Britain stands no longer where once she stood. I am convinced that such people will hardly be able to tackle the problem of England with unprejudiced minds. Other Germans, splendid patriots, are all too easily inclined to designate as hypocrisy any form of English policy of which they disapprove and simply to ascribe it to the influence of "Jews and Freemasons." They have too slight a knowledge of history and allow their vision to be dimmed by non-essential symptoms. In short, all such German critics attach insufficient importance to the factors of history, to the peculiarities of the English character, political methods and institutions. While the German usually follows the goal he has set up for himself in his own straightforward way, he often finds in the Englishman an apparently easy-going empiricism, a policy which, as Sir Arnold Wilson recently and humorously remarked, occasionally takes one step in some direction or other, and then declares afterwards, the end of the step is the goal.

Ought we to give up our efforts in the face of such criticism? Decidedly not! Just because of it we ought to redouble them to discover the best way of becoming friends.

What actually does "friendship" mean between two nations? Let us glance at a few instances. The one nearest at hand is England's intimate friendship with France. To us Germans it would appear first of all co-ordination of interests. This friendship originated in 1904. It lasted through the War, and is, even now, despite many vacillations, a political reality sufficiently clear for Germany to look upon both nations almost in the light of a unity. What is said and written in England and France on common love of liberty, of democracy and ideals would appear to us of far less importance than the "expediency" felt by both countries. Consider too England's friendship with the United States of America. In this case such a relationship has been encouraged by history, language, culture and economy, recently also by steadily increasing signs of common political interest which are always at hand to smooth over occasional difficulties.

France's system of making friendship is totally different. Historically considered, it dates back to the days of Richelieu, consisting of changing methods mainly based on numerous friendships and alliances to be placed round Germany, and, at the same time, on a system of playing German States or Parties one against the other. The second part of these methods has been definitely stopped by recent events in Germany. So only the first method, with the hope of drawing the "English friend" into European "entanglements" as much as possible, remains. Apart perhaps from Belgium, the friendship of France for Poland, Czechoslovakia, Rumania and Yugoslavia is planned with definite aims in view, therein much resembling the alliances of pre-war days, which were made in a spirit of antagonism towards other States. On these dangerous friendships France formally invoked the blessing of the League of Nations, that is to say, to a great extent her own, the crowning-point being reached in the Military Alliance with Moscow, the repercussions of which have already proved disastrous to her internal conditions. Characteristic of the real aims of this kind of friendship was the outspoken confession of a French politician made while negotiations were taking place regarding the Pact with Soviet Russia. He frankly said France would even make a pact with the "Devil" if he could guarantee her the status of 1919, i.e. French supremacy in Europe. No, such instances can never serve as models for a future friendship between Germany and England. Let us think again. What other way would promote Anglo-German friendship?

Besides the German claim to Colonies there is no actual divergence between Germany and England which would first have to be made the subject of negotiations, and on the satisfactory settlement of which we should, like England and France in 1904, fall into each other's arms, overcome with emotion. There is no third State against which an Anglo-German alliance could be formed, as was the case in the past, when Frederick the Great helped to win Canada for England on the battle-fields of Europe or when Blucher and Wellington defeated Napoleon at Waterloo. Nor is there definite community of interests between our two countries. There is something else. Two great and proud nations face each other. Neither of them wishes a second war with the other, but each is charged by Providence with a special task to perform in Europe and in the world, and each has to contribute in her own way to make peace a reality. What then ought to be the basis of Anglo-German friendship? I see three foundation stones on which we might build that friendship:

The first is respect on the part of each for the dignity, strength and efficiency of the other. Inevitably after what has happened, and we being as we are, for a long time to come we shall frankly criticise each other. This, however, must be done without malice and paltry polemics that hurt. Let the guiding principle here be fair play and an effort to understand the other's point of view.

The second foundation stone is the clear, firm determination on the part of both Governments to promote mutual understanding. Pacts, agreements, or even alliances are not required for this. The policy of the Governments, however, ought to be publicly defined so clearly as to prevent its ever being concealed by passing moods, obscure press campaigns or even by the intrigues of outsiders.

The third foundation stone consists of a common adjustment of the views concerning the future of Europe. Germany is aware that England is bound first and foremost by friendship to France, secondly to the United States of America. Germany, on the other hand, can boast of a well-tried friendship with Italy, and to an increasing extent with other countries. A permanent guarantee of the peace of Europe would thus appear impossible without a certain balance of interests, a minimum of mutual adaptation in the policy of the four Great Powers mentioned above. No hegemony of any of the Great Powers would ever be tolerated by the rest of Europe. They are bound to come to final agreement or keep up a dangerous tension. I know that I have now arrived at a most important point. The very ties existing today between two pairs of the above mentioned Great Powers suffice as a warning - when we think of the pre-war period - against a new formation of groups destined constantly and systematically to pursue a policy of antagonism to each other. Serious happenings in the past have taught us above all that no agreements ought to be made which either prevent freedom of independent action or dangerously limit it in the moment of a European conflict.

The more England becomes involved in dangerous entanglements such as desired by France and astonishingly enough recommended by certain outstanding politicians in the House of Commons the greater becomes the resemblance with the conditions of 1914. "General settlement" seems to be the latest enticing slogan for the elimination of all difficulties. It can perhaps be explained by England's wish at last to safeguard a permanent "peace in Europe" twenty years after the War. But did not the predecessor of the present Prime Minister, Lord Baldwin, before leaving the political arena, publicly declare that in his opinion a generation would pass before the World War would be finally liquidated? I should like to say in all frankness that we in Germany do not believe in the blessings of a "General Settlement" in the near future, one that will fulfil the wishes of all concerned. We must first of all stick to what is most important and will be most necessary in the years to come. This book is most certainly not the place for advice to statesmen on political decisions. Let us rather bear in mind the solemn assurance given by Neville Chamberlain that the preservation of England's existing friendships, and an understanding with Germany and Italy, are the aims of British foreign policy. Beside it, let us place the desire recently expressed by the Fuhrer, which admits of no misinterpretation, for co-operation with every State, and most certainly with England, that is willing to work together with us for the preservation of peace and the increase of happiness and prosperity among the nations concerned. But the wider one's range of vision, and the more clearly one recognises the difficulties confronting us in Europe, the more insistently must one demand that, whatever the development of the friendships and alliances of both countries may be today and to-morrow, it is not only the right, but also the duty of both great nations to place their own national aims first in everything calling for consideration and decision.

What does England want? First of all peace, preservation and consolidation of the Empire, and security for the connecting routes within it. What else she thinks and wishes has been expressed in the carefully worded declaration on Foreign Policy made by the Prime Minister in the House of Commons on March 24th.

What does Germany want? She wishes to give her people security within her frontiers, assurance of work, economic activity and food. To accomplish this she must have additional possibilities for economic activity, for exchange of goods, and for food supply. Amalgamation with the former Austria, special agreements with countries in Central and South-East Europe and Colonies come primarily under this heading. Furthermore, Germany requires a thorough revision on a large scale of all her private obligations incurred before the Crisis of 1931, for she wishes to be a "good debtor," and has no desire to be excluded from the circle of world-wide trade in the future.

Germany will continue the fight against Bolshevism, that menacing spectre close to her frontiers and elsewhere, which never relaxes its efforts to recover the ground it has lost since the 30th of January 1933.

Last but not least, is the demand made by a strong, united nation that all those of like race living beyond the borders of the Reich should enjoy the protection of their culture and the full rights of the country they live in. This is first of all the now famous problem of more than 31 millions of thorough Germans in Czechoslovakia. England knows what the Fuhrer has said on it and Mr. Chamberlain appreciated in his above-mentioned speech the recent declaration of the German Government in the sense of non-aggression against the Czechoslovakian State as a contribution towards peace.

Such in brief are the aims of both partners. Is it not possible by means of mutual understanding and good-will to find a path with the finger-post pointing to Friendship? Is it not an English proverb: Where there is a will there is a way?

Does not England's recently declared wish to solve present and future problems with "justice" and - should it be necessary - in "peaceful revision" show that way?

Germany cannot alter the fact that owing to the loss of the War and to a long period under the dictated, entirely unjust and insane Treaty of Versailles, she has still to put forward certain claims today. But on the other hand, what can she contribute towards an understanding with England? I should say first of all this. The British Empire is a reality, yesterday, today and to-morrow. It has a great mission to fulfil in the world. Germany ought therefore to take an interest in this mission so that it may continue and realize the blessing of a just peace.

Is it possible, in the face of the greatness of such aims, that the divergent methods hitherto employed by both States in their foreign policy, will prove a serious hindrance to an understanding? On one side we see the League of Nations, many friendships, the remains of "collectivism" and a policy of clear defence of national interests, on the other a policy of direct understanding with all the States that wish for it; repudiation of Geneva, repudiation of "collectivism." I should like to add only one remark to what I have already said on this subject in two previous sections. When France claims the right to form alliances and friendships all over Europe, when England comes to special agreements with Ireland, with France, Belgium, Holland, and Portugal, ought not Germany for her part to have the right to regulate for instance her relations as she pleases, in direct negotiations with her neighbouring States? Should not the so-called "interest" evinced in these relationships be restricted so as to prevent the use of force and maintain peace in Europe, as well as to make sure that the States directly concerned approve of the measures decided upon? Has not in certain cases "collectivism" been a hindrance for loyal collaboration and for settlements based on justice between neighbouring States?

Are there not signs everywhere that it is high time to put an end to a certain restless policy of interference or prestige and substitute instead a calm adherence to plain facts, and acceptance of the principle of "a wise moderation of interests" recently laid down by the Fuhrer in his great speech on the 20th of February. Would not an affirmative answer to these questions be just the proper course for a new and constructive European policy to adopt? But come what will, Germany demands fair play. Not two standards, but one, and equal rights and privileges for all must become the rule of Europe. This rule is no less applicable to armaments. As a naval officer I watched the growth of naval armaments in Germany and England up to the Great War. I had the bitter experience of witnessing the collapse of my country. Later on, I took a personal part in these long and wearisome efforts to bring about general disarmament and then a fair adjustment of Germany's military power by means of international negotiations. These negotiations have broken down. As for the present situation I am perfectly aware that the rearmament race between nations involves grave dangers. It is just this practical experience and personal knowledge, however, which have made me believe that neither divergent methods of foreign policy, nor the strengthening of national defence undertaken by both Germany and England for very good reasons, need be any real obstacle in the way of friendship.

And now I come to my last point. What ought the nations men and women, contribute themselves in order to set out on the road towards friendship? A whole book could be written on this subject. But that would be too much. I should like instead merely to quote a sentence taken from a letter of mine to *The Times* of 9th August 1937:

> We Germans and you Englishmen will, notwithstanding many good intentions, never become really good friends, if we continue to criticise the internal conditions and the methods of government in a way that must hurt the feelings of the country concerned. Let us rather recognise and appreciate what is good and what is great in the other nation!

Yes indeed, there is much that is great and good in Germany just as there is in England. This book contains quite a number of contributions dealing with the achievements and aims of Germany in the most varied fields of activity. A strong will from above directs, organises and plans everything, both for the present and for the future, and it is only recently that the concentration of the nation's energies has been carried further, as was clearly evidenced in the Fuhrer's long report on the 20th of February. In England too, the State today has extended its control in many ways. The period of "laissez-aller, laissez-faire" is irrevocably past and gone. Let us glance around. We see, also in England, in regard to education, hygiene, road-making, sports, labour service, air raid precautions, food supply in case of war, control of industry, co-operation with trade unions, building of houses, eradication of slums, and countless other things, the firm hand of the State - and shall see it more in a near future. And why has England applied these modern methods of "leadership"? Because happiness and joy in life, the standard of living among the masses could not otherwise be improved. Germany is working vigorously to solve her own problems in this direction. There is ample opportunity here for each country to study the work of the other as well as for friendly competition. Let each country work therefore on its own lines, according to its own methods and then in all friendliness let them compare the results. In doing this there will be little time for criticism, and no feelings will be hurt. On the contrary, when one considers what both nations have done in their internal spheres of activity there certainly ought not to be any opposition at all, but only mutual respect. Today Germany is a State directed and governed by National Socialism. England has her own particular form of democracy. It is, let us not forget, also the basis of the solidarity of the British Commonwealth of Nations. It would be sheer madness to assert that because their forms of Government differ, these two Powers cannot exist side by side and co-operate in friendship for the realisation of European and world peace.

As yet the future is still open. As yet no momentous decision has been made. But most essential - and I should like to stress this point very strongly - is goodwill in equal measure, on the part of each Government. Economic arrangements, political agreements for the appeasement of Europe, a stopping of the gigantic armaments race - for these tasks there is no catalogue of negotiations and no order of sequence.

There is only one natural solution in peaceful evolution and the gradual drawing together of both countries guided step by step by the firm will of their Leaders. Let both of us, Germans and English, look forward with clear eyes into the new era in front of us. Hard work awaits us both. Let us put aside old and new prejudices. Let us learn from the past and overcome the difficulties of the present.

Let each country fulfil the great demands of the future in its own way, and by its own methods. Let us march together, not against each other, into this new future for the benefit of our two great countries, for the benefit of Europe, for the benefit of the World.